To Mary and ....

Enjoy !

THE VALBONNE MONOLOGUES

THE VALBONNE MONOLOGUES

CHRIS FRANCE

Dedicated once again to that Nice Lady Decorator and my two expensive children, James and Charlie France

THE VALBONNE MONOLOGUES

First published by the author 2012

THE VALBONNE MONOLOGUES

Book formatted by www.bookformatting.co.uk.
Printed and bound in the EEC

ISBN 978-0-9575678-0-1 (cased)
ISBN 978-0-9575678-1-8 (limp)

Contents

FOREWORD
BY JOHN OTWAY

This is the sequel to Chris France's Best Selling book *Summer in the Cote d'Azur*

The two words "Best Selling" which Chris uses to describe his first literary outing have been used very erratically by this author.

I first heard him them uttered when world-wide sales of the book had just hit the 200 mark and he was forced into the position of having to order a reprint.

However his selective use of this phrase can be illustrated by the fact that many years ago - after Chris had invested a few thousand pounds in one of my records - he would not accept the same description for twice as many sales of the single *Misty Mountain* on the *County Recording Services* label.

Even though in the past thirty years nearly five hundred copies of this 7 inch piece of vinyl have now been sold (a number he can only dream about) , he refuses to preface the word "selling" with the word "best" for my work whilst at the same time applying it liberally to his.

Chris is a great friend and I would like to wish him all success in the world with this new book and with luck he will, over time, be able to call it the "better selling" *Valbonne Monologues*

PREAMBLE

After the success, in my own mind, of my first book with sales approaching 200, I decided that it was such a triumph that I had to write the second. I thought the elite who read my first serious (not really) literary offering which was called "Summer in the Cote d'Azur", and took a look at the lives of the idle rich in Valbonne, just north of Cannes on the edge of Provence, deserved another episode. Valbonne is one of the most beautiful places in the world to live and where I am lucky enough to own a house with my wife Issy. She is referred to as that "Nice Lady Decorator" after taking me to task on her previous descriptions which have included "the in house plasterer" and "the future ex-Mrs. France". We have two dogs, an amiable easy going obedient springer spaniel called Max whom I adore and Banjo, owned by that Nice Lady Decorator, a calamitous 35 kilo cocker spaniel that I abhor. He is smelly, an inveterate dribbler, a thief, disobedient and malevolent. His ability to go for a walk for an hour and retain last night's dinner in order to deposit on my freshly mown lawn was never going to endear him to me. Our two children, James and Charlotte (Charlie) are referred to as Sprog 1 and Sprog 2 respectively.

I say "idle rich" but when it comes to enjoying themselves the often well heeled ex- pat community in this area is far from lazy; indeed it is generally very industrious in its pursuit of leisure and there are any number of activities that can be undertaken, the most popular of which is eating and drinking in the sunshine. It was suggested that my second book should be called "Winter in the Cote d'Azur" as it could then comprise part of a series with at least two other seasons to be similarly abused, but I decided that it should contain Valbonne in the title for no more reason than the English Book Centre in Valbonne, the Waterstones of the south of France operated by the lovely Lin Wolff, told me that if Valbonne were in the title she would sell a lot more, and as sales are at a premium, I took the decision to follow my commercial nose.

Talking of noses I realise that many will be holding their noses aloft at the idea of my producing another book. The first one has been ritually burned, publicly defaced, torn into strips, then made into paper planes, as well as lending support to many a wobbly table and has creating amusement for many as a result, albeit not in quite the way I'd intended. I do hope readers will derive some enjoyment from it and I don't really care how as long as they buy it!

I am lucky enough to be able to make the time to write after a reasonably successful career in the music business during which time I was able to work with artists as diverse as The Artist Formerly Known as Prince to The Clash and from Rolf Harris to Ice T. I still retain some music business interests and remain at the helm of Music Of Life the award winning record company that I co founded with Simon Harris in 1986. Also, I still look after the estate of the late and immensely talented Steve Marriott, the driving force behind The Small Faces and Humble Pie. One of my oldest friends is enigmatic pop and film star John Otway for whom I have performed many services over the last 40 years: doubtless I will still be seen as a charity by him until I die. Actually maybe afterwards as well, he will want to inspect the will.

Being resident for much of the time in the South of France and earning much of my income in sterling means that I am forever exchanging currency. Some years ago I came across a currency conversion company called Currencies Direct. They did such a good job and were such good chaps, that they asked me if I would recommend their services to some others in the same position as myself. In return, they offered to pay me a commission and as a result I am now Regional Coordinator for the Valbonne area. It was they who first suggested that I write a daily blog, something of which at the time of writing I am still guilty; www.valbonnenews.com. It is therefore their fault that I now consider myself a writer.

This time I have included pictures, absent from my first book and deemed a mistake by that Nice Lady Decorator; hence production costs will be higher and a break-even of nearly 200 may make this my last, although with an ego the size of Devon don't bank on it.

ACKNOWLEDGEMENTS

The people with whom I have been lucky enough to mix over the past few years deserve the greatest respect and credit as, without my being able to witness their antics, disgraces and poor behaviour I would not have had a subject about which to write. I must say a special thanks to so many people who are listed roughly in the order in which they feature including my wife Issy "That Nice Lady Decorator" France, Peachy and Suzanne Butterfield, the Naked Politician and wife Dawn, John Otway, Stephen Frost, Master Mariner Mundell, Alistair Mcfaddyen, The Wingco and his lovely wife Maryse, Matt "Cornish Tsunami" Frost and his carer wife Viv, Paul and Jill Harris, Mr. Clipboard, aka Mr. Clipbeard and wife Ashley, Paul "Slash and Burn" Thornton Allan and his steely-eyed wife Lisa, Cubby Wolff, Ingeborg and Peter "Blind Lemon Misted, Pat and Tony "I invented the internet" Coombs, Lin and Marc Wolff, Steve and Nancy Weston, the Boltd-Christmas family, Mellissa and Nigel Graves, Ieuan Dado, Jude "Where's my Bailey's" O 'Sullivan, John "800 years of repression" O 'Sullivan, Peter and Judy Lynn, Jerry Shirley, Roly and Poly (Lesley) Bufton, Lin and Marc Wolff, Pippa Maile, Gerald Gomis, David Baumann, The Reverend Jeff, Hugh Grant, The Frost family, Amanda and Anthony "Dock Of The" Bay, Pat Toohey, Dave "Tripe" Goddard, Maria Carr, Mick Pedley, Nick Kail, Pauline Bull, Wild Willy Barrett, Neil "Mr." Humphrey (s), Helen Humphrey, Cathie "The Culture" Van der Stehl, John Coward, Dave Rogers, Mike and Nancy Allen, Nigel and Lesley Rowley, Dave Maskell, Ben and Mary Dobson, Sarah and Simon Howes, Soraya and Bill Colegrave, Christine Bryant, Lindsey Weskar, Chris and Mrs. Chicken, Simon

Harris, Largy, Meg and "Dancing" Greg Harris, Nick Goult, Pauline and Gordon Cato, Nigel Davies, aka Al Yiddley, Julie and Peter Bennett, The Ratcliffs, Karen and Iain Hockney, Francis Wilson, Fiona Macleod, Dr. Patrick Ireland, Jez Dean, Paul and Ellen North, Wayne Brown, Simon Asserati, Marina Kulik, Sophie and Rupert Scott, Suzie and Norman Philpot, Great Aunt Pam, Robert and Christine Angeli, John and Rachel Surtees, Douglas Mac The Knife" Mcgeorge, Carol and Dave Wurr, Janie and Peter Savin, Debbie "the Naked Forker" Frost, John Gilchrist, Julie Faux, Lise and Nick Davies, Sandra Seymour-Dale, Wim Teunissen, Fiona Biziou, Brenda Moorhouse, Lucy Butterfield, James Hensley, the Daily Mail, Daily Telegraph and Private Eye.

Special thanks to my unpaid proof readers and editors, Lin Wolff, Viv Frost and that Nice Lady Decorator. If there are mistakes, they are to blame!

Chapter 1

OCTOBER 2011

Seagull Delivers Bill On Trip To St Tropez

It is very important to make the most of living in the Cote d'Azur and if one does not own a boat, it is vital to have friends who do. Drinks started at just after 12 in Antibes aboard D5, the very nice boat owned by the Naked Politician and his lovely wife Dawn (does that make her Dawn naked or Dawn politician?) with a few others including old pal, John Otway down in the Cote d'Azur for a couple of days rest and recuperation. From there we adjourned for lunch to the very lovely Petite Plage, one of my favourite luncheon haunts in Juan les Pins.

Juan les Pins as a venue was chosen by Mr. Otway because he regularly destroys an old song by Peter Sarstedt called "Where Do You Go To My Lovely" in his "musical" set which mentions the town. You will see that I have placed the word musical in inverted commas. This is because people who have witnessed Mr. Otway's performances in the past will know what I mean but if you have not yet experienced that treat, a simple YouTube search will reveal the true scale of the horror that will befall anyone expecting either good musicianship, or a decent singing voice in his (albeit wonderfully) funny performances.

That fact that I have been a fan for over forty years is illustrated up by the number of times I have been persuaded to invest in his dodgy self promoting schemes, but the full story will have to wait for my autobiography, which will see daylight when I can find somebody to write it for me.

It was another warm and sunny day with swimwear to the fore, but some beach attire obviously has different effects on the bird population than others as my picture below shows.

The Naked Politician, thankfully not naked at this moment

Exactly what this sea-gull had in mind is open to debate but I think if one were to describe a bird in this position without recourse to the photo, one might have been forgiven for thinking that the Naked Politician might be worried. The exact nature of the seagull's interest is open to debate, but I do hope its bill was not too much of a shock.

Planning for the book launch is at fever pitch and is almost sold out. I would like to think that this is due to the quality of my writing and the entertaining content but I suspect that the special guests - John Otway and Stephen Frost- may prove more of an attraction. Blackadder fans will remember Stephen as the jovial firing squad leader in one of the best episodes of the final series, or one of the two lads in the series of Carling Black Label adverts in the eighties.

Practical issues need to be settled, Arrangements such as the menu, the wine (and the whining?) and how the whole event will work and what the output will be from my very special guests, or more especially how will they upstage me, a man with no stage presence or experience of public speaking upon which to fall back. We have seating for around 80 and I know of at least 90 people I think will want to attend, so first come first served system has to apply. You know the old adage, the early bird gets the worm, and this case the worm is me. I just hope I remember to buy my own ticket in time.

Another yacht trip in D5 from Antibes to St Tropez for lunch seems to me to be the perfect way to spend a Saturday, particularly as the plan is to then to have lunch in Cinquante Cinq the well-known restaurant for the rich and famous with a patchy reputation for its food. You will guess that by the time we had motored down the coast, a rather large amount of good wine had been consumed allowing bizarre concepts to be discussed. Once such mad theme was what would happen if my book was ever turned into a film? I said I would have liked it to be a bit in the style of "Sex In The City" whereas the general opinion was that it was more likely to be more "Paunch in Provence".

St Tropez in October is as good as it gets. The burn over to the best known flesh pot in the south of France was reasonably flat, something of a surprise after the wind of Saturday, and the suitable administration of "Quells", a sea sickness relief remedy ensured that the bacon sandwiches, handed out whilst those irritating French decided to upset the English Rugby World Cup aspirations earlier in the day remained in one's stomach rather than decorating the superstructure of D5.

I am certain that he just got a little too hot as we sped back from St Tropez burning 400 litres of fuel per hour and that was the only reason he felt it necessary to disrobe. To start with I was concerned about his carbon foot print, but after he sat on that Nice Lady Decorator's knee to wrestle the steering from her, I became concerned at another kind of err.... imprint and the effect it may have on her nice white leggings. A quick inspection after we returned to port laid this particular worry to rest, together with about 20 bottles of champagne and rose which were also laid to rest on the trip.

I had to crop this significantly in order to remove the face of the Naked Politician. I also had to enlarge it somewhat for other reasons that I cannot into here.

I was looking forward to a quiet recovery day that is often the norm on a Monday. That this did not come to pass was the result of a fallible memory brought on by age and alcohol abuse. It seems that whilst out on the boat on Saturday I had instigated a "gentleman's lunch" at the Auberge St Donat for midday yesterday.

It seemed such a good idea to introduce the Naked Politician and Peachy Butterfield to the Wingco and fellow boating person Master Mariner Mundell and (to keep feet firmly on the ground) Alistair the Air, my new BA long haul pilot friend. It is a long-held tradition in winter (and with the temperature dipping dangerously into the low 20's yesterday, the arrival of winter was confirmed) to adjourn after lunch at this particular venue to the Wingco's house located conveniently nearby to sit on his terrace, drink brandy and listen to loud music. Being a traditionalist at heart, I felt it was my duty to respond positively to this post lunch invitation, which I had issued. Here ends the case for the defence.

When we arrived (by this time without Alistair the Air who had, quite sensibly as it were, bailed out – can I say that about a BA pilot?) the gentleman's lunch party encountered the opposite sex for the first time in the shape of that Nice Lady Decorator and the lovely Maryse, or Mrs. Wingco as she has come to be known, who were enjoying a quiet glass of wine on the terrace.

Cinquante cinq in St Tropez. Is it called that because the minimum you can pay is 55 euros?

Downhill From Lunch

When one is at play amongst the idle rich of Valbonne, and of a certain age, one can ask forgiveness for less than 100% recall. That is my position and I am sticking to it. Thus the pictures that I discovered on my phone this morning may or may not have been taken by me. It is not that I deny taking them; it's just that I can't damn well remember.

That I recall retiring to the Wingco's terrace on Monday, after lunch at the Auberge St Donat, to drink brandy and listen to him play accompanying guitar to some obscure Mississippi blues artist at considerable volume cannot be denied as I reported on it yesterday, but I cannot remember taking the pictures on my phone of him being joined by the Naked Politician. There are other photos that I cannot show here which fall into the same bracket.

I am all for the pursuit of knowledge, even knowledge of the weird and wonderful customs that are prevalent in the frozen wind-swept desolation that epitomises the north of England. One of the miscreants who was at lunch, Mr. Peachy Butterfield, is unfortunate enough to have to return periodically from his dream existence in the South of France to look after his investments in property nestling in the moribund tundra that exists north of Birmingham. His property empire, consisting as it does of several houses in various states of construction, represents a considerable portfolio running to perhaps as much as several hundred pounds in value. Food production up there must be very difficult (although from the size of the man mountain one would hardly believe it) and

The Wingco and the naked politician get on down

techniques to sustain food production have clearly required considerable development to survive the harsh weather that is the norm in this deeply uncivilised northern outpost. Thus expressions such as to "puddle your collies" have entered into the daily vocabulary of these hardy folk. It seems that this expression means to water ones cauliflowers, although it is often used colloquially as a euphemism for going to the loo. Sayings of this nature according to Peachy are widespread and apparently known as "allotment slang".

This got me to thinking about what other expressions one could come up with in the same vein; what about "to tickle your tripe" or "strumpet your pigeons"? Maybe "frolic you ferrets"? I would hesitate to use the expression "whacking my whippets", but can we be sure this phrase does not exist?

I have often gently wound him up about that part of his life spent in the north of England and his fondness for this tundra strewn wasteland. So it was a shock to discover that he had, on occasion, ventured down to grimy civilisation in London to find out how the other, more fortunate half of the English live. I was even more surprised that he had eaten at one of Gordon Ramsay's restaurants somewhere near the Thames, but not at all surprised at his admission that he had eaten pigeon breast at this worthy establishment. Furthermore, he revealed that it was his dream one day to open a restaurant (probably so this man mountain of an eating machine could sample its delights), but with the codicil that the vegetarian option would read "Fu*k off". I have a picture of him saluting the feeding of pigeons in his home town of Chester.

Launch Latest And Tennis

In the evening to The Queens Legs to meet one of my book launch sponsors, Matt "Cornish Tsunami" Frost who, according to his friends never tires of referring to the Queens Legs as being "open" or "closed". He expressed concern about the possibility, nay, almost certainty of heckling at the event, and the noise that the attendant throng might be making after a few complementary glasses of champagne. He was also concerned that we may have gate crashers, given that the event has sold out nearly a month before the launch and clearly ticket touts will be looking for opportunities. It was decided that a strong doorman would be needed, and who better than that Nice Lady Decorator. This is because, many years ago, she was employed by me to take the entrance money at the door for some of my gigs, many of which were during the punk boom in 1976. One gig in particular featured punk icons The Damned. The local chapter of Hells Angels who were pathologically opposed to all things punk arrived in force at the gig and many of them were inside before I was aware of what was happening. When I went to remonstrate with her as to why she had let them all in, as I had no security staff, she pointed out that they had all paid. I fleetingly considered suggesting to the biggest one, their leader, that he had spelled "Angel" incorrectly on his jacket, and that being a Hells Angle was not quite as fearsome, but thought better of it. Matt Frost then suggested that having this kind of chapter at a book launch was not a good idea, and he has a point. As some of my better educated friends would most likely agree, some of my chapters are far scarier.

After a sumptuous lunch it was back to the Pav, our Thai style pavilion, to make serious inroads into my store of Rioja and that Nice Lady Decorator's Chablis wine lake. I know that my more sympathetic readers in the UK reading this whilst huddled close to their radiators (or peat fires further north) will have been thrilled for us that we were able to sit out until after dark in shorts and short sleeved shirts on another spectacular autumn day.

On Friday night before the Wales versus France World Cup

rugby match, the plan to stay in and prepare for the early start for the game yesterday morning was thrown into disarray by that Nice Lady Decorator who demanded a pint of Guinness early doors.

This began the dismantling of the evening's plans as, also in the Queens Legs, were old friends and former local residents Paul and Jill Harris on a flying visit back to civilisation from the dank and dreary Midlands. Paul is an insolvency lawyer specialising in fraud, at least, that is what he told me. Now call me old-fashioned but a lawyer an expert in fraud? What chance do we have? What next? A policeman, expert in theft? A doctor, expert in death?

Also enjoying a pint during happy hour were John and Jude "where is my Baileys" O'Sullivan, all on their way to the Valbonnaise, the villages favourite pizzeria, so it was inevitable that we were destined to join them all for dinner.

Over dinner the accuracy of some of my reporting in this column on the lives of the idle rich in Valbonne was called into question. As regular readers will know, accuracy is not the watchword for my column. It will almost always be replaced by opinion, my opinion, and that opinion will always be influenced by what I consider to be a good story. This was described by John "800 Years Of Repression" O 'Sullivan as an unfair use of poetic licence but the general feeling amongst the assembled diners was that my licence should have been revoked long before now. On a different note I cannot remember who it was during the course of the evening who described the Yoga courses in Valbonne run by the lovely Faye as "fanny stretching" with Davina? However, Peachy Butterfield may have some recall.

As many who have been pilloried in this column can testify, my BlackBerry is always at the ready to record moments of stupidity or to remind me of something that has amused me during the course of the day or more often the evening. However, this often means that I have a lot of what turn out the next morning to be incomprehensible notes which I then have to attempt to decipher when writing the daily treat. Today is no exception, unless you have any other ideas, the note that says "fish and strip" can only relate to someone with an idea of combining a fish and chip restaurant with a strip club, however I know not who, or I am not prepared to say. I also have a note saying "slots of fun in Cleethorpes" which I think referred to the name of a penny arcade, but it may have been a brothel in the frozen north. The relevance? No idea.

My picture today shows the very first attempt by the French to build the Channel Tunnel. The earliest prototypes threw up a number of problems. As you can see this is more of a bridge than a tunnel and it also starts at St Tropez in the Mediterranean, so the designer seems somewhat geographically challenged. I am also less than convinced about the quality of materials being used in this particular construction, but all's well that ends well.

I like the idea of the small plastic table

Crimewatch Never Pays

Last night we went to the Thornton Allan's for dinner with Mr. Clipboard and his stunningly attractive wife Ashley. With the impending publication of my book, the launch lunch for which is now sold out, and thus confirmation of my status as an author, I have decided that I need to pay some attention to my public image as Johnny Rotten may once have said.

Thus, to that end, I have decided to grow a goatee beard which, even though I say it myself, is already luxuriant and admired by almost nobody except rather surprisingly by that Nice Lady Decorator. Mr. Clipboard describes it as "very annoying facial hair" and has spent a fair degree of time recently plotting with Mr. Thornton Allan and indeed last night with the alluringly attractive Mrs. Thornton Allan plus slightly less alluring local estate agent Cubby Wolf to try to remove it, without my permission. This has involved a number of very dangerous maneuvers, mostly involving scissors, to attempt to set back its growth by several weeks. Now I am all for a little judicious pruning when required and it may be argued that it needs a little tidying up, but what they have in mind, and last night were trying to carry out, was more akin to scalping or, to be more precise - chinning.

Thus the evening was a little less relaxing than I had hoped but I (and the goatee) escaped just about intact, but there is a real danger that someone will get to it before the big launch lunch on 7th November. Three weeks is a long time to be vigilant and will be quite wearing as I shall have to be on my guard at all times. As I now beginning to realise, impending fame, at least in my own mind, can have its drawbacks or should I say scalpbacks?

Rugby World Cup

It seems that after the charming management of The Source decided it had seen enough of the antics of the some members of our nation who had been defeated in the quarter finals by the French, and proceeded to shut, not unreasonably, some two hours after the end of the Rugby World Cup Final; thus I issued an invitation to a handful of my fellow countrymen to continue the revelry back at our home.

Amongst those accepting was the Master Mariner Mundell who, for some reason of a higher order than I will ever understand, decided in his infinite wisdom to collect a large lump of snow-like ice that he discovered outside The Source and bring it back to the web (as our outside bar is known – easy to get stuck in, very difficult to escape). He then proceeded to mould it into a miniature snowman and amused himself by dressing his new creation in various guises by the inventive use of natural items available in the close vicinity. Quite why some photos show Mr. Snowman with an unfeasible large erection is something that I do not recall but at least I know it was a he.

Now to the wrestling, at least I think it was wrestling, perish the thought that the picture in my possession depicts anything other than playful err...play and no connection must be made with earlier erectile references to Mr. Snowman. I cannot explain why the miscreants had taken to what I hope is playful public schoolboy jolly japes. Perhaps it was the excitement of the Manchester United versus Manchester City football match on the TV?

Tuck your shirt in boy

I did take this next picture. On the right the Wingco is in normal guitar posturing position, but who is that brunette beauty on his right? Obviously she is alluring and has raised his temperature sufficiently for him to be seen cavorting on the floor in a most unseemly manner later in the afternoon. I had considered her very attractive myself at first, but my ardour waned somewhat after she took up with the Wingco in a most unladylike, one may even say groupie-like manner. He truly is a rock and roll giant and I salute him. His far more beautiful wife was I think it is fair to say, slightly less amused, but as she has married a rock and roll god she must have seen this kind of thing before.

Winter Approaches

I had scheduled to meet old pal and the best joke teller I have ever met, Peter Lynn at home for coffee. He brought with him a curious and entirely ridiculous substance called decaffeinated coffee, assuming correctly that I would not give such an obviously useless concept space in my house. Decaffeinated coffee seems like an oxymoron to me. What is the point of coffee unless it is for a decent shot of caffeine? No sober man could ever like the taste of coffee without the proper amount of poison included. What does he put in it? Un-sweetened sugar? I only wish I had some quiche to test him more fully as everybody knows real men don't eat Quiche (unless it is served up by that Nice Lady Decorator, in which case an obvious exception needs to be made).

This piece is especially for my readers in England. Although summer has gone, the autumn days are still warm enough to sit out and sunbathe and perhaps to read a book in the sunshine. I took a picture yesterday of the lounger in which that Nice Lady Decorator had been sitting a few moments before and guess what she was reading? She was reading an early proof of my first book.

This could go either way. Either she likes the idea that her lazy husband has actually got around to nearly publishing his first book and she will pleased and happy, or, on the other hand if she focusses on the contents, which is a more or less a compilation of the err....best bits of my daily column she has mostly not read, and the contents do not find favour then I will be in the dog house. So far she is on page 9 and the jury is out.

Next Saturday is Fireworks night, November 5th when I shall be playing golf with the REGS at St Donat, but in the evening I shall now be considering staging a firework party. This is because dear old Max, the amiable and gentle and not smelly family dog has just been confirmed as stone deaf. Whilst this is very sad and nothing can be done, it will enable me to buy some very loud fireworks to celebrate this momentous day in British history without worrying about his being frightened. Banjo, the appalling giant, smelly, loose bowelled cocker spaniel, a disgrace to the doggy fraternity has wonderful hearing, and although I do not like him, I accept that he will inevitably eventually take over as senior dog in the household. Thus I have decided to try to work anew on our relationship. With that in mind I have invited him to come and witness the firework display. I do hope he will enjoy the spectacle and sheer exhilarating sound of fireworks being let off at close quarters. I realise however that he may get over excited by the event so I plan to tether him to a tree nearby so that he gets the best possible view. I do hope this will cement a new era in relations between us.

Yesterday afternoon, Tony "I invented the internet" Coombs and his less than adoring wife Pat dropped around to pay for their tickets for that literary lunch, and Banjo proceeded to make himself unpleasant by attracting a rake of mosquitos and refusing to obey the simplest of commands. I know I said "sit" but he obviously imagined a silent "h" and did just what it says on the can, or rather what you do in the can if you are American.

Storm Imminent

With the onset of winter in the form of demonic thunderstorms marking our departure from summer and a rather nice autumn, attention will soon turn to winter sports, and with the ski resort Isola 2000 opening in under a month, I picture a couple of grown up children eagerly practicing their snowman making skills ahead of the season.

Two little boys with a new toy

So to dinner last night at literary HQ in old Valbonne at the home of Matt and Viv Frost, who, together with Lin Wolff from the English Book Centre in Valbonne are the stalwarts and founding fathers (mothers?) of the literary events which will shortly become the sort of occasion that require attendance for the chattering classes in the village.

Viv's husband, Matt Frost is a larger than life figure who is often to be seen in the Queens Legs, the Vignale and La Kavanou and was resplendent in a Welsh rugby shirt, which he was wearing in celebration of the recent win in the Rugby World cup for this small mining, as opposed to small-minded, nation. He claimed that as he was from Cornwall he was almost Welsh, as Cornwall is nearer to Wales than the rest of England, and to prove it produced a lovely meal based on a leg of Welsh lamb.

Of course, according to folk law, the Welsh have a number of usages for this poor animal, of which cooking and eating it is only one. Having spent some time earlier in the day with Steve Weston from the Riviera Ex-Pats Golf Society, who has form in the sheep area, (see my first book) I was reluctant to apply my mind to the wide range of uses and indeed "entertainment" that this pretty fluffy animal can allegedly provide. By that, before any of my readership gets the wrong idea, I was referring to sheep dog trials, where sheep enjoy being herded one way or another for the enjoyment of the Welsh community, because frankly if neither the Welsh nor the sheep enjoy it, what is the point?. Luckily for us, only eating it proved to be on the rather menu. I love beans of any type but that Nice Lady Decorator is a tad reluctant to serve them in our household so Croatian Bean Soup to start was the first sign that methane production was likely to increase in the short-term, but when another favourite of mine, brussel sprouts, appeared with the lamb, that Nice Lady Decorator began to fidget in her seat. Later it was I doing the fidgeting in my seat as the combined culinary offerings were quickly threatening the kind of methane carnage that she fears.

When I was at school I was required to spend one period a week studying British Constitution with a teacher who was so right wing his views were just to the right of Attila the Hun. He contended that England should spend 50% of its gross domestic product to do three things; to build up Hadrian's Wall so high it would keep the Celts out, dig out Offa's Dyke to 200 metres in width in order to keep the Welsh, with all their sheep loving foibles out, and thirdly blow up the two bridges that connect Cornwall to the English mainland, and then have Cornwall towed into the Atlantic and torpedoed. Needless to say, as Matt is fiercely proud of his Cornish heritage, I did not mention it at dinner.

Tennis – A Contact Sport

Tennis is a game that requires a certain commitment. Some of us have become utterly committed (or we should be) and the more committed one is, the more likely one is to overcome an opponent, even if he is nearly a decade younger.

So I greeted the invitation to play tennis with the naked politician at the very salubrious Sophia Antipolis Country Club yesterday with an air of a man with a greater commitment to the cause than his opponent. That my opponent did not have that the same despite his considerably more tender years sent out a message to all us oldies, but exactly what that message is, is not clear to this country bumpkin, I just know there is a message.

Life has its winners and losers. Some of us are winners, some not so fortunate. From this information the more perceptive regular readers of this column may be able to guess the result, I myself am, as you know by now, far too modest to reveal the winner or the exact size of the thrashing administered, but if you see the Naked Politician in the next few days, you may see some grazes on his knees which were sustained during one of the two games he won in two sets.

To celebrate or in some cases to commiserate over the result, lunch was taken at the fabulous Lou Fassum, a Michelin star restaurant about 100 metres from the very different but equally good it its own way Auberge St Donat. We were joined by Peachy Butterfield, his lovely wife Suzanne and that Nice Lady Decorator whose enthusiasm for lunching at Lou Fassum is matched only by her antipathy for lunching at the Auberge St Donat.

Mower Theft

During the summer, I featured in my column a well-trained battery operated mower which automatically came out every day, cut the grass and then returned to its hutch to recharge itself. I liked it because I fondly dreamed of how Banjo the grisly canine would get on with it. I imagined him cowered in some corner howling, waiting for it to shave some fur from him, That at least might make him smell a little less. This little fellow, (the mower not the dog) owned by the Boltd-Christmas family (I know, crazy name, crazy people) in Biot, has been stolen. It seems to me that the thieves may have a bit of Irish in them. It won't work without its charger, it needs wires set in the grass to stop it mowing flowerbeds or committing watery suicide in swimming pools and it is a rather boring shade of green. So if anyone sees something that looks like a vacuum cleaner out on its own, let me know. Maybe it just left home?

Yesterday we had some rain. It was not forecast, and it is the first since July. I did not move to the south of France to be rained on in

17

summer, so I want my money back. I know it only lasted for 40 minutes, but it seemed like an English winter for nearly an hour before the sun returned. I know it is sunny again today, but there is a point of principle here.

I am supposed to be being dragged kicking and screaming this morning to some obscure rugby match being televised at La Source Restaurant in Le Rouret. The French and the Welsh are due to commence battle in the also ran World Rugby Cup. Why I have to be there instead of being allowed to languish in my comfortable and pungent pit, I have no idea. Oh yes I have, it's because that Nice Lady Decorator thinks it will be a decent chance to get an early drink. My suggestion that she drives herself and leaves me to sleep was met with that usual no-nonsense expression, and once all the bedding had been put in the wash leaving me naked on the bed, I thought perhaps she had a point. At least she had made a point.

My picture today was taken in Valbonne earlier in the week. The car should not have been parked there, but I think leaving a guard cat on it roof is an interesting thief deterrent: I wonder if that would count as an alarm for car insurance premium purposes?

At a dinner party this evening, one Ieuan the Welshman, the Graves' family gardener, may be in attendance. Now, on the one hand, if the French give the Welsh the walloping the English would like to, then I will delighted to see him, but if by some miracle they overcome the French then I may myself be overcome by sickness or something and cry off. The very idea that Wales could appear in the Rugby World Cup Final is as preposterous as it will be sickening. On the other hand, the wonderful French side, of whom I was admittedly slightly dismissive until last week when England handed them the game on a plate, deserve wholeheartedly to get the chance to get ripped to shreds by the Kiwis, who will no doubt dismiss Australia's challenge tomorrow.

Monday sees the return to the Riviera of Mr. Clipboard and I have already received my red marked schedule of activities for Tuesday, his first full day back in charge of everything. I shall report for tennis at 10.15 and then arrive promptly at the Auberge St Donat for lunch, and will of course have had a haircut as ordered before he arrives.

So as we were both feeling rather shabby yesterday morning, we decided to forego the pleasure of seeing France overcome Wales at La Source and instead stayed in to lick our metaphorical and wine induced wounds, and prepare for another night of revelry. We were at a dinner party last night, I should not reveal the name of our hosts, but seasoned readers will know who it was that was photographed with her mouth sellotaped up to ensure she did not say anything stupid. If you need further hints, then Ieuan their Welsh gardener was also in attendance. A full report on the atrocities will have to wait until Monday, when I have hopefully regained an upright position.

Chapter 2

Print Run?

As we sat enjoying a Sundowner in the Pav after a long lunch, when discussing how many copies to order for the print run of the first edition I said to that Nice Lady Decorator "I don't suppose you are going to pay me for your copy of the book?" "No, I don't want one at all, fu*k off" she said. This seems to represent an under stated market reaction to the quality of my writing, but a reaction to which I must apparently expect to become accustomed. Despite almost inevitable fame on my doorstep she still calls my daily column; "writing silly stories for my friends".

Lunch at the Auberge St Donat after tennis at the Vignale was the usual lively affair. Tennis earlier in the day had been the usual triumph despite a new pairing. After the first set when myself and Master Mariner Mundell, my new partner for the day, had cut the opposition (in the jointly rotund shape of the Wingco and Mr. Clipboard) to shreds, winning by several clear points on a tie break, there may have been a slightly anti-climactic second set, the result of which I cannot recall.

What I do recall is that I once again had to fight to retain my goatee, the Annoying Facial Hair or AFH by which it has become known, and which I am cultivating for my book launch on 7th November. I am told that the reason I am tending and protecting this luxuriant growth is a vain attempt to appear more interesting than I actually am. But as I pointed out last night and again at lunch, if one is prepared to enter into the world of vanity publishing with the gusto so clearly evident, then the growth of a lowly beard is as nothing in comparison.

My picture today shows the ugly face of jealousy in the shape of Mr. Clipboard armed with some garden clippers, clearly intent on removing an amount of my AFH which probably equals or exceeds the entire amount still growing on his head.

A picture worthy of Crimewatch?

Take yesterday for example. We are full for the launch lunch 7th of November at the Auberge Provencal, but yesterday a film director and his wife asked if they could attend, so what self-respecting (this is a considerable understatement) writer, or should I say author, can resist the tantalizing possibility of having his work turned into a film? After all, I have first hand experience of someone close to me turning their life story into a film with Otway the Movie.

So, after struggling to stay awake and watch some old episodes of Foyles War on the TV, I retired to bed to consider the wonderful possibilities of a cinematic future. Lunch today will be taken on the delightful terrace of the golf course at St Donat, between Mouans Sartoux and the perfume capital of Grasse, after which we shall play 9 holes of golf, assuming the possibility of thunderstorms has abated by then. That the golf after a nice lunch is unlikely to be of a high standard is a given, but at least we will have some time in which to formulate a wager of some kind.

Before that I must concertina a full days endeavour on behalf of Humble Pie or more specifically for the groups drummer Jerry Shirley and the late Steve Marriott, the singer and guitarist in this legendary group who were huge in the 1970's especially in the USA, the estate of which I still represent. Jerry Shirley also has a book released this week in USA called "Best Seat In The House". We authors must stick together.

Rogues Gallery

I have received several calls and a number of emails claiming that they have seen the person claiming to be Mr. Clipboard (whose rather gruesome picture I featured above) on Crimewatch, the popular UK TV programme designed to expose crooks.

When I confronted him yesterday at the golf course about his alleged appearance on the UK's most notorious crime show, the golf itself having been abandoned due to the unscheduled appearance of a thunderstorm, he admitted that he had previously been featured on this prime time show in a starring role some years ago. It seems that he was the estate agent for whom Suzie Lamplugh worked before disappearing, and was asked to take part in a reconstruction of her last hours for TV. I had thought that his mug shot may have featured in the Rogues Gallery.

Due to the success in selling out my book launch at the Auberge Provencal on 7th November, I have been appointed acting promotion manager for The English Book Centre Literary Events. When I revealed this snippet of news to Mr. Clipboard he was aghast, claiming that it was like making King Herod president of Save The Children.

This is of course a scandalous charge but if Literary Events are normally high brow events, then I do get his point. I would not be comfortable organising such gatherings-; indeed the launch of my book, whilst clearly a stirring event in the publishing world could not be described as highbrow but, more populist, more Eastenders than Euclid.

Once again yesterday in the restaurant before golf and in the bar afterwards at the rather wet St Donat Golf Course, I had to battle to protect my honour in the shape of my "Annoying Facial Hair" (AFH).

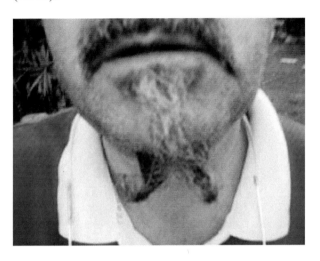

so called Annoying Facial Hair, I think its nice

There must have been at least six occasions when scissor welding maniacs in the shape of Mr. Clipboard and Slash and Burn Thornton Allan, attempted forcibly to trim my rather splendid beard. That I managed to keep it looking in decent condition, with just a very slight trim of the split ends, was mostly down to my judicious confiscation of the golf course's scissors from the miscreants. Such is the opprobrium generated by the AFH that I was told that if I collapsed on the golf course, first they would remove the beard, secondly they would call emergency services, after that, they would as they so tastefully put it "shag me up the arse", steal all my money and golf balls and look innocent when the ambulance arrived. Public schoolboys, don't you just love them?

Today, Mr. Clipboard departs for the UK, and not before time for my liver, but before he does we have one last tennis stand off later this morning at the Vignale followed by lunch. Then, glory be, a few days with nothing in the diary; in fact the next social event for which I have received my orders in triplicate, seems to be the watching of the French rugby team being carved into tiny pieces by the All Blacks on Sunday morning, in the final of the Rugby world Cup at La Source restaurant, on the way up the hill to Le Rouret, followed by lunch at this establishment. In order for this to be the next time we go out and drink alcohol assumes a giant leap of faith in that Nice Lady Decorators determination to avoid it. I am not confident.

The Mona Lisa Lives

That I have now finished with drink and socialising for a few days is, in my mind, a certainty. A very long lunch after tennis with our party being the last to leave by a very long chalk was the perfect way to set up a period of abstinence, which is the state you will find me in for the foreseeable future. Obviously the notion of "foreseeable" is something that for the more myopic amongst us is a fleeting concept, but let me be clear here, I will respect the wishes of that Nice Lady Decorator, even if she should decide to break the self-imposed vigil of abstinence.

Talking of that Nice Lady Decorator, today's picture was taken last weekend whilst she was at play with the Mona Lisa, aka Mellissa Graves, sadly on this occasion bereft of her Welsh gardener Ieuan, however no sign, as far as I can see of her husband Nigel either.

Today then, my nose will be against the proverbial grindstone. What a stupid expression. If you put your nose against the grindstone you would very quickly have no nose, and if that sentiment were expressed about a dog then the Revered Jeff would have the riposte here in a jiffy "A dog with no nose?, how does it smell?.....terrible". Shall we instead say that a little more attention to work is required for a day at least after the vicissitudes of life when Mr. Clipboard is in town?

But let me cast my mind back to lunch at the Auberge St Donat, post tennis. Mr. Clipboard left at 3 20 precisely to make his next appointment but that unfortunately was not the trigger that it should have been for myself, Master Mariner Mundell and the Wingco to leave, oh no. That would have been too simple. Instead we remained, discussing matters of great import no doubt until sometime after 4, by which time most of the doors and windows were shut and no more wine was forthcoming. At this stage even the Wingco got the hint and we left.

By this time, talk had turned to the fanciful notion of a chap's only skiing holiday in early December to Val d'Isere. I say fanciful because with the Wingco a committed non skier, and that Nice Lady Decorator no doubt a committed non believer in such a concept, the idea would never get off the ground (is this the correct expression?) except in the Master Mariners household where, it seems, his word is law as long as his wife does not get wind of it. Thus I expect to hear no more of this tantalising prospect, at least until the next time it is after 4pm in the Auberge St Donat, the place where dreams can live, albeit fleetingly.

Abstinence Beckons

So the first hurdle to a few days of abstinence, indeed attempted temperance leading up to the rugby on Sunday was mounted and successfully negotiated-; no lunch out for either of us yesterday, instead a meagre and rather worryingly healthy salad, but with the return of the prodigal daughter or more likely profligate daughter for half term yesterday evening, from possibly the most expensive education ever known to man, that Nice Lady Decorator agreed to take her to the Queens Legs to meet up with friends she has not seen for months. Thus, I could see the jaws of temptation in the form of an open ditch protecting the hurdle (is this taking the hurdle analogy a jump too far?) opening up in front of me.

You know what happened; we went to the Queens Legs for a pint as well. Just the two though and then back to, I think the word is "enjoy", that Nice Lady Decorator's cooking. I received a cryptic comment from Peter Lynn today wondering if the she had any comment to make about yesterdays photo, but she did not because she did not see it. The same will be true today, she will not read today's episode, so once again I am safe until she possibly sees it in the inevitable second book which, as you are reading this, you will know has come to pass.

Today is set to be a gardening day. Maintenance of the outside areas as summer departs is vital and I have in mind rigorous testing of the hammock and garden equipment, such as the sun loungers, to ensure that the have survived the summer in good condition.

Ego Mania Lives

40,000 hits. That's what we are talking here. Since its inception a mere two years ago, there have been 40,000 hits on my blog website. This is a graphic illustration of how literary standards have dropped over the last two years. As the Wingco said to me the other day: "when you were actively making records, if there had been that many hits on your label you could hardly have been happier"

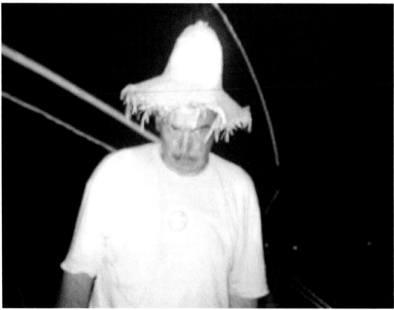

Talking of the Wingco, over lunch last week at the Auberge St Donat I mischievously congratulated him on seeing the light and attending my book launch lunch, bearing in mind he considers the daily column "ghastly" and thus the book that it has spawned would be viewed in a similar light. That moustache of his bristled with indignation: "I am going to lunch, nothing to do with any book", he exclaimed and then he went on to say (rather forcibly I thought) something along the lines of hell freezing over before he bought such an item. It was at this moment that I suggested that perhaps it would make an interesting gift for someone he did not like, and from the look of his expression, I have a sneaking suspicion of what I may find in my Christmas stocking. I have a brooding picture taken of him with his head unaccountably stuck in a lampshade. Perhaps he was looking for enlightenment?

So the dreaded gardening could not be avoided, the bad back excuse having been flushed out early. It was very unfair for that Nice Lady Decorator to put that one euro piece on the floor and then as I stooped to pick it up triumphantly say "there is nothing wrong with your back". My back does genuinely ache now, after spending a good part of the day slashing and macheteing my way through the undergrowth but I drew the line when she said there was room for more on the trailer.

Last night was another failure on the abstinence front. I was nursing the bad back in the hammock when that Nice Lady Decorator suggested a sun downer, and I only agreed because I thought I might get some relief. However, all she had in mind was a drink in the late afternoon sunshine, and like a man with no willpower I agreed, although my suggestion to her that she bring me a cold beer to the hammock as I was comfortable did not find favour.

Book Launch, The Heavens Speak

Who was it, over the weekend who was complaining about the lack of rain because his lawn was still requiring watering? I do not recall who the guilty party was but I hold them entirely responsible for the deluge that has descended on us in the last 24 hours. I took the picture below of my lawn yesterday morning, receiving some rain as requested by my guest at the weekend. Maybe now is the time to turn off the automatic watering system?

On a day such as yesterday, there is very little one can do except office work, planning, and I think our Americans friends call it brainstorming? So the opportunity to brainstorm and plan over lunch at Auberge Provencal in Valbonne which was offered by Valbonne's very own ex-pat mortgage broker, Matt Frost, was timely and welcomed by both myself and that Nice Lady Decorator as time out from her decorating duties. But with the Auberge Provencal shut for reasons unknown, lunch was transferred to the ever reliable Auberge St Donat. The planning aspect of the meeting over lunch was the most difficult to agree. Basically we have too many people coming to the book launch and not enough room for anything else, so lunch in situ at the venue was designed to enable us to consider what was to be done. But no matter, a few glasses of wine and we could imagine anything.

God overdoing the rain bit

So dear readers, I do not want you running away with the notion that I was squandering time on lunch, oh no, decisions of enormous import were at least considered. The conclusions? They are secret.

So secret that I cannot remember them, or more likely I have deliberately forgotten them due to an invitation to extend lunch at the Buftons (of which more later), but I am sure any actions required were successfully delegated to whoever will be in charge.

What I do remember was a discussion between Roly Bufton (who was celebrating his wedding anniversary with the lovely Lesley) who joined us as we sat down, and Matt Frost about Napoleon. You might think that this would be a perfectly acceptable discussion, deep in France about one of their most historically important leaders? Well, what seemed to be exercising their minds more than his march across the Alps (or was that Hannibal?) was the Radio 4 programme about a supposed on-going conversation between Marengo and Copenhagen. In case you did not read the classics, and here I must declare an interest, you may not know (as indeed I did not) that Marengo was the name of Napoleon's horse and Copenhagen was the name of Wellington's horse. It seems that Radio 4 were broadcasting or were about to broadcast a programme that suggests that the two horses were in contact and that they exchanged views prior to the battle of Waterloo or whatever it was they were fighting over. This seems to me to be an entirely acceptable use of the tax payers millions; people can die of starvation in Africa, but the BBC can still spend money on a latter-day version of a re-enactment of a variation on Mr. Ed, the talking horse. Splendid!

You will remember I mentioned during the deluge on Tuesday, and the emergency decamping of the meeting about the book launch to The Auberge St Donat, that after lunch we were invited back to Roly and Lesley Bufton's hilltop palace to avoid floating off into Valbonne? They were also in the restaurant so, the invitation to drink champagne and watch the rains was too much for that Nice Lady Decorator to refuse, and I have to say she did not care whose anniversary it was in any event, if champagne is on offer then she will be there and it is my duty to follow.

I say decamped, and I hope I will not be misinterpreted here (or should I be saying Mr. Interpreted?) but there was no sign of Mr. Humphrey's, so perhaps he will have decamped in time for church at Café Latin on Friday.

No No At Nounou

With the sun shining and the air still surprisingly warm, and it being a Sunday, lunch on the beach beckoned. I had heard that Nounou on the coast at Golfe Juan was highly recommended as a seafood establishment, with the speciality of the house being bouillabaisse -basically fish stew. What I did not know until after we were seated and it was too late to escape was that although it was very good and very comfortable right on the beach, it is also very expensive, and I had to talk that Nice Lady Decorator out of ordering the lobster bouillabaisse at a price a little over 90 euros, this is about £79. I should have known, with no way to see in to the seating area and no menu to peruse outside, the trap was beautifully laid. The meal however was exemplary, John Dory in a wonderful lemon sauce for me whilst that Nice Lady Decorator tucked into Dorade Supreme baked in salt. The surroundings were also very pleasant although there were one or two pieces of furniture and er..."art" which perhaps would struggle to find a place in my house.

The memory of the bill was sufficiently engraved on my conscious mind to ward off sleep at siesta time, which was a pity as sleep was more necessary than normal as we had a dinner engagement later.

Earlier in the day I had taken my morning constitutional into Valbonne to collect the Sunday Times. The questions lurking in my mind at the moment concern the speech I must make at the launch of my book, which will be attended by actor and improvisation artist Stephen Frost and the enigmatic John Otway. That I must follow Stephen, a professional and brilliant comic, to speak is something that has exercised my mind somewhat recently. I think the idea will be to say something short and sweet and sit down before the heckling gets too intense and allow the self-styled rock and roll failure Mr. Otway to say a few words and play a couple of songs and get the flak.

Pieces Of Eight

If anyone before today had suggested that the Nice Lady Decorator had the look of a pirate, I would have had to fight them. However, after managing to stick a plant into her eye yesterday and her now sporting the resultant eye patch, her piratical nature is evident for all to see. Any suggestions concerning parrots on shoulders will be dealt with summarily, if she ever gets to hear them.

I thought she said "pieces of eight" when discussing the seating plan for my imminent book launch but it turns out that what she was saying was "places for eight" an entirely different concept, and one that she illustrated by attempting to give me a black eye when I mentioned it. It was a mistake anyone could have made. She really got her hook into me. Anyway, she amused herself last night by watching half of Midsomer Murders, the left half.

Recently, The Master Mariner discovered on my phone a number of photos taken after the recent Rugby World Cup where a happy collection of well-greased rugby fans were invited back to our house by that Nice Lady Decorator. As you can see things got a little out of hand. Perhaps it was the sight of all those big strong men that stirred up long forgotten emotions in a couple of public schoolboys, both old enough to know better. I cannot name the miscreants but Blind Lemon Milsted and the Wingco may be squirming a little when they see this. The Master was particularly keen on this picture and I must admit it is rather intimate and touching? Although who is doing more of the touching is something I do not want to delve into as you must appreciate.

The Master Mariner also has a touch of the pirate about him, claiming that he was going to sail into Cannes this week to lunch despite the G20 summit meaning the whole town is just about locked down. He has a scheme in mind that I cannot reveal but from what I recollect it involves flares, fertiliser orders, men overboard and a three-pronged RIB attack on Cannes harbour. However, I am reasonably certain he awoke this morning and imagined it was a dream. I certainly hope so, but I will go and visit him in prison if he goes through with it.

Two older chaps who should know better having a cuddle on our living room floor.

Look Behind You Mr. Wolff

Many nicknames have emanated from this column, mainly as a result of my feeble attempts to protect the drunk, the depraved and the guilty after their being caught out doing something stupid or worse, but I am not responsible for naming "Wonky eyed Pete", apparently well-known in the less salubrious establishments in Valbonne. No connection can be made with the nice wonky eyed lady decorator, still sporting an eye patch and dark glasses after mutilating herself in a friends garden earlier in the week. I told her she has to look out for herself and keep an eye out for dangerous plants. It seems that I am not as funny as I think I am.

John Otway calls to give me the exciting news that the BBC is re-screening on New Year's Eve his epic Top Of The Pops appearance in 1977. He will apparently be interviewed to discuss the inner meaning of "Cor Baby, That's Really Free" (the title of his first hit) for the programme but I suspect he will use this as a shameless opportunity to promote Otway The Movie, the feature film he has made about himself on a tiny budget. How tiny? For instance, he has asked me to cost a helicopter shoot over Lake Geneva, to get an aerial shot of his playing his epic song of the same name with a small orchestra, aboard a boat on the lake as it enters the harbour in Geneva. I think he thinks we can do it for about thirty quid. My good friend Marc Wolff who lives nearby has organised and flown many aerial stunts for major feature films including most James Bond, Blackhawk Down, Harry Potter etc. so I have asked him to cost this out. I am awaiting Mr. Wolff's quotation and for some reason, probably the fact that involvement in any of Otway's amusing but crackpot schemes over the years has cost me money, I am reminded of a childhood game which involved saying "look behind you Mr. Wolf".

Chapter 3

Cannes Canned

With the G20 summit taking place in Cannes and horror stories reaching me of almost lock down in the centre of the town, plus warnings that some lanes on the motorway were going to be closed between Nice Airport and Cannes to allow presidential types to avoid the motorway tolls, I thought I should leave plenty of time to get to the airport for my flight to misery (England) yesterday. Eighteen minutes after setting, off I was at the airport, two and a half hours before my flight. No one had told me it was a public holiday in France and the roads would be empty.

So the joys of EasyJet were once again visited upon me and I will suffer similar ignominy this evening when I fly back, parental duty done for this week. However with two children to clear up behind, I will have to do the same thing all over again next week for Sprog 2. There are many things from France that I always miss when I am away, but one thing that I do not miss is their love of gaudy decorative items, and one that I would never miss, especially if I had a gun, is most of the decorative items in the renowned fish restaurant Nounou at Golfe Juan at the weekend. Indeed Nounou is exactly what I would say if I go there again and I am paying.

It is hard to believe that whilst we have been enjoying this rather warm and very pleasant weather down here in the South of France that the skiing season will be upon us in a month. It is much easier to believe that skiing would be available near Guildford considering the weather greeting my return to the old country. I had arranged, or rather, Mr. Clipboard had arranged, for us to have lunch at an Argentinian steak house in Guildford at 2.20 after meeting at the Angel Post House as long as I caught the 13.41 from Gatwick to Guildford and it was not delayed. Doubtless he would have had a contingency plan had this not worked out. He is particularly good at organising anything, especially when it involves eating food, at which he is a master. Caucaucau was the name of the restaurant I think, and cow was what we ate.

Sadly I was not accompanied by that Nice Lady Decorator on this occasion, as she is still doing her Long John Silver eye-patch act back in France due to stabbing herself in the eye etc. That of course required me to drink more beer than I had originally intended, ably assisted by Sprog 1 who more than stood in for her in the beer drinking stakes.

Exciting news arrived that I have been invited to sign and sell copies of my book at The France Show in Earls Court by Currencies Direct, one of the lead sponsors of the show which takes place in January. Some may consider that the book launch next Monday in Valbonne could also be loosely described as The France Show, but I could not possibly comment. This great opportunity to spread the news of the lives of the idle rich in Valbonne is tempered by the fact that I will have to spend several days in London in mid-January in deepest winter, but there it is: The price of fame. I must be strong.

Book Launch Preparations In Tatters

I think it was after the fourth time that Nice Lady Decorator had torn up my proposed speech for my book launch on Monday, that we got the call confirming that the deputy mayor of Valbonne would be delighted to attend the sold out low-brow literary event. I now have a speech in tatters and she has to undertake a desperate reorganisation of the table plan to see if we can squeeze her in. Yes the deputy mayor is a woman. That she was very late in replying can have nothing whatever to do with her gender.

Actually, I am enormously impressed that the mayor's office

decided that this bench mark event should be sealed with mayoral approval. The mayor's office in France carries much more power than back in England, covering most aspects of daily life including granting planning applications; With our grandiose plans sitting on the mayor's desk as we speak, you will understand why it will be important to accommodate his deputy.

This is one of the scariest things I have ever had to do. Standard advice, if in doubt, is to err on the side of caution, but on the run through this evening there was so much umming and erring, it looks like I shall be taking caution to new levels. I think I must have been a member of the rock group Golden Earing in a previous life (you need to say earing in a Merseyside accent for that joke to work).

As one storm began to abate, the next storm is due to blow into town today. Thunderstorms of immense intensity over the past few days have flooded roads and gardens (mine) and filled up my swimming pool to the brim, but I suspect that the intensity of the oncoming storm, this time in the shape of John Otway and various Frosts, including Stephen Frost the actor from Black Adder and Mr. Bean, who are both guests of honour on Monday at the Auberge Provencal in Valbonne, will be of equally biblical proportions.

Yesterday after a particular violent weather outburst, that Nice Lady Decorator and I braved the tempest and headed down to the Brague, which was running through the Valmasque forest with astonishing power and majesty. Perhaps I should not have taken a tennis ball with me, but with Max the faithful family retainer, the amiable English Springer, safely tied up on his lead, I felt that the calamitous canine Banjo, the dog that no one except that Nice Lady Decorator wanted in the house, might benefit from a bit of extra exercise, having been unable to be out much in the recent weather.

Swimming is one of his favourite hobbies (in my swimming pool) but I suspected he had always wanted to try something a little more invigorating. Unfortunately for both Banjo and I that Nice Lady Decorator put a stop to our little game before it could even start, so he was forbidden to pitch his strength against the river in pursuit of a tennis ball and thus sadly, once again, he has survived. If it had all gone well, given the speed of the water, he would have been all at sea within about 10 minutes.

The rehearsal of the speech was once again a disaster and I am fast coming to the conclusion that its successful delivery will only to come pass if I have had several stiff ones before getting up to speak. I suggested this to that Nice Lady Decorator but from the look in her eye she had misinterpreted the expression ""stiff ones" and was thus not entirely convinced that this method would work.

Frost On Fire

Before the great lunch launch today at the Auberge Provencal, I thought it would be good to spend some time with my lead sponsor, Matt "Cornish Tsunami" Frost, and host to several other Frosts including one of my special guests for the launch, Stephen Frost. From the times I have seen him on TV on "Whose Line Is It Anyway", and after meeting him at Glastonbury, and then meeting his and Matt's brother Simon the evening before, I quickly formed the impression that a Frost gathering might be a slightly noisy affair. When one adds to this potentially cacophonous ensemble, the arrival in town of my other special guest and oldest friend, John Otway, I suddenly realised that if I wanted to be sure to be welcomed back to my favourite local restaurants, then avoiding them altogether for such a potentially rowdy Sunday lunch might be quite a good idea.

The decision then to lunch at Capriccio in Chateauneuf was an inspired one. A party of 9 including three large and ebullient Frost brothers was just never going to be a gentle affair and there was the potential to destroy a quiet Sunday lunch for a large number of people in a very short time. As it was, I think we got away with it, just, and the large tip seemed to placate the management and staff that had to wait for a full hour after the other less than happy diners had left to rid themselves of the exuberant Brits.

So, nicely oiled, we picked our way through the rain ravaged countryside and returned to the Pav (where else?) in order to drink copious amounts of wine and plan proceedings for today. At least that was the intention and I am certain that arrangements were made and the details sealed later at The Queens Legs in Valbonne; and if I remember any of them then I am not entirely certain they will aid my fragile confidence in my ever shortening talk today. I took this picture at the post prandial discussions were nearing their peak. You may notice that it appears to be dark, indicating I think the great detail that was discussed and the intensity of that planning process.

John Otway and Stephen Frost plan my downfall in the Pav

The massive deluge which seems to have engulfed half of southern Europe has at last abated, but yesterday morning, before collecting the chaps from the airport, was spent mopping up the river that had decided to flow through my living room last night. At least it had the common decency to leave as quickly as it arrived; I just wish it had taken all the leaves and Banjo with it. Thank God for tiled floors, and being married to a Nice Lady Decorator.

Tomorrow it will all be over and from the Wingco's perspective the unthinkable will have occurred and I will be able to call myself a published author, or better still, a novelist.

The Launch Floats

It seems that I got away with my speech. The fact that I left out half of it and got some of the rest of the content muddled up, mainly because I could not read my notes as vanity (already on display in the publishing sphere) precluded my wearing of reading glasses. However it seemed not to have been noticed by the happy assembled throng.

Matt Frost, one of my sponsors for the book launch lunch, introduced his far more famous brother Stephen to introduce me. Stephen is a seriously funny man. His ten minute talk was a fearfully difficult act to follow, especially for a nervous public speaking debutante. The day before at lunch at Capriccio, apprehensive at the prospect of speaking to nearly 90 people, I had sought his advice about what to do on the day and whether he could offer any tips . He replied "Keep it short and convince yourself that everybody wants to hear what you are saying". As a confidence booster this was not a great deal of help. Well, I kept it short, mainly for the reason stated above, as to the convincing part, well, I remain unconvinced.

John Otway was in inspired form, playing a handful of songs including the 7th best song of all time (according to the BBC) but I am not entirely convinced that the small French contingent, including the deputy mayor of Valbonne, quite understood the lyrics of "Beware Of The Flowers 'Cause I'm Sure They're Gonna Get You, Yeah".

A staggering number of books were sold on the day, including 5 bought by Peter Bennett from Blue Water who took my advice about buying some as Christmas presents. I had suggested that they might make a good present for people you don't like, but I suppose customers may come into that bracket. The alternative interpretation is that he wanted to give some of his customers something brilliant and witty to celebrate the forthcoming festive season, and very good value at just 12 euros, and one with which I am sure the Wingco would take exception.

Yes, the Wingco was there to witness the "ghastly" publication being born, but as he had previously made clear, he was there for the lunch rather than the book. There will however be no respite, no rest for a weary but happy novelist. That Nice Lady Decorator has a plan to stop the house being flooded and I am fearful that the cement mixer will be pressed into service, which can only mean that a man, who was yesterday enjoying huge literary success amongst his friends, will today be labouring at the cement mixer. How the mighty have already fallen. One final note, and here I must raise a note of concern; some people in attendance managed to avoid purchasing said item at the lunch last Monday. I know where you live and am prepared to name names and reveal indiscretions of those who fail to heed this warning. The Wingco however is excused.

They Think It's All Over

As I awoke Mr. Otway from the deepest of slumbers yesterday morning, to get him to the airport in time to catch his plane back to England, I spotted the brandy glass beside his bed, with still some brandy left in it. It was a reminder that, after a long lunch, a serious session in La Kavanou, peeling off to The Queens Legs and then falling out of there for a late night drunken curry at the Kashmir, that, rather unbelievably, we were still thirsty when we got to my house and considered a brandy as a suitable and necessary night-cap. John was pleased with himself because he had not drunk all of it. What willpower!

A day such as Monday would have been enough for a mere hard-drinking mortal for a week, but of course we had done something similar on the Sunday in the company of Steve Frost and his brothers Simon and Matt in Valbonne this week.

I now have some pictures from the launch and show one of these today. You will see that it is of a celebrity, a man who has appeared alongside some of the greatest living comedians and in some of the best sitcoms ever made holding a copy, one may even say clutching lovingly a copy of a certain book launched successfully this week.

THE VALBONNE MONOLOGUES

Is it just me or does Stephen Frost look like he could be Alistair Darlings love child? He has good literary taste don't you think?

Startlingly, the Deputy Mayor of Valbonne, laughed when she should and we now have a meeting with her to discuss future events. This represents the opportunity for a great breakthrough: We have grandiose plans, although I admit some of these were formulated under the influence of a post book launch alcoholic haze.

So by the time most of the regular readers of this column are reading this, (it is Wednesday, the launch was on Monday, Otway departed yesterday) I will have been up at the crack of sparrows to board a plane for the glories of Gatwick. It is my parental duty to go to Sprog 2's parents evening and then to drink loads of proper English beer and feed both as Sprog 1 is coming up from Guildford for the evening.

It is a struggle because I am still feeling the effects of the weekend and Monday despite not a drop passing my lips on Tuesday. That was made more possible by staying in my bed for most of the daylight hours, and managing not to read the texted invitation to join Stephen, Matt and Simon Frost for lunch at the Auberge St Donat, which was a very fine decision.

In the carnage that has enveloped me over the past few days, I have managed to forget about the ubiquitous notes I make on my BlackBerry when I hear something weird or stupid. So yesterday, whilst on the train from Gatwick to Victoria, I had a look back at the notes I had made and there are some gems.

Last Saturday, before alcoholic events depleted reason and memory to minuscule levels, I popped in for an early evening glass of wine with the Cornish Tsunami himself, Matt Frost, who was busily trying to tidy the place up before the arrival of his brothers. Perhaps surprisingly for these huge man mountains, they are very well-educated and very well-read but then common sense does not automatically go hand in hand with intelligence. Consider this; I caught Matt polishing his fridge and cursing that the grey metallic surface of it was not very bright, certainly a lot duller than when he had purchased it new. It was at that moment that I spotted a small imperfection on the surface which looked like a hole, and discovered that it was indeed a small hole.....in the protective plastic coating the fridge had arrived in when it was bought. Yes, he had been diligently polishing the plastic coating. After I had stopped laughing, which admittedly was some time later, I asked how long ago he had purchased it. The answer;-Six years! Bright indeed!

There was another story about him building a home-made guillotine in his garden to chop the vegetables on Bastille Day, which did not impress his French guests in quite the way he had hoped, but he has had enough stick for one day, so I will not mention it.

Parents Evening - Nasty

So then, Last night to parents evening after a couple of pints of London Pride to settle the nerves. After receiving the customary telling off from the teachers because of the poor attention to detail and general lack of respect exhibited by Sprog 2, clearly the-off spring of a certain Nice Lady Decorator, we adjourned to feed the wolves or children as that she prefers to call them. I say wolves because it seems to be a teenage trait, perhaps even a higher form of nature for a teenager who has been away from home for some time, to be hungry and thirsty as soon as parents arrive, and to develop tastes hitherto undiscovered, especially if they are expensive. I am a struggling author for Christ's sakes (this last bit especially for the reverend Jeff, whose claim to fame is that the Daily Mail has published a number of his poems). Anyway, the telling off evening was enlivened by a generous supply by the college of quite decent Bordeaux designed to ease the pain of hearing about one's expensive children's activities, before departing for that fleecing by my Sprogs at a Chinese restaurant in Earls Court. Locusts could not be more destructive, mosquitoes no more determined to snare their prey; Me. We then retired to bed to be awoken at 4am by the fire alarm. A hair dryer. At 4am. That was the reason given for the fire alarm at our squalid hotel near Earls Court going off. Who is using a hair dryer at 4am? And then again at 6am? I wished with every fibre of my being that they had been in the bath at the same time with very soapy slippery fingers.

Santa Clause falling on hard times?

Yesterday morning I was subjected to one of my least favourite activities; shopping in London. I was not looking forward to witnessing the lack of Christmas spirit that is encapsulated in Oxford Street in London's West End, but even I was shocked by the picture I took of Father Christmas selling the thrusting left-wing magazine, created to help the unemployed; "The Big Issue". As you can see, times must be hard for Santa, he has clearly lost a great deal of weight either through recessionary pressures, or perhaps the frankly, much needed, gastric band had been tightened a couple of notches too far? I also like the nice touch with the dog, or is in an emaciated reindeer?

Some London Pride was required at lunch time to help take off, indeed I have been flying for so long, at least two weeks without much respite, I guess I should be more concerned with the landing which will commence today as I wind down towards the weekend.

Return To Valbonne

Meetings yesterday in Valbonne allowed me the rare opportunity to drop into church, aka Cafe Latin. I had with me several unsold copies of my book "Summer in the Cote d'Azur" which sadly remained unsold despite my best efforts to change their status. Obviously people don't want to buy Christmas presents too early. I had hoped to encounter Mr. Humphrey's to see if he was free, and he was. I was, however, rather alarmed to see that my style guru was wearing the same leather jacket as he been wearing on Monday. How can that be? Also, after I had asked if he was saving up for the collar I thought perhaps he might rethink that particular item, but with the misplaced conviction of a man who knows when he looks good, he dismissed my comments with an imperious toss of the head, much in the style of Larry Grayson.

Earlier in the day, that Nice Lady Decorator and I had set off for a walk along The Brague River, but she slipped over and landed in the mud (normally a fleeting concept down here but still much in evidence after last week's deluge). I suggested that I took a picture of her in her full muddy glory but the laser beam eyes were employed and a total sense of humour failure followed, so I changed the subject and took a picture of the level to where the river had risen to last week, although I think inadvertently I did get a bit of the rear view of her in by mistake.

Gardening: A word that strikes horror deep into my soul. It dawned bright and sunny yesterday morning and I was just beginning to contemplate taking the new John Grisham novel out to the hammock for a little rest and recuperation, and to ensure that his writing standards had not slipped below mine, when I was intercepted and suddenly presented with gardening gloves and various wicked looking implements, apparently often used in outdoor areas. Was it Winston Churchill who, when describing golf, called it "an activity invented in hell with implements designed by the devil"? He got it wrong; this statement sums up exactly how I feel about gardening.

On the left edge of this photo is some wood washed up showing the level The Brague reached last weekend, on the right is the more normal level of the river

So as the late great rugby league commentator Eddie Waring used to say, I went for an early bath after my garden exertions. At least my exertions in the garden bring a more positive result than the exertions of that faeces filled fido, Banjo. I was asked, and under pressure, had agreed to take a trailer full of cuttings and garden refuse to the local recycling depot in Valbonne, but the attempt by that Nice Lady Decorator to smuggle a bucket full of his calling cards into the trailer that she had collected before I could mow the lawn came to nothing. It is her dog; she can dispose of his droppings.

An Early Frost

Winter will soon be upon us, so today I have a picture of some early Frosts, these were photographed in Bluebell the camper which had to be pressed into service last weekend during the rains as that 4×4 decided to get itself a bit wet and refuse to move.

That Nice Lady Decorator with Matt, Simon and Stephen Frost, who appears to be doing an Artful Dodger move.

I wondered why it was that Matt and Stephen Frost call Simon, their little brother, Walking Eagle. It seemed to me that Bald Eagle might be a more suitable nickname given the lack of hair in the picture above but Stephen said that there was a time when that was the case but that nowadays, he was so full of shit he would never get off the ground, so they had decided to call him Walking Eagle.

The signs are that there is some kind of gathering for Sunday lunch. As I have no executive power or authority in this department, I am eagerly awaiting news. I wonder where we are going. It is so exciting. I just know that Peachy Butterfield will be involved due to overhearing a chance telephone conversation, so one way or another

I shall be subjected to his latest find, a cheeky little Cote Du Rhone for 1.39 euros. I can feel my stomach cramps already.

A meeting with the mayor's office on Tuesday may open the door for a series of exciting events emanating from the modern comedy world here in Valbonne, but then again given my previous experience of trying to book the commune's facilities in the past, when I received a very De Gaulle like "Non" when I wanted to stage an event last year, I do not want to read too much into this; however, reports seem to indicate that the deputy mayor loved the book launch event and by all accounts seems to understand the value to the village of empowering the local ex-pat community for the good of village commerce. Rather interestingly, she has a brief to involve herself with the ex-pat communities.

Sunday, the traditional day of rest dawned bright and sunny, it was only later that the metaphorical clouds created by alcohol descended, but as usual, that was after an especially bright period. Lunch without knowledge, my knowledge that is, was about to take place. If I had cared to look, the signs were there; the enforced gardening yesterday, the especially long trip to the supermarket, the ridiculous bill for that Nice Lady Decorator "just popping out for a few things". However, I had my Sunday Times, the hammock, a tantalising view of snow on the highest mountains, warm sunshine and a coffee, and all was well with the world, until around 2pm when people started arriving.

Firstly (as usual) Master Mariner Mundell arrived early as is often the case. The Master must have misread the tides or there was a following wind or something, or perhaps a man who has been religiously circumcised (and that docs not mean he had sailed around the world if you get my err…drift) wanted to ensure that he extracted the maximum value from any situation.

Suzanne Butterfield appeared and then her husband Peachy hoved into view, although given his gargantuan size, hoving is perhaps a misnomer as there was not much of a view of anything else left. He was clutching a magnum of 2011 Cote du Rhone, so fresh it was still warm from the summer and with which he was particularly pleased. He seems to have eschewed the Mancunian

Merlot and the Accrington Stanley Asti Spumante and the other wine gems he has visited upon us in the past, having at last discovered cheap French wine, which is a move forward - however small. He did spend some time bemoaning the fact that the Cote Du Rhone he has found recently (which he considers a bargain) had apparently sold out, not being on the shelves. I think it is more likely that it been moved to the paint stripper department.

But then, just as I had come to terms with the probable destruction of my wine stocks, Matt Frost and his carer and wife Viv also appeared and I knew then it was going to be a big day. In situations such as these my faithful BlackBerry will record many a quip, jest or misplaced comment, which will often result in producing a gem for my research, and today is no exception. Some hilarity was heaped on Matt because of my piece earlier in the week where I had revealed that he had been cleaning his fridge and become frustrated that it would not polish up nicely, until I suggested he remove the protective plastic coating that had been in place for 6 years.

This morning I found a veritable treasure trove of interesting and sometimes embarrassing information on the BlackBerry when I finally had a chance to look at it. Did you know that more than one person it our midst thinks the Wingco looks like Joseph Stalin? However the best story emanated, perhaps inevitably, from Peachy Butterfield. It seems that when at a barbecue in the semi-frozen north of England last year, on the one day where the temperature reached double figures, Peachy was entertaining his mad Aunt and her friend. They had set up a kids' paddling pool in the garden, the equivalent of a swimming pool in the Cote d'Azur, in case they were overcome by the heat of the English summer and Peachy, after feasting on his usual diet of suet pudding, lard, tripe and road kill, and never being one to hold back, stripped to his love heart embellished underpants and jumped into the paddling pool. One would have thought that most of the water would have left at the same time, the displacement numbers being fairly clear; however, his 79-year-old aunt, not to be outdone, whipped off her dress to reveal she was topless beneath and joined him in the paddling pool.

Worse was to come- His aunts friend, a mere stripling of 77, decided to join in, to Peachy's (expressed) horror, she removed her dress to reveal nothing whatsoever underneath and also jumped in. Just to be clear about this, the result was that Peachy ended up in a paddling pool up north in the cold with two ladies averaging 78, with no bras and only two pairs of pants between the three of them. Perhaps it is best that I do not have a picture of that event, but to give you an idea, I have a picture of Peachy in his underwear accompanied by the Naked Politician.

Twins?

Comedy In Valbonne?

The beautiful deputy mayor did not stand a chance. Losing her voice on the day she was taking a meeting with myself and Matt Frost ensured that she did not get a word in edge ways. Suffice to say that she did not put up one word of objection to our proposals, and some exciting possibilities may eventually emerge...

The day's work done, we headed to the Vignale Tennis Club in the late morning for a doubles tennis match conceived over a few drinks on Sunday; despite myself and Master Mariner Mundell sailing to victory, there seemed to be some dispute about who won. 4-6, 6-1, although being nominally a draw at one set each it was in fact a victory for us on the count back. That it was not seen that way by the losing pairing, the Wingco and Mr. Frost, is a matter of some regret for me, but I am sure I will get over it, as must they.

Promotion of my book took up much of the afternoon; at least it took a great deal of thought, which I thought was best undertaken with my eyes closed whilst swaying in the hammock in the sunshine. I find I do some of my best thinking there, even although I often cannot remember what it was I thought. A press release was prepared later on and is now ready to tear into the literary maelstrom which will become my natural spiritual home in the future. From 50,075 to 29,500 in the Lulu best sellers list is a meteoric rise by any standard; a rise of over 20,000 places in one day? if you draw the graph on that one I will be in the top 10 by the weekend.

I shall be at The English Book Centre in the village on Friday to sign those personal copies as Christmas presents. I do hope you will not be put off by the rush. I hear that the crowd barriers will be in place early and that seems a wise precaution. Any suggestion that these will be used to keep people in until they have bought a signed copy is as heinous as it is true. Life has seldom been so good. Pat Toohey was delighted with her freshly signed and dedicated copies of Valbonne's latest and possibly greatest literary sensation (until the one you are reading now) my first book. Pat revealed to me that she has only once before sought personalised written dedications from an author and that was from the little known Peter Mayle who wrote a novel of similar standing to mine, "A year in Provence". OK, so my book only covers six months rather than a year, but that does not mean it's only half as good; No, it's much worse than that.

The picture below was taken at the book launch and features Tony "I invented the internet" Coombs making Stephen Frost laugh with his claims to have been the father of all modern technology. I think I overheard him telling the great improviser that he had just invented the I-lie, a do it yourself lie detection application. Apparently it kicks in as soon as you open your mouth.

You invented what?....... hahahahahahahahahahaha

After the mob that will undoubtedly be absent from today's signing, it is possible that I shall break my three days of temperance with a small lunch, perhaps at the Cafe des Arcades if the sun remains in evidence as it has all week.

A week today I will be heading to Africa and Kenya in particular. You may think that this could be a holiday, but even if purely for tax reasons I shall be working throughout. Medina Palms is a wonderful development on Watamu Beach which according to the Sunday Times is one of the top 10 beaches in the world. As an agent responsible for sales of units at this wonderful development, it is my irksome responsibility to test and if necessary to criticise any shortcomings I discover. Clearly to be able to do this effectively I will have to try all the facilities and spend some time on that beach ensuring that it is of the high standard reported.

Book Signing A Triumph

So after the excitement of the signing event at the English Book Centre in Valbonne for my book had subsided, and the crowd control barriers had been removed, quite a long time before they were deployed, we adjourned as I had predicted to the Cafe des Arcades in the village square for a quiet and well deserved lunch. I wanted to savour the sale of all three books sold at the mornings signing; However, if one is to be diverted from a quiet lunch, after a walk in the Valmasque forest in order to build up an appetite for lunch, who better then Master Mariner Mundell and the Naked Politician to create that diversion?

There are a number of characters at whose feet I would always like to be able to lay the blame for such diversions so to encounter the Naked Politician together with his lovely hand brake wife Dawn, also lunching in the sunshine in Valbonne Square suggested that luncheon was not going to be either short or simple. I sensibly made notes on my BlackBerry during the afternoon of some of the conversations that occurred before things got out of hand. It was the Master who persuaded us to stay longer at lunch and then and afterwards to go back to one of his residences. Initially I resisted of course but once that Nice Lady Decorator had granted tacit approval (by not forcefully confirming we were due to return home) then my post luncheon fate was confirmed. Before that, the Naked Politician seemed to forget that I write a daily column much read by his peers, and revealed rather too much information about his current activities. He is a very successful commercial property developer, so successful that he now resides in the errr...advantageous tax zone of Monaco.

He is well-known for being naked on occasions, as pictures that have appeared from time to time in this book will testify, but he is also a politician for part of the time, and a property mogul for the commercial part of his life. I made the mistake of questioning him about one particular property owned by one of his companies in Deansgate, Manchester which housed a snooker hall. I am a great lover of snooker and have a long standing affection for old snooker halls, having spent some of my early twenties in one of these where one of the artists I used to manage, Wild Willy Barrett, did some of his best work. The news that one of these venerable old establishments had fallen out with their landlords and were being closed down filled me with sadness. Yes, the Naked Politician is that landlord. But with every cloud there is a silver lining, so the closure of one of Manchester's most famous snooker halls was tempered with the knowledge that the venue would give way to what he described as "the biggest lap dance club in Britain, perhaps Europe." So, the Naked Politician will now have an excuse, nay a reason, to be in close proximity and with certain inalienable rights as a landlord to a lap dancing club? I also foresee possible problems.

I think I could write another book entitled "The Joys of Castorama, on a Saturday" after yesterday's debacle. Why that Nice Lady Decorator chooses a weekend to go to the busiest and worst laid out do-it-yourself store in the world is completely beyond me. What is wrong with the other days of the week, when most of the great unwashed are safely at work or looking for it? It seems that we needed some boards to repair the floor of my kennel, aka my office. I did not need them, she needed them, which is fine by me, but then suddenly I become involved simply because she needed someone to carry them, and so my weekend got off to a very poor start. You could say that I was board stiff, but I would not as that would be a very poor joke and one that you would not be right in thinking I would avoid.

REGS golf today at the wonderful St Donat will be the scene of another feeding frenzy of people battling to buy autographed copies of my book "Summer in the Cote D'Azur". I have advance orders for 3 copies but it will not stop there, in fact I have a target of an additional 4 copies to be sold on the day meaning that I shall soon be closing in on a century, more than half way towards breaking even just 2 weeks after the launch!

Rather disappointingly I have been told that Mick Pedley will not be wearing his German Shooting Trousers which will come as a bit of a relief to our token German member Klaus. I would have so loved to get a picture of him (Mick) wearing them, ideally accompanied by a shotgun. Amongst the regulars I am expecting to see at this Taylor Made sponsored event was Dave "Tripe" Goddard and sheep loving Steve Weston whom I will try to "fleece" on a wager. Just to show that the golf is played in the best possible spirit I have this picture of Nick Kail, one of the golfers, who seems to have forgotten to apply suntan lotion.

Chapter 4

Kenya

Kenya, and in particular my visit to Medina Palms which is newly featured in Country Life is rapidly approaching. This time next week I shall be there and, internet access permitting, I shall bring a you a daily run down on the lives of the idle rich of Kenya rather than the Cote d'Azur for a couple of weeks. It seems churlish not to take in a safari experience whilst there, and the shortest trip we could find was a half day, in part due to that Nice Lady Decorator's opposition to spending a night in the jungle. This seems to be the perfect stage for a rock chick brought up in the world of rock and roll but there you have it.

The tournament at St Donat was a success, mainly because of the sheer numbers of my book "Summer in the Cote D'Azur" which I sold, a massive and projected 7 sales.

The golf itself was crap and I don't want to talk about it, save to say that I must have been disturbed by the media hype about my book that may have existed only in my own mind. Most of the usual suspects were present, Mick Pedley was however without his German Shooting Trousers, but still our token German, Klaus was a no-show. Sheep loving Steve Weston was also notable by his absence, but he has already purchased a book and it was obviously going to provide him with great reading material on his way to the Dominican Republic, where he was holidaying, I forgive him. Anyway, the way I played, he would have fleeced me in any wager. Pauline Bull, the beautiful former Miss England and an active

REGS member not only won the ladies section but organised and directed the photo shoot for the Taylor Made management – (which was the very least we could do in return for their sponsorship) - one of the results of which I feature today. Her experience of appearing on TV and especially "The Generation Game" proved especially useful when dealing with the older generation which comprises most members if this golf association.

Taylor Made for Miss England

Serious preparations are being made now for my trip to Kenya as we leave on Friday. Before I can contemplate that though, I must once again engage in the joys of emptying the trailer at the local tip in Valbonne. Every time I empty the trailer that Nice Lady Decorator fills it up again. There is thus, in my opinion, nothing to gain from emptying it. Needless to say; the request to empty it, which is accompanied by that laser beam eye expression, changes everything. I did have the temerity to think that if I left it full all the time then it could just stay in position and that she could no longer pile stuff in it, but this thought did not reach my mouth. I am, of course, at the very least a coward of the highest order.

They say the darkest hour is just before dawn, (although my old mate Wild Willy Barrett used to claim the darkest hour was just before the next darkest hour) but she was not even in the picture adorning this column yesterday, and anyway I will not have a word said against her.

No such claim to darkness can possibly be levelled at the subject of the photo below, well, certainly not to the photo itself anyway. Of course there is always likely to be some darkness wherever the shadow of this man mountain is cast. It is of course Matt Frost, Valbonne's very own mortgage broker in the village. There seems to be some kind of sartorial cry for help going on here. I like the shirt and I like the hat, but combining them? I have no pretensions to good taste; in fact I have heard it stated that I have absolutely no taste, however, even I would not be as daring as to attempt to combine a brightly coloured Brazilian shirt with a cricket hat when invited to lunch. It is a pity we cannot see what are on his feet - Flippers perhaps? The picture was taken at a recent luncheon at my house before the customary degeneration in standards of behaviour, and clearly before my style guru Mr. Humphreys had expressed an opinion.

No, no and no.

It cannot now be long before I get the expected call from Marina Kulik to be a model in her popular painting classes held in Plascassier. I have been working on the bulges and wrinkles that her class apparently find very rewarding to paint and am actively looking forward to receiving the 22 euros an hour that I shall be paid for doing nothing. Doing nothing for money is what I have often been accused of during my career in the music industry and the ensuing royalty flow that helps cover my daily expenses, but I put it down to meticulous planning and careful use of the existing mechanisms in place to pay songwriters and recording artist for their work. This must be the reason I am drawn to the idea of getting paid for doing nothing more than making a spectacle of myself like the man in the above shot. Now there's a word that could be used in the context of this picture, and with more than one meaning: shot.

I popped into the Queens Legs in Valbonne last night for a pint of Guinness with that Nice Lady Decorator and when I came out I saw a Gendarme issuing a parking ticket. I asked him if he could take pity on an old man but he would not listen, so as anyone would do, I questioned his parentage, and then threw a few more insults whereupon he issued another ticket for bald tyres. He was just getting quite nasty when my bus arrived. You have to find your amusement in different ways as you get older.

Earlier in the day, in late afternoon I was sitting quietly in the lounge cursing the intermittent internet connection, when suddenly there was an ear splitting crash and just about every drinks glass in the house smashed to the floor.

That Nice Lady Decorator has been working on a new glass cupboard for a couple of days, repainting it and generally repairing it to ensure it was fully functional, but it appears that the glass shelf supports were not as strong as she had hoped and the whole edifice succumbed to gravity in a spectacular fashion. It was vital that she was there in the room when it happened and that I was nowhere near the cupboard; otherwise there is no doubt in my mind about who would have received the blame. Despite the fact that I was there when it happened but on the other side of the room and could not possibly have had anything to do it, I have still caught a glimpse of that look that implies I must be in some way to blame.

Actually it is a godsend on one level as before this tumultuous event, we had such a mish mash of unmatched glasses in the drinks cupboard, left over from sets from which one or more had been broken, that now she will be able to go and buy some that match, or more likely I shall be delegated to go and restock our glass cabinet on her behalf.

I mentioned a dodgy internet connection, but help will soon be at hand. Tony "I invented the Internet" Coombs is due to come round this evening with his lovely wife Pat, so before he gets as much as a glass of wine I will get him to fix his infernal invention. Actually it may be more like a tumbler of wine or even a cup unless I am forced to go shopping this morning before tennis, which has been rearranged for 11am due to constant backsliding by several of our party on the scheduled 6pm kick off.

The amply endowed (sorry Lin) and smouldering Maria Louisa Santos Carr sends me a message via Facebook correcting my report about who won the ladies grouping of the REGS golf tournament at St Donat last weekend. It seems it was she, rather than former Miss England, Pauline Bull, as I had reported yesterday, who was victorious, but when one has two such dazzling ladies in close proximity one tends to forget one's own name on occasions. I use the word smouldering as it also reminds me of Dave "Tripe" Goddard, leader of the Landlubbers off shoot golfing group, with whom I must state she has absolutely no connection, – I must add when I think of him smouldering it is more in terms of a smoky peat fire which most people from Yorkshire still use for heat.

Lunch was taken at the Auberge St Donat after an exhausting game of tennis yesterday morning in sparkling autumn sunshine. The result is not in doubt; the MOGs won. That's an end to it. During lunch it became clear that the Wingco objects forcefully to being compared to Stalin, and is of course, the sole reason for me to continue with the comparison, a fact that I think he is gradually coming to terms with, especially after I told him that was the case. As to the tennis, it was one set all when luncheon loomed up on us was but if you look at the scores, 4-6, 6-3, tennis aficionados will have calculated that although nominally a draw, one team secured more games than the other; Thus on the count-back principle, that I am proud to have established, there is a clear winning team, and by definition, a pair of losers. That I was part of that winning team might be construed as blowing one's own trumpet, but let's face it, facts are facts.

My honour is being impugned. Pat Coombs, who arrived at our house last on Tuesday evening with her husband Tony "I invented the internet" Coombs, is convinced that the photograph on the front cover of my book "Summer in the Cote d'Azur" in part exposes my manhood, the right one as you look. Indeed can there be a wrong one? My position is that it is clearly a part of my knee, but I can see that in certain lights and with the benefit of a magnifying glass, that this relatively benign pose could be misinterpreted.

This is the only reason that I again show the possibly offending front cover, and in no way could this featuring be construed as a cheap marketing opportunity to sell more books in the run up to Christmas. That will happen a little nearer the festive season.

Left knee or left gonad? you decide

Kenya Here We Come

Yesterday afternoon it was my duty to meet with the very beautiful Cathie the Culture, the cultured Australian, in Cafes Des Arcades in Valbonne to complete the necessary documentation to open her account with Currencies Direct. Part of this process requires me to secure a copy of a passport and a utility bill, quite easily obtained from home by use of a scanner, or if that was too technically challenging for La Culture we could meet up for a drink after I get out of Africa... I suggested that she may be able to scan these and email them to me, but received a blank expression, the sort you receive when asking a 5-year-old to explain Einstein's Theory Of Relativity. I explained how to do it but later received an email saying that she felt she was "technically challenged" and was looking forward to that drink.

Today we leave the wonderfully sunny south of France for a night in the tender hands of a hotel near Heathrow before heading off to Nairobi on Saturday. The hotel is called the Jury's Inn, but frankly, until we have experienced the hotel itself the Jury is out. Peter Lynn, who recommended this hotel, kindly remarks that he hopes that all traces of the recent typhus outbreak there have been eradicated, but I said I only ever drink Earl Grey tea so it should be all right.

I have five British Airways pilots as friends, all of whom are long haul specialists. It is no secret that I have acquired economy class tickets from BA for my trip to Kenya, the land of vultures and predators (so a bit similar to Valbonne then) with the near certainty that one of my five close friends would be flying the plane or at the very least will do the decent thing and secure us an upgrade. Even if there is only one upgrade to be had, I know that the Nice Lady Decorator would insist that I received the benefit. As I write, there are 5 pilots all scurrying around doing their best to ensure that there are no slip ups. None of them will wish to risk failure in the clear duty and the subsequent punishment that would inevitably follow in this column. Messrs Warner, Coward, Macfadyen, Rogers and Allen, you have been warned.

It was a tough decision. After arriving at the faceless square grey box of a hotel called The Jury's Inn at London's Heathrow Airport, a recommendation from my old friend Peter Lynn, a decision had to be made. It was late afternoon; either take a late siesta, or go straight to the bar and go straight through to an early dinner and then bed? There was never really going to be any doubt, so we headed to the bar.

It's not that the hotel was uncomfortable, the wine undrinkable or the food inedible, it's just the mind numbing blandness and total lack of warmth that characterise these airport hotels that gets to me, and drives me to drink. After all, what else is to be done in this situation? What possible entertainment is to be had?

So an early start today, the reason we had to stay near the airport and by the end of the day we shall be in Africa. The Reverend Jeff comments that he will be expecting a number of terrible puns in the coming two weeks along the lines of "safari so good" and I told him that he was absolutely correct.

A very long day awaits us as we fly to Nairobi in Kenya for the trip down to Medina Palms on Watamu Beach south of Malindi. Regular readers will know that this trip cannot possibly be construed as anything else but work as I am an agent for this beautiful development, which was this week named in the Top 10 overseas developments in Country Life. That I have to see it with my own eyes is a given and we shall be staying at the showhouse "Alhamra", owned by old pal and cricketing pal Nigel "mad as a box of frogs" Rowley and his lovely wife Lesley.

My accountants will therefore not be surprised to know that I have the most solid grounds for submitting the expenses as a bone fide business expense. Clearly it will be necessary to have secretarial support in the form of the very beautiful Nice Lady Decorator, who has been complaining recently that I never have anything nice to say about her, which is probably true but does not reflect how I actually feel about her. However, before the real work commences on Monday, there will be time for a little relaxation, and this will take the shape of a "big cat experience" at the Nairobi National Park early on Sunday morning.

We are talking the real thing here, we are hoping to see some extra-large tabby cats, and if we are lucky enough to witness them it will be, as the Reverend suggests, safari so good. Sadly, work commitments will allow us just a short trip into the bush before flying down to Malindi from Nairobi on Sunday afternoon

We were already comfortably seated in economy, had given up all hope of an upgrade and I had started to plan my revenge on all the BA pilots who had failed in their clear duty, when suddenly a steward arrived and said that on the captains orders we were to collect our things and follow him. The people in the row behind gave knowing looks, thinking that we had been responsible for some misdemeanour and were being escorted off the plane, but we knew what it would presage, an upgrade! But delight turned to incredulity when we were taken through the Club World section into the First Class cabin. I was given seat number 1F, and that Nice Lady Decorator 2F. Any nearer the front and we would have been in the cockpit.

So I enjoyed the following - an excellent Grand Cru Classe Bordeaux from Lafitte, several glasses, followed by an Australian Mudpie desert wine that I had always wanted to try, and followed that with a XO Cognac whilst eating some divine food. That Nice Lady Decorator found an excellent 2008 Chablis which she proceeded to drink at such a speed that the captain had to keep retrimming the aircraft as the nose kept going up as the Chablis stock was depleted.

The Fairview Hotel in Nairobi was a good choice and I managed to get my first pictures of African wildlife, albeit on the walls of the hotel restaurant as it was dark by the time we arrived.

There was one person who was disappointed. Cathie The Culture wanted the following scenario visited upon me; to be seated next to three screaming kids, all snotty and full of cold being fed another can of full fat coca cola with added sugar and e numbers, just to ensure they were able to sustain for the whole nine-hour flight the cacophony that was already at full throttle in the departure lounge. Throttle, now there is a word that I would have happily put into practical use had this projection come true. It continues; the first toy was to hit me on the head as I was drinking a cup of tea. Hot tea. That tea was then to drop all over the nice white chinos I had worn in the vague hope that one of my pilot friends had stood up and been counted and had secured us an upgrade.

Thereafter, snot laden food, mostly crisps and chocolate stuffed with all the e numbers that coca cola had missed was consumed noisily and constantly, and the youngest of the three horrors would manage to drop some chocolate on to the by now almost ruined trousers. Had that been the case then I fervently hope that all three, and their shell suited perma-tanned parents die horrible slow lingering deaths in a lion's den in Africa.

Apart from a couple of short trips to Marrakech, a nightmare 3 days in Lagos, this is my first trip to Africa and I am looking forward to it as much as one can look forward to work, and work it was. As I said thank you to the pilot and gave the crew signed copies of my book, I managed to mention Currencies Direct, and they all took my card and expressed interest. My missionary work in Africa has begun.

It seems we were lucky as the Nairobi National Park had suffered four days of torrential rain before we got there, and it seems the heavens opened again later in the afternoon, but I suspect that as the writing gods knew that one of their peers was in their presence, that was reason enough for us to be greeted by pleasantly cool temperatures and some sunshine during our game drive.

A game drive, now there's an interesting expression. It could refer to the Wingco driving me home to Valbonne having imbibed well, or it could have either shooting or computer game connotations, but as we are in Africa I suppose it will mean a drive into the bush to seek wild game. And just to satisfy the Reverend Jeff (who had predicted a string of lousy safari puns) we were lucky the wind had died down and we were not in a giraffe. In a single morning we managed to see giraffes, buffalo, a rhino and some sleeping lions, impala, baboons, and even some warthogs. There were also some vultures trying to sell us overpriced icons, but that was later.

Dave Maskell, our guide and big cat specialist enlivened the drive with colourful stories of lions and his work with them, including being mauled by one in 2003 leaving him badly injured. I noticed that he carried a gun in a holster and assumed it was protection in case a predator came too close, which in part was true, but more recently it had been used to dispatch two intruders from his house one night. He knew they were coming because his dog had been poisoned two days earlier. In Kenya it seems that you can defend your house in any manner you deem fit. I have a picture of some ostriches which crossed the road in front of our game drive vehicle, an ancient Mercedes Jeep with an open top and a large shelf to stand on.

A few birds I found on safari

The flight from Wilson airport to Malindi in the afternoon was punctuated by a stop at Lamu, which we were not sure was scheduled, but hey, this is Africa and eventually we arrived in Malindi where we were met by old friend and madman, and the inspiration behind Medina Palms, Nigel Rowley. Buying about 50 mango's on the way for a little over £2, he then transported us to heaven in the shape of Alhamra, his house which is a showcase for Medina Palms which we visited briefly on the way and of which more later in the week.

Staff took our bags, staff welcomed us with a glass of

champagne, staff cooked dinner and served wine, staff did all the clearing away, staff tidied and sprayed our room and secured and set the mosquito nets, so vast that frankly they would not fit into any room in my house, whilst we had dinner. I have thus deduced that I need staff.

Also staying at Alhamra is Ben Dobson, who despite being from up north somewhere (Southport?) is something high up at Adidas, high enough to have secured tickets for the Adidas box for myself and that Nice Lady Decorator at Lords for England versus India in the summer. Yesterday then, as our hosts were otherwise engaged on site meetings, and after a leisurely breakfast, we all headed along Watamu beach in search of a restaurant located on the sand at which to have lunch. Ocean Sports was its name and very pleasant it was too.

Lunch revolved around a very long meeting and subsequent meticulous examination of the merits of an investment at Medina Palms. The conclusions were extremely positive,- The place is amazing, by Valbonne standards incredibly cheap, wonderfully spacious and with a new International airport to open at Malindi in the near future.

Having arrived at the restaurant a little after midday, where one could and did order the finest fresh fish, served on a shady sundeck, watching the tide come in from the Indian Ocean over the white sands of Watamu for little more than £4, we left, well fed and watered at around 4pm in tuk tuks to the supermarket. Tuk tuk is the colloquial name given to those 3 wheel monstrosities made mostly by Piaggeo, which I guess must be Italian as they seldom work properly.

Under the influence of a good lunch, a mohito and a large cognac to finish, a race back to the house was a certainty and those of my regular readers who are aware of my competitive edge will know that the very fact I am prepared to report the event can leave you in no doubt as to who was the victor, although as usual modesty restrains me for confirming the result publicly. The co-winner, that Nice Lady Decorator, had already taken her back seat driving responsibilities seriously before we had even got off the grid.

We arrived back in time for afternoon tea in the simply vast upper deck of our room, a massive covered terrace over 50 square metres square, overlooking the Indian Ocean before sundowners at 5 30pm. Obviously the whole days meetings were a very valuable aid to understanding the Medina Palms project

The supermarket was an interesting experience. Nothing is paid for; a bill is delivered to the house at the end of the week. The highlight was the purchase of the one vital ingredient missing from the fantastic cooked breakfast created by the very friendly Kenyan staff, baked beans. Surprisingly, and possibly for the first time in my life, I was in agreement with a northerner Ben Dobson on this point. He did not say it, but I could tell that, emboldened by the discovery of Heinz finest, he went searching for tins of tripe, black pudding, whippet and pigeon garnish, but am glad to report that he was unsuccessful. At least I hope so otherwise a nasty shock may await me at breakfast this morning.

Last evening we went to a lovely little sun downer restaurant and bar a short distance from Alhamra, just south of Malindi called Piripan. It stands on an archipelago, with the Indian Ocean on one side and a little more than a quarter of a mile away from a tidal inlet. After spotting some gecko's, small lizards, lurking behind the bar as we put away a couple of wonderful cocktails, it was suggested that what the bar needed was a gecko blaster.

Earlier in the day after a trip into Malindi I had some made to measure shorts made for a little over an ill octopus (that is six quid at today's exchange rates) the Reverend Jeff had predicted dire puns and I guess that was something of the sort. They say that only mad dogs and Englishmen go out in the midday sun, but with half an hour before lunch was served, I decided on a short walk. Alhamra, where we are staying in staggering comfort and looked after by the most attentive staff I have ever encountered, is two minute's walk along a lane to the beach.

There are permanent Masai guards at the gates, not necessarily for security as crime is rare, but to ensure guests feel safe. James, our day guard wears a Manchester United shirt under his traditional Masai Robe.

The discomfort,, the cocktails and the matchstick coloured face should have forewarned me that I had overdone the sun, so I took to my bed early with a rehydration drink and several pints of water inside me. You would think that my swarthy appearance and having lived in the Cote d'Azur for seven years may have prepared me for the strength of the sun, but even although temperatures were somewhat below those that one accepts as normal in the south of France, the sheer power of the equatorial sun is something I had never before experienced. Today, I must collect my tailored shorts from Malindi and then we are going to explore nearby Turtle Bay, where no doubt hundreds of anxious traders will attempt to get us to part with our cash. The Kenyans are lovely smiling people with a great sense of humour, football mad and although the traders can be persistent will back away if you ask, this is best done with a joke. The place and the population remind me of Barbados twenty years ago. Golf is on the horizon on Friday and already the wager discussions have commenced. It seems that lost balls may be a problem because even the caddies supplied are reluctant to go too deep into the bush due to the danger of not coming back. Apparently we will see baboons and may even see a giraffe foraging in the jungle. There may be some other animals on the golf course, but I will be playing with them.

Men will know and sympathise straight away with that situation where one is not feeling ones best and one is then dragged into at least 16 shops (and here I use the term loosely, scruffy little caves might be nearer the mark) in equatorial heat with air-conditioning a thing of the very far future to search for cushion covers. My continual bleating about stopping for a coffee was ignored, and so I found myself slumped in various chairs in a myriad murky corners of Africa whilst that Nice Lady Decorator searched for that perfect purchase.

There is a stronger Arab African influence here than in Watamu which, like much of Kenya, is broadly Christian. That means there is a wider range of shopping available, from Masai beads through African carvings to Italian goods, because many Italians have also made their second homes here, allegedly due to monies gleaned from involvement in the Italian "insurance" business if you get my meaning.

There are also a number of material shops and eventually in one of these, Ali Baba, she found the items she required. A more fearsome haggler he can seldom have encountered. If he had 40 thieves to start with, the number would have risen to 41 had he taken on that Nice Lady Decorator, such was the level of discount she extracted from him. He honestly looked like he had seen enough of tourists by the time we left.

Talking of thieves, Somali pirates have had an effect on the outside perception of safety in Kenya, but now I am here, I can see that it amuses the locals rather than posing a serious threat. Actually the only threat is the damage the story does to the tourist industry.

We returned to Watamu to collect my new-made-to-measure tailored turquoise shorts (don't tell my style guru Mr. Humphreys if you see him and he is free). So pleased am I with these items, which cost me 900 Kenyan shillings, a full £6.50, I promptly ordered another pair in lime green, together with a matching hand-made shirt which I shall look forward to showing off at the REGS golf tournament, weather permitting. They will pick up the green trim on my silver golf shoes perfectly.

Although Somali pirates are certainly not a problem down here on the Kenyan coast, there are other diversions that suggest a different kind of danger, the danger of impressionable girls having their heads turned by alarmingly languid and attractive chaps clad in dresses as my picture below indicates.

These Masai warriors are much used locally by the bigger houses as security guards and they can be quite scary. The cost of hiring them, at around 500 Kenyan shillings a day (about £3.50,) is almost irresistible as they also add a certain local colour, with their brightly coloured robes. It also of course gives the house guests a degree of comfort. However, how much comfort do they provide? And to what extent do they have the opportunity to personalise the service? This thought came to my attention when that Nice Lady Decorator found this particular specimen on the beach at Watamu yesterday afternoon.

Has he any idea how much trouble he is getting into here? Not with me, with her.

We had walked along the beautiful white sand beach at high tide, and at a small village of local craft stalls had purchased a wide range of fabrics, jewellery, a hand carved ebony chess set, some curious African ashtrays, a carved sandstone elephant and various other bits of detritus for the grand total of around £15, when her eyes lit on James, a charming Masai, rather too charming in my opinion, although that charm dissipated somewhat when he demanded 50 shillings for the photo, about 35p. Had there been cushion covers available on that market I would have been certain that she would have added to her collection, which stands almost waist-high in our bedroom.

At dinner, a most fabulous crab thermador produced by the smiling Kenyan kitchen staff at Alhamra, there was a discussion about the nature of the wager at golf today. We are due to play at Vippongi Ridge about 45 minutes' drive towards Mombassa, and which looks astonishing in the brochure. I for one will be attempting more than usual to keep my ball on the fairway as over dinner increasingly embellished stories of wild life, especially at the wilder end of the spectrum of the word wild, were disclosed by our host Nigel Rowley, a Kenyan veteran of 25 years standing. It seems that giraffes, pythons, monkeys, and warthogs are just some of the animals we may witness on our round, and although we will have caddies for those errant golf balls that refuse to stay on the fairway, those least accurate of balls may have to be declared lost, unless we want to risk losing a caddy.

The Kenyan staff has been exemplary, always smiling, unstinting in the efforts to make your stay comfortable, nothing is too much trouble, but the food they consume themselves locally is largely based on maize and chilli and differs somewhat from the food we tend to eat and which they prepare.

This allows the occasional howler to emerge from this warm blanket of conformity to high standards of English service. Last night, after an excellent celery soup, enlivened as ever with a little chilli, as indeed the cream of sweet corn soup had been the night before, followed by a very good pepper steak, we were all looking forward to desert. What followed was right out of The Vicar Of Dibley, where Mrs. Cropley had an eye for unusual food combinations. The chef had clearly not quite understood the concept of black pudding, and its unsuitability as a desert, and the piece de resistance was the carefully cooked egg placed on the top. Our dear host was not amused, either by the desert or the mirth that followed, but it was a completely understandable and charming mistake.

I said that I could not be certain how much room I would have to report on the golf yesterday, and that cynics may suggest that if I lost there would be little or no mention of it for reasons of space. Well I am glad to be able to refute that suggestion. It is not about who wins and loses but about how you play the game, and some of us play the game better than others creating winners and losers. The more enlightened of my regular readers may by now have guessed the result, but once again my sense of innate modesty will not allow me to confirm something which must be an obvious fact, supported by some pictures I now have of me wearing a 1000 Kenyan shillings note on my forehead.

Suffice to say that I have never been beaten at golf in Africa, and I played for the first time yesterday. The golf course at Vippongi

Ridge was truly as astonishing as the brochure suggested. It has been carved from a sisal plantation, the plants looking exactly like the yucca plants we have in the garden at home in Valbonne, and indeed they look identical. The fairways were immaculate, but what was mind bogglingly impressive is that each blade of grass on the fairways and light rough (I will come back to the ladies golf contingent a little later) was planted by hand. Imagine that? Hundreds of Kenyan mamas on their hands and knees planting every seed by hand, amazing. The result is a superbly crafted magnificent golf course high on a ridge looking down to the distant Indian Ocean, as close to heaven as I have ever been. Renowned Welsh golfer Ian Woosnam OBE has built a house on the course.

Lunch at the golf club preceded the drive back to Watamu, but due to the quality of the lunch, a few too many beers and too much wine I dozed off and missed the Hotel Titanic in one of the local villages for which I had seen a sign on the way up. With my comments yesterday suggesting that Pythons could be amongst the wildlife we may encounter, I was half expecting to see a Pythonesque reenactment of Fawlty Towers at Hotel Titanic.

What would Christmas be without M and S? Well the simple answer is Chrita. There are a number of collections of beach traders with Christmas merchandise here at Watamu in Kenya, where we have just three days left before returning to the tender embrace of the south of France. They enjoy giving themselves famous names and the claiming to be the official Kenyan outlet for, amongst others, Harrods, Peter Jones, Fortnum and Mason (didn't know they had shops?) , Debenhams and of course Marks and Spencer's. The most believable though was the guy who rushed out from beneath his roughly thatched open fronted establishment claiming to be the local Tesco's. He was more convincing because he was proudly displaying his Tesco's staff badge with his name; Tesco Dave.

They have any number of bargains on offer and in fact I think I am going back to Harrods in the morning to get that carved ebony giraffe which was on offer at 500 Kenyan shillings, about £3.50. It is amazing how much cheaper Harrods Kenya is that Harrods

Knightsbridge.

The shopping in these outlets has been a revelation. I have been lucky enough to buy Oakley sunglasses for under £2 and even some Nike shades for around £1.50, both pair's originals, at least, Tesco Dave told me they were. There were a few more top quality outlets just below Mapangos, our venue for lunch yesterday, in the next beach just past the headland to the north of Medina Palms.

Mapangos at Turtle Bay, Watamu

Mapangos is set in a beautiful horseshoe bay of white sand with two large islands in the mouth, the biggest of which is accessible by paddling over at low tide. I took this picture from the pool area looking out on to the Indian Ocean. My chosen repast of lobster linguine was divine as was its price, some £6. Catering mostly for the Italian ex-pat community and holiday makers, pizza and pasta loomed large, but every restaurant to which we have been has also had fantastic seafood available.

After lunch, a dip in the warm Indian Ocean was preceded by early evening cocktails, eschewed myself in favour of a gin and tonic of the highest quality. I suspect that neither the Gordon's gin nor the Schweppes tonics had been sourced from Tesco Dave.

Last night, dinner at Alhamra was taken under the stars watching the anvil shaped clouds, hovering on the horizon; expel the occasional flash of lightning. Another culinary triumph of the most delicious fish cooked in a ginger sauce, this time sadly without being offered black pudding for desert.

Yesterday, despite a short-term reverse in the tuk tuk wars where I was just about to take an unassailable 3-0 lead before an appalling blunder by our driver, Terrance the Tuk Tuk, who, under pressure mistook right for left, I will still leave Africa having royally "Tuked" up the opposition. Whining and whingeing is to be expected but nothing will change the fact that a draw later on, when we shared a bigger version leaves us in the lead by three and half to two and a half, so unassailable.

Christmas In Valbonne

Well, there are now 5 BA long haul pilots off my Xmas card list. As suspected, having grown quickly accustomed to the quality of the service in First Class on the way out to Nairobi, by way of contrast, we were left to languish in economy for the flight back. It was not all bad as the plane was half empty so we had more space than expected, but those promised complementary copies of my book, contingent upon the right treatment being applied, hang on a shoestring.

Arriving back in France in mid-morning, it was very gratifying that my diary, which had been left clear in case of a delay on my way out of Africa was, within an hour, filled with a celebratory mid-day drink with Paul and Lisa Thornton Allan and then further adorned by an invitation to lunch at Auberge St Donat, my old favourite.

Present were the usual tennis suspects, The Wingco, Peter "Blind Lemon" Milsted and Dancing Greg "Thirsty" Harris. Tennis was at least discussed, if not played. The Wingco, excellent wordsmith that he normally is, inadvertently made a rather thoughtless comment about breast cancer, specifically suggesting that a sufferer might like to "get it off her chest" but otherwise it was reasonably uneventful, yet great to be back in the bosom of the south of France ex-pat humour.

I have so many pictures from my trip to use in the coming weeks, but this was one of my favourites, showing some local Kenyans repairing a roof of their home. I did not know that Thatcherism was rife in Kenya.

Roof repairs, Kenyan style

Last night then my annual brush with religion, I went to church, the proper lovely old building in Valbonne as opposed to my more usual form of "church" at Cafe Latin on a Friday morning where a number of the locals go to worship coffee on a Friday morning, that's today, and where I expect to be this morning.

The occasion was of course the annual carol service staged by the International Riviera Singers, supported by the Mougins School choir, at a proper church where they do all that hallelujah stuff, singing about our Lord, and I don't think they mean Voldemart. Continuing the stream of consciousness, could that be a good collective name for an American chain store? Voldemart, anything you need for the mystic man in your life? But I digress.

As many of you know I do not have a religious bone in my body and as I have not heard from my old god-bothering pal the Reverend Jeff for some time this seems as good a time as any to air my views on religion at Christmas; I am always up for a good sing-song, and the Valbonne Church carol Service is a great event for that, particularly as they serve free vin chaud to the congregation afterwards, although I think they should serve it before hand to get the atmosphere really charged up. The village church is cosy and packed - I would venture to suggest that the only time it is full is for weddings, funerals and the carols - and it is quite a social event. I took a photo of the interior whilst people were gathering without being struck down by a thunderbolt.

Is it me or can I see the ghostly form of ET? look at the picture on a small screen and you may see what I mean

Many of the attendees, including myself, would not be seen dead in a church, and I mean that literally. When I head off to infinity and beyond, the last place I want my passing to be celebrated would be at a church, No, I intend to leave strict instructions for a large party to be held, with loads of drinks and where black apparel is banned. The reason for avoiding church events, apart, of course, from my status as a confirmed non believer, is the normally po-faced seriousness of it all, and the fact that Darwin proved them all wrong with his theory of evolution being at the root of life rather than the old tall story about Adam and Eve.

Anyway it was a jolly gathering to sing some traditional Christmas carols with a few mates and then after a couple of vin chaud courtesy of God, to wander up to The Queens Legs for a couple of pints of Guinness, courtesy of Arthur, and to catch up on the Christmas spirit, which to be frank, was quite hard to capture in the heat of Africa last week. Suzanne Butterfield and her man mountain husband, Peachy Butterfield, were propping up the bar alongside Simon and Sarah Howes and a mystery was solved. Simon is renowned for stocking Chateau Gloria as his house wine, and when we were all singing the long refrain of that fine old Christmas carol "Glorrrria" at the pause at the end of that word, I could have sworn I heard a cork popping from a bottle. It appears that I was not imagining it and indeed Peachy was enjoying himself by catching Simon's eye and sticking his finger in his cheek and making a cork popping noise at the end of the line. This was until Suzanne put an end to his childish (but very funny) antics.

Also present was my style guru, Mr. Humphreys. When I saw him in the congregation I asked if he was free and he was. His namesake in the popular TV series "Are You Being Served" was constantly subject to his sexuality being questioned, and indeed the answer was there for everyone to see. Of course any similarities between our Mr. Humphreys and the rather camp shop assistant in the TV series are entirely coincidental, in fact a more heterosexual specimen in our Valbonne version I have yet to see, and that is precisely why he can get away with wearing a yellow suede jacket, although wearing that kind of item at any other time of the year than Christmas and I suspect questions might be asked, even of him.

Golf At Charistmas

Talking of doubtful clothing choices, there was a real danger that I had left it too late to get a place in this Sunday's end of year REGS golf tournament, but a quiet word with the secretary and space was found. However, I received a rather direct note from him claiming that the committee had met and come to a decision that no lime green or pink outfits being worn by any of the participants would be deemed fit for play, but as the golf get up I intend to wear (as long as it is warm enough) is not entirely lime green, I think I will be

OK...

With only barely two weeks to go until Christmas, the weather here is beautiful. I watched the hurricane force winds in the UK on TV last night and said a silent prayer as I was out walking this morning in the Valmasque forest.

As it turns out, a tee off time of 8.30 at this time of the year ensured that it was just a bit too chilly to wear my lime green made-to-measure golf ensemble. This in no way can be attributed to that Nice Lady Decorator who I saw describe me in an email yesterday in connection with this splendid attire as "The Jolly Green Giant". Insults like this are like water off a ducks back. I will not be downcast and I will use the fortitude exhibited by my style guru Mr. Humphreys, which he often uses when faced with people who do not understand style and individuality.

She has been a little under the weather since we returned, a touch of African tummy if I am not mistaken, but it did remind me of a sign that I saw when in Watamu in Kenya last week, pictured below.

Yesterday, Tony "I invented the internet" Coombs kindly came around to fix the internet again. I asked why he invented something that was patently so fallible but answer came there none. Perhaps its fallibility is the reason he refused to take the official credit for its invention? Talking of fallibility, I see I had the usual long boring argument in my comments section during the week from The Reverend Jeff. It always seems like good fun to goad him about his religious beliefs but as soon as I have read the first sentence (that being the operative word) of any response, I begin to lose the will to live and want to slash my wrists. Christmas is of course named after me and is a time for fun and parties; it is only ever dragged down by those religious sorts. It's a bit like The France Show at Earls Court in mid-January, a big celebration in my name.

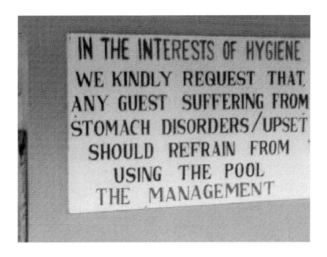

Wise words indeed.

The Party Season Commences

I am accused in the comments section of being a dipsomaniac, but this is untrue, I have no interest whatsoever in checking car oil levels. To be honest I have little interest in anything today, as I had been to a particularly wearing girl's lunch that I inadvertently gate crashed yesterday, and which was still going strong at 10pm last night. I do have an excuse for gate crashing, quite a good one really. The lunch was taking place at my home and I knew nothing about it until I returned, otherwise I would have stayed and had a couple of drinks at the golf club where I suspect I would have had some more meaningful, although perhaps less interesting, conversations. I may also have managed to retain most of my clothing, but that is another story, suffice to say that my wearing of lime green seems to do something to the ladies bereft of their menfolk.

It is not that it wasn't fun. It just wasn't very high-brow as was amply illustrated by the 18 empty bottles of wine and Bailey's I had to recycle yesterday. Well, at the peak there were 9 girlies, although a hard-core of 6 were mainly to blame. Anyway, the working week has commenced and that Nice Lady Decorator has gone to the UK with a huge hangover ready for another nightmare, Christmas shopping.

As usual after events such as these, I awake to find a number of photographs on my phone for which I can find no rational explanation. What is happening here for instance? And what are two of my Christmas oranges doing in Lisa Thorntan-Allans cleavage? And why is the amply endowed (sorry Lin) Mellissa Graves involved? I think we should be told, but I suspect it will forever remain a mystery.

Christmas oranges will never be the same again

I had been so gentle with him, after his revelations about his documented fondness for sheep, but Steve Weston, a prime mover in the REGS, with his publication of a picture of me yesterday on their website in my Kenyan made-to-measure lime green golfing outfit, together with a disparaging, some may say jealously-motivated comment, must now accept that the (kid?) gloves are off. It is amongst my most popular stories from the summer before last when Steve talked frankly about his love of sheep in front of an increasingly incredulous golfing gathering. I am sure today he is a little sheepish, particularly as long-suffering wife Nancy made a point of telling me at the weekend that she wanted a sheepskin coat for Christmas. Perhaps Steve should suggest he buy her a mink coat instead? That would at least rescue at least one lamb from the slaughter.

Yesterday I received a call from venerable Valbonne estate agent "Cubby" Wolf from Riviera Realty asking what he had to do to get a mention in this column. I suggested that as a Currencies Direct affiliate for some 2 years standing, sending me a client might be a good starting point, but after he claimed to have no clients at present, I decided that his purchasing a copy of my book "Summer in the Cote d'Azur" would suffice. He agreed rather too readily (I am not accustomed to soft sales) and then tried to avoid the moment of truth (payment) by saying he would probably see me some time over Christmas, but made the mistake of telling me he will be in his office in Valbonne this afternoon, so I will deliver it personally.

The relative peace of the last few days will then be shattered when I collect that Nice Lady Decorator and Sprog 1 from the airport in the evening, I have hidden my beers but I know he will track them down with that dogged determination so lacking from his studies.

It is not often when one gets a bit of information that is so juicy one cannot wait to write about it. Many of my regular readers will know that my local style guru is a certain Mr. Humphreys, a Justice of the Peace, a magistrate who can bang his gavel with the best of them and who, like his namesake in the popular TV series "Are You Being Served", is usually free.

I was at a Christmas lunch at in Valbonne yesterday, courtesy of Lin Wolff when fellow guest, Matt Frost (on this occasion allowed out without his minder, Viv, who is in the UK) revealed that he had witnessed my sartorial hero, Mr. Humphries, languishing in a "washeteria" in Pre Du Lac, near Chateauneuf, being served as it were. It seems that once recognised, Mr. Humphreys panicked and demanded that his presence at a do-it-yourself washing emporium would not be revealed to me, his most devoted disciple. I cannot understand why he would be so determined to deny me knowledge of his need of washing facilities outside the home. Perhaps he thinks I may reveal this fact to my readers? Nothing could be further from the truth, I would never, on principle, report a fact that might in some way belittle one of my hero's, so I want to assure him that his guilty secret is safe with me, I would never knowingly disclose such a clearly sensitive fact. I would also give no credence to other claims that were made at the same time involving his use of curlers, or indeed exactly how they were being used.

Luncheon conversation ebbed and flowed, and I learned a thing or two by listening to my superiors. Nancy Wilson, the only Irish person I have ever met who claims she cannot drink, taught me that sharks sting, at least I have witnesses who can testify as to what she said. I don't quite know what she was driving at, but I suspect she had muddled up sharks with jellyfish, a mistake I could perhaps have forgiven her had she partaken more fully of the prosccco. Actually, now that I come to think about it she is probably technically correct. If one was bitten by a shark it may well sting somewhat. Actually you can get stung by a shark; Wayne Brown may well know what I mean.

One other theme that was explored was the possibility of a Muslim bathing costume, which I realise is a difficult concept to grasp (not that I would ever want to grasp a Muslim women, I am far too much of a coward for that) and what it might be called a burquini seemed to hit the nail on the head.

Another book signing today in Valbonne. There is always the chance that I shall bump into someone who has not already done the right thing, but do you really want to experience the Chris France hard sell on the streets of Valbonne? Wailing, moaning, whimpering, tears, gnashing of teeth, I will try anything to make a sale. Better to turn up today and take the medicine and buy a copy. There really is no shame in it. Well there is in the book obviously but that is a different matter.

Last Night to drinks at Bastide St Matthieu, the fabulous boutique hotel near Grasse owned by the beautiful exotic and dusky Soraya and the rather white and, dare I say it, less attractive fellow author and host Bill Colegrave, whom I once found asleep at a party as my picture below depicts. I joined a discussion about a new book detailing the life of Dickens.

Guess who?

It seems that the book being discussed, a newly released and earnestly researched book, delved deeply into his life and the influences that conspired to allow Dickens to create some of his work. A comment was made that he was effectively a diarist of his time, observing life and characters with whom he had come into contact, and using this experience to weave stories for the benefit of his readers. I ventured the opinion that this was much like me and this column, and someone who shall remain nameless agreed rather too quickly in public with this observation without, for one second, taking on board the full horror of what they had said, and the literary ammunition they had unwittingly supplied me. So now it is official, my writing has been mentioned in the same sentence with, and has been compared to Dickens, but for some reason when I asked what Dickens surname was, I received some sharp glances and formed the opinion that I may have said something stupid. Later in the evening when I was regaling that Nice Lady Decorator with my new-found literary fame as a diarist, she expressed the opinion that my output as a writer could perhaps be better described as the "outpourings of a diarrhearist". This is a bit of a pain in the bum for me.

Christmas In Valbonne

Sprog 1 has arrived back from Guildford, and immediately I have seen a significant depletion in alcohol stocks in my various fridges. How is it that children today have an innate ability to carry out open wallet surgery? Where do they learn it? Why were my parents always too poor for me to perfect the technique? Another way of putting it is to use an expression I heard yesterday, "bung removal". A bung is an east end colloquialism for a wad of cash, and also something that is put into a hole to stop leakage, so removal of it tends to be fairly catastrophic, and likely to worsen with Christmas still over a week away.

Sprog 2 has not even arrived home yet, she is due in this evening, but she also has a very thirsty way about her, indeed it was in a pub in London last night that she happened across Hugh Grant and sent me the picture of herself and several of her friends helping Mr. Grant reconnect with the younger generation.

So to the English Book Centre do some signing of copies of my book, "Summer in the Cote d'Azur" in time for Christmas. One potential customer was initially scared off after having a look at the content which after some consideration she described as follows; "sounds like a lot of bitching to me", a comment which I thought was slightly harsh but fair, but to my delight she then returned and bought one for her "miserable" husband, whom she thought "deserved it". I have been encouraging reviews of the book on-line, and this is at least a review of a kind. Another review of a more ethereal kind manifested itself in the form of a power cut during proceedings which I am sure the Reverend Jeff would interpret as divine intervention.

My favourite crossword clue relates to the forthcoming festive period; "Postman's problem at Christmas?"; "How many letters?" Answer; bloody millions. Given that backdrop it is perhaps not hard to sympathise with the postmen when they are on their rounds at this time of year. So with that in mind, I would not like to criticise our own postman for abandoning his motorbike in the middle of the road into Valbonne, which stopped all the traffic for 10 minutes today.

Friday tends to have a traditional ring about it. That ring being the roundabout at Plascassier where the Auberge St Donat is situated. At first, I thought the excitement of the book signing, would conspire to send me directly to my office to plan my ever burgeoning workload, but I was wrong. The combined persuasive powers of the Wingco, Peter "Blind Lemon" Milsted and 60's play boy Anthony "Dock Of the" Bay was sufficient to lure me to lunch with them at our traditional Friday venue, and I am glad, because of the entertainment provided for me in the shape of the immense chagrin of the Wingco (he describes this column as "ghastly", which by simple extension applies to the book), I sold two more copies of the book in the restaurant, which I was asked to autograph at the very table where we were having lunch. Oh for the delicious irony of having a customer asking the Wingco to sign the section featuring him, as happened at the launch last month. Happy days.

Whereas the sky was clear, almost everything else in my world on a Saturday was muddled due to the arrival home of both Sprogs. Much as I enjoyed seeing them, the novelty wore off after about five minutes. Older parents will recognise the ominous signs of their return to the fold; unwashed dishes, the kitchen a disaster area, dirty washing piled up to the ceiling, no room on the sofa because of a steaming pile of late teenage indolence. As soon as they arrive home every friend from miles around turns up to drink my beers, turn my house into a pigsty, commandeer the Sky TV remote control and generally do all manner of things to force myself and that Nice Lady Decorator out of our house. Don't you just love them? Under this intolerable pressure we sought refuge in The Queens Legs and that is the case for the defence.

Even there, solace was temporary because having drunk all the beers in my fridges, they suddenly woke up to the fact that it was Happy Hour at The Queens Legs until 8pm, and the great unwashed hordes descended upon the place, forcing us in the opposite direction.

Today, being a Sunday, lunch is being prepared. I know this to be the case because that Nice Lady Decorator has been wrestling with an eleven kilo leg of pork for a couple of days (now there is an interesting concept) and I am quietly confident that even the starving student hordes, and a few of their parents, will not be able to finish that at a single session. I have found a couple of magnums of a grand cru St Estephe, so will seek solace in red wine induced sense-obliteration this afternoon.

The Office Party

Dinner in Nice with the new Managing Director of Currencies Direct is the French equivalent of an office party. There are, I think, 6 of us attending and we have all been asked to wrap up a present, with a value not in excess of 10 euros, to exchange on the night. I think there was a message in that request, because what item do I now have on sale at the seasonal reduced price of exactly 10 euros? Why, my book of course, so someone is going to get a real surprise treat when they open that, especially as it is signed by the author himself.

Christmas is a weird time of year, when sights you would not normally see, or would immediately report to the police, are common place. Where, for instance, and in what circumstances other than at Christmas time would one be happy to have ones young child bounce up and down on the knee of a weird old man with a long nose and, a red shiny suit? Especially if he was offering sweets for some indeterminate reason?

In that context, I invite you to examine the picture I took in the Queens Legs of a figure languishing behind the bar. I am told that it is supposed to be a representation of old dead crooner Bing Crosby in a Father Christmas outfit, and indeed when pressed it did sing a rather poor version of White Christmas, but one has to consider the appalling possibility which sprang into my mind. Could this really be a caricature of the former president of France, the scourge of the

British economy, our very own former president Sarkozy? And why is he holding a ski pole? Perhaps it was one Guinness too far.

Was Bing Crosby's secret lovechild really the president of France?

Yesterday, the Sprogs instigated a lunch for their friends and the parents of their friends at our expense, and at our house. This effectively means that we were invited to a lunch at our house, at which we were expected to cook and provide sustenance of both a solid and a liquid kind, and to which what seemed like every teenager in Valbonne decided they had been invited. Amongst the token parents who were in evidence were Simon and Sarah Howes, who brought as a gift a traditional poinsettia which was slightly bigger than our house, and which probably required a crane to deliver to our home. I forgave them as they also brought 3 bottles of Chateau Gloria, two of which fell by the wayside during the afternoon. The other I have secreted for entirely selfish reasons and will be opened when I am not surrounded by teenage vultures that want to try it.

Also present were Tony "I invented the internet" Coombs and his loving wife Pat. I asked him what he expected to invent over Christmas but he said he had not yet decided. He has however decided to take two weeks off over the festive period, something that he has never done before. Bearing in mind his claimed importance in administering the internet, I asked what would happen to it over Christmas if he was not at his post ensuring that his invention was functioning correctly. He dropped a bombshell by revealing that the internet will close down on Christmas Eve and remain closed until 6th January for routine maintenance. I think you can tell by this slurred statement that the combined effects of Chateau Gloria, a Grand Cru St Emilion, a Sauterne and perhaps even a Bailey's had begun to magnify his megalomania.

I have been endeavouring to secure reviews for my book over the past few weeks with varying amounts of success, but yesterday Matt Frost told me that he had lunched with one of my contemporaries (whose identity he would not reveal) who has described my book thus; "as intellectually challenging as reading The Dandy with a hangover".

Well, is it?

Has anyone ever heard of this book "A Dandy with a Hangover"? Or who wrote it? I am afraid I have not but if it is that intellectually challenging, then I must seek it out, even if it has as its subject a gay chap with a drink problem.

Today could have been described in those terms as well. It was a lovely day, fine and dandy but the inevitable Monday hangover spoiling the splendid if rather cold weather. The problem with a hangover is that one does not always enjoy the day as much as one would without it, and one tends to begin to question one's very existence, a fact summed up beautifully by this picture that I nicked from old friend Lindsey Wesker's Facebook page.

Robert Degan, who is credited with writing the Hokey Pokey or the Hokey Cokey as it is known in England, died about two years ago in USA. In the funeral parlour as the undertakers readied the coffin they tried to put the left leg in, and that's when the trouble started.

Last night to Nice to a very nice Italian restaurant called La Favolae, in the Cours Saleya in the old town, to meet up with the Currencies Direct team for the first annual company Christmas dinner. As a nod towards the fast looming festering season I dug out a sparkly black tie, that I have not worn for over ten years, to go with my black jeans and my black dominatrix shirt, and thought that I was looking quite good, until our Currencies Direct leader in France, Pippa Maile described my outfit as "Madonna meets Men In Black". I had not realised just how good I looked, I should have taken photographs for my style guru Mr. Humphreys to see (if he was free).

When it came to exchanging those 10 euro gifts, the tell-tale shape of my book was spotted by almost all delegates who were all understandably keen to get their hands on it, but in the end the lucky recipient was the new Managing Director of Currencies Direct whom I know was delighted.

The annual hunt for Christmas presents worthy of ones friends and family is a constant challenge. Inspiration can come from anywhere, and personally I find shops are not the most fertile of places for ideas. Sometimes, when one is least expecting it, one sees something and one knows it is just perfect.

Granny Racing looks like it could be great fun, but I wonder what it entails? Does one race against a granny or does one back one's own granny against someone else's? I wish I had received that gift if only to find out what it was all about.

Pictures allegedly exist of the evening but due to a day spent threatening, cajoling and bullying, I am reasonably confident none will reach the public domain. My excuse for consuming what an ex-girlfriend used to call "an elegant sufficiency" apart from the fact I was not paying, was that my driver for the evening, the diminutive Christine Bryant, had earlier revealed that her night vision was really quite poor. When, you may ask, did she reveal this quite pertinent fact? Just as we reached 80 miles (120 km's) per hour in the middle lane of the A8, our local motorway on the way to Nice. Some justification then I would contend for attempting to block out the return journey.

On an entirely unrelated theme; Somerset Maughan once described the Cote d'Azur as a "sunny place for shady people", so it was rather ironic to discover last night that Wayne Brown, the creator of on line magazine FR2day, has rented a flat in Somerset, otherwise there could be no connection between Wayne, Somerset the writer and Somerset the county, and I will fight anyone who suggests there may be.

Church At Christmas, Surely Not?

On the way across from the parking in Valbonne, I passed Cafe Latin where I encountered a large gathering for "church", the last chance to worship coffee on a Friday before Christmas. Amongst those in the congregation was my style guru Neil Humphreys who I discovered, when I asked, was free. He immediately honed in on my purple cashmere (effect) sweater which I had put on in a fit of colour-blindness earlier. He was very impressed and drew attention to my comments in past columns about his rare ability to wear purple and not be considered camp, at least by a few people. I told him that I was in awe of this macho ability but he seemed unimpressed. He did however introduce me to a local builder whose name is, and I kid you not, Chris Chicken and his lovely wife Mrs. Chicken. I asked after his brother, Kentucky Fried but I am afraid to say I received the sort of look that said I should be up before the beak. Being in the soup I took stock of the situation and with ruffled feathers decided that should be enough chicken jokes for today.

With the Sprogs inviting hordes of friends over again last night, an escape route was required, so we tunnelled out and headed up to the Queens Legs for a pint, with a quick look in La Fontaine du Vin on the way, to ensure it had not improved, before remembering that we were invited to the Wingco's town house for a festive glass or two.

Within a short time, his guitar was out and we were regaled with improvised Christmas versions of old rock classics, the most memorable of which was "Hey Santa" with more than a passing nod to the Jimi Hendrix Experience "Hey Joe", the Wingco's version enshrining the immortal line "what you doing with that sack in your hand". That led to the tasteless and unfounded suggestion that Gary Glitter is well-known for leaving children bedrooms with an empty sack. It was at this stage I decided I had heard enough and headed to bed.

Who the hell was it that gave that french bloke a microphone? Once again we felt it necessary to enjoy the unseasonably warm sunshine and take lunch in Valbonne Square, which was lovely except for the French guy who had found a microphone from somewhere and proceeded to cast a cloud of noise and feedback over proceedings.

We had been enjoying a festive lunch with Mellissa Graves, her husband Nigel, their Welsh gardener Iuean and some parents, but the parents of who was not immediately clear. Over lunch Mellissa told me that she always enjoyed this column, especially as she always used to get the blog just before tuning in to the Jeremy Kyle show on the BBC, but she found this column just as addictive. I was not certain how to take this comment as I hate the Jeremy Kyle show with a fierce loathing, but to be bracketed with a very successful programme by probably the best known broadcasting company in the world was, in some ways, a double-edged sword.

There was a small problem when sale no 119 of my book was about to complete to the parents in question at lunch, as a result of the brilliant sales pitch about it I had made to the older Graves, but the penultimate step towards break-even was impeded by the young Mellissa who absolutely forbade me from completing the sale for reasons I cannot reveal until after Christmas. All I can say is that it seems that Father Christmas may be bringing a very special present for some lucky visiting parents this morning.

Tired out from recent celebrations, I went to bed to dream, but for some reason I dreamed of the lovely Maryse, wife of the Wingco, and what she told us recently about playing around with notorious Liverpudlian footballing icon Kevin Keegan at the height of his Reverend Jeff, curly-perm like days. When I interjected to clear up any misunderstand about what "playing around" might mean. I was fixed with a manly stare by the Wingco which I thought I should perhaps read as a warning. It transpires that according to Maryse, she played a round of golf with the mega-permed footballing hero, but as she claims never to have had a golf lesson, I have my suspicions.

Christmas Arrives Eventually

Any suggestion that I had ever in the past described the Apple iPad as a nonsense piece of brilliant marketing for a new fad that was absolutely useless, and was a triumph for hype over value (a concept that many suggest would amply demonstrate my self-orchestrated promotion of my first book "Summer in the Cote d'Azur"), is entirely without foundation. The iPad is of course the most wonderful invention ever known to man and Steve Jobs its creator, should be ordained as a saint immediately at this very festive and religious time of year.

If I have inadvertently in the past ever conveyed any opinion to the contrary, then this was clearly either a mistake or has been misinterpreted by my readership. Hence the very generous and completely unexpected gift of that self-same item, that vital piece of technology, from that Nice Lady Decorator to me for Christmas, was some kind of recognition that, as a thrusting entrepreneur living in a difficult economic environment in a foreign country, I must keep abreast of the latest technology .

With two iPads now in the family, and with that Nice Lady Decorator now receiving, and reading, my daily column every day, she can now be certain that there will never be a disparaging remark about her and my undying love for her as my life partner and best friend. Her vivacious, outgoing personality and her great figure and classic good looks will be trumpeted regularly, certainly until she becomes bored with reading the daily drivel. I give it a week.

The weather has remained stunning, allowing us to partake of champagne in the web before lunch, Sprog 1 and I both resplendent in our Kenyan lounging trousers, gifts for Christmas which marks a radical and welcome change from the woolly pullovers of dubious design, which have been visited upon as in years past. Cognac for me sums up the Christmas spirit, accompanied by some of Cuba's finest, a Montechristo No 2, the king of cigars, followed by a descent into sleepy contentment, although waking up to find the lounging trousers covered in brandy and ash holes was a little less welcome. My father used to blame ash holes in his shirt as damage caused by fire-breathing moths. I think I shall do the same.

Christmas at home in Valbonne with the family was the usual drinking and eating affair which I love. That Nice Lady Decorator tucked into an eye-wateringly expensive Mersault which even I, a very fussy white wine drinker, was allowed a sip, whilst a red, a magnum of Grand Cru St Estephe marked out my area of special responsibility. The Sprogs were blissfully unaware of the quality of that Nice Lady Decorators' preferred tipple and I am sure they were both happy with a rather nasty chardonnay, with a bouquet reminiscent of cats piss and a taste of old cats fur, which pretty much sums up my feelings on most chardonnay generally.

"Happy drunk, I'm Christmas" was the best comment I saw on Xmas day on Mellissa Graves Facebook page and I think it had a resonance with many of my friends. Happy drunk seems to sum up a number of my friends, indeed some of my family, so the ideal antidote to the usual Christmas excess was a stiff walk, preferably involving some steep hills. Mellissa once took drastic action to ensure that she said nothing stupid at a dinner party for me to be able to publish. Those extreme lengths included sellotaping her mouth closed as I have captured overleaf.

Cipieres is a beautiful village in the hills above Gourdon, and below Greoliere where, despite no visible signs of snow from where we were, it seems Greoliere Les Neiges, the small ski resort above the old village has a couple of ski runs open. The walks are breath-taking, and by that, apart from being very beautiful and dramatic, I mean so steep they take your breath away, so the final piece of the antidote to walk-induced thirst was to buy a beer in the sunshine at Les Ormeau, one of the restaurants in the village.

Few of the locals were out and about, Boxing Day not being a holiday here. I tried to think of anywhere in Britain, given the sunny weather, where such a beautiful place with a sweet local restaurant or bar could be so deserted on Boxing Day but answer came their none.

I wonder what the artist or creator of this piece of artwork below was consuming? It is a mural (or muriel as one of my oldest friends always describes them) which has been etched onto the walls of popular pizzeria the Valbonnaise in Valbonne. I have yet to work out its full meaning but the positioning of the meat cleaver is a worry. Also what is the significance of the words "French house" in English in such a parochial though charming place, one of the few places in Valbonne where little or no English is spoken?

Post Christmas Warm Down

Perhaps I will spend the day with the new love of my life, the iPad, a Christmas present from that Nice Lady Decorator or iWife. I don't know what made me think of it, and it is not something that could apply to me, but when a marriage comes to an end, could that be construed as the limit of her shelf wife?

At least I realised, before I made the call to Apple to complain about my new iPad camera not working. Every photo I tried to take was black, but luckily, before making that call I realised that the rather nice black cover was still on it and covering the camera lens. It is a mistake which anyone with my limited affinity with technology will sympathise.

I have history when it comes to new fangled technology. My run in with the iPod reminded me of long ago when I took delivery of my first fax machine at my office in the west end of London in the early 1990's. The delivery driver had to dash in and dash out being on a double yellow line, before I had a chance to ask him how it worked. Cursing, I reached for the instructions, the first of which was to remove all packing tape. I ripped out all this white tape that was in the machine, plugged it in and didn't work. I rang the supplier angrily, who calmed me down, and then asked me exactly what I had done. I told him I had followed the instructions and removed the tape, but he said "there was no tape to remove, it was ready to plug in and use". Then I could hear him holding the phone up to his amused factory audience and saying "so you ripped out all the control leads in the machine and now it won't work?" I can still hear the huge guffaw that rang out around the factory.

I was also guilty of saying to my former partner, and co-founder of Music of Life, our record company, Simon Harris when he installed email into our office at around the same time; "what a complete waste of time, I will never use it". Wrong.

Later at home in Valbonne in the evening and with no social engagements for once, (hurrah!) we were treated to the spectacle of the lovely Stacey Solomon, in intelligence terms several sandwiches short of a full picnic, appearing on Celebrity Mastermind. There was the delicious prospect of the bubbly and vivacious Stacey, winner of various TV talent shows and "I'm A Celebrity, Get Me Out Of Here", where she has constantly exhibited an endearing stupidity that seems to have struck a chord with the great British unwashed. She got off to a great start answering questions about The Inbetweeners TV series and film. I doubted that she would take the works of Keats as a subject and her chosen area of expertise suited her well. I am a big fan of that series and watched the film on Christmas day with my kids. Only people who have seen the programme can know who excruciating my teenagers found the experience.

Stacey's classic answer came in the first question of the general knowledge section; "name the area of northern France famous for its sparkling wine" intoned John Humphries the presenter. After a little prompting, the answer came; "Jacobs Creek?" This was for me a comic highlight of the Christmas season.

As predicted, as soon as some Brits jet in to the Cote d' Azur, the beautiful weather we have been experiencing for almost a month suffered a slight hiccup. Yes, there were some clouds in the sky yesterday, even a little rain, and a very unwelcome departure from the sunshine festival we have been experiencing. Mr. Clipboard and his family have arrived, however it seems that after a blip yesterday, normal sunny conditions will return in time for tennis this morning, when the MOGS, in the shape of me and the Wingco, will once again stamp their authority on the tennis court, before adjourning for lunch at Auberge St Donat in Plascassier.

We are nearing the end of the first phase of festivities with Christmas behind us, and on to the madness surrounding New

Year's Eve to come. I was sent this picture recently by a regular reader of this column, which seems to sum up Christmas by this time in the proceedings. He insisted I did not reveal its source and used it only after 29th of December when the festively festooned miscreant had left to return to the UK ,as he was less than keen to be identified, so I promised Peter Lynn that I would not mention from where this came, or whose step-son was the culprit. Nothing I have written here should be misconstrued as a potential clue to unmask the subject of this photo, My New Years Resolution concerning inappropriate use of information has not yet come into force.

Just as I had sat down to enjoy a quiet night in, the phone rang and Mr. Clipboard and lovely wife Ashley were at the other end claiming that their boiler had broken down. They were cold and wondered if they might pop in for a glass of wine and a warm. I am nothing if not warm-hearted, and overcome by the festive sprit and the need to extend goodwill to all men, even Mr. Clipboard, I welcomed them in to feed and water them. Later, as news of my largesse extended, some other poor unfortunates arrived hotfoot from windy and wet Britain. The Thornton Allans had been spending Christmas in Cornwall (why?) and were in need of some decent wine. Thus my whole quiet evening was thrown into disarray, and not for the first time. Given the short notice I made the mistake of not hiding several bottles of a grand cru St Emilion that I had put aside for New Years Eve, and the eagle-eyed Mr. Clipboard spotted them during an inspection of the kitchen facilities, and set about them with the thirst of a man who has been in the desert for too long. By desert of course I mean the UK where he resides, happily, he assures me, through gritted teeth.

The tennis lunch at Auberge St Donat yesterday reached an undreamed scale of atrocity. Having won the tennis, as predicted, against Mr. Clipboard, on the basis that at one set each when lunch beckoned, the MOGS had secured victory under the Chris France scoring system, by dint of winning the first set by a larger margin than losing the second set, the scores being 6-4, 6-7. This victory was confirmed by a simple count back (12-11 in case there are any

public schoolboys reading this who still find arithmetic a dark art).
I also managed to sell another copy of my book to Mr. Clipboard.

One up to Santa!

However, delight at the sale that turned honest endeavour as a
writer into success, crumbled to horror when he decided to set fire
to his purchase as we enjoyed cognac and grappa after lunch. I
knew it was a hot literary offering, but quite how hot I had not
appreciated until the flames licked into the content as my picture
below captures.

Much amusement was afforded the attendees to the much-
superior tennis lunch home leg, as opposed to the very boring away
fixture last Friday at La Source at Le Rouret, by the ritual burning
of this volume of my work, but the real pain I felt later when I
discovered that I had been robbed of the 10 euros (already in two

pieces a result of previous tortuous negotiations), which was stolen from my wallet in broad daylight. I say now that I know who is the culprit and would have suggested that I turned out the light and invited the thief to return the money, but with public schoolboys and their pre disposition towards buggery, I decided I would prefer to take the financial loss rather than risking the loss of considerably more dignity should any of then want to revisit their childhood habits.

The Nazi's were infamous for burning literature, but as you can see the practice is alive and festering in the public schoolboy fraternity

From this you will have come to accept that at lunch I was surrounded by a number of public school types who had all managed to avoid working for much of their adult lives in complete contrast to yours truly.

Indeed today as I metamorphosed from ordinary author, like a caterpillar into a butterfly, and became a successful author, as my book turned into a profitable enterprise as a result of four more sales, jealousy of the most green-eyed kind reared its ugly head in a variety of forms. Not only was one of my books summarily burnt as evidenced by my picture above, but also my luxuriant goatee beard, a deeply hated sign of virility, much maligned by the largely balding contingent of public schoolboys who surrounded me, was reduced to a mere shadow of its former self by an unwarranted physical assault on my person. I will now forever be aware of the deep hurt suffered by Tom Brown in his school days, as I was roasted on the fire of jealousy which has built up ever since I, a mere council house boy, had his book published.

The more literary accomplished (but only in their own minds) coterie of public schoolboys simply could not bear to witness a poorly educated upstart eclipse them in the literary stakes, so they had to revert to public schoolboy bullying of the most unpleasant kind to assuage their own lamentable lack of literary achievement. I suppose it could have been worse. One of them, in an alcoholic haze, made the statement that "the rich boys will lay waste to your bottoms". Old habits die hard (so to speak).

It was an entirely democratic decision. The most we can seat indoors for a dinner party is 14, if we raid some outside garden furniture, so that's seven couples. One might think in the modern world that the more chivalrous amongst us, still clinging to age-old conventions of fairness, might expect that the Nice Lady Decorator would choose four couples and I would choose three to invite for New Years Eve. What I had not bargained for was her invoking a little known local rule that says the division of choice takes place only after she has invited all seven couples.

Thus amongst the revelers last night not invited by me to welcome in the New Year, were several people who had abused both myself and my book on the day before. By way of illustration I give you today's picture once again of Mr. Clipboard and my literary output being subjected to rather contemptuous public school boy antics. At least he had the good heart to return the 10 euros he had stolen from me, but given that the money came in the shape of some seventy coins in a mean plastic bag says something about the spirit of this gesture.

Chateau Gloria, Grand Cru St Emilion, champagne, Baileys, all were spilled on my floor before the old year had finished and at about 2.40 am this morning, after "Won't Get Fooled Again" by The Who was replaced on the Ipod by The Bee Gees "Staying Alive", I was overcome by a bout of extreme tiredness and headed to bed, however before that I distinctly recall the lovely Maryse, who bears the burden of being married to the Wingco, telling all and sundry that she was a regular reader of this column and found it highly amusing. The Wingco himself, of course, found this revelation un-amusing, which, given his constant description of this column as "Ghastly" and his stated principled refusal to read it was not a surprise..

Now, what is happening here?

We had fireworks as well, some of the funniest and pathetic examples I have ever witnessed and probably more entertaining as a result. These were thrown into fine contrast as the night sky over Valbonne was alight with a myriad of fireworks being let off all over the village, but not even the rockets we had made it much more than 20 feet into the air, and many went off in the bottles, prompting one party go-er to say it reminded him of how deliveries arrived at a sperm bank. The inspiration for this display had clearly not come from the magnificent London firework display which we had on the TV at 1pm, midnight back in the UK.

Chapter 5

New Years Day

Despite twice getting lost or, "misplacing the route" as that Nice Lady Decorator chose to put it, a large group of hung-over New Year's Eve revellers tried to do the right thing and work off some of the excessive consumption from the night before, or even from the preceding week, or indeed in some cases the previous year, by having a good walk up the beautiful area in the hills behind Gourdon, between the almost snowless southern alps and the warm and sunny hinterland of the Cote d'Azur in the hinterland of Cannes.

There was still a great deal of discussion during the walk , which had a good turnout of about 12, many of whom had been with us the night before, about the events that had been visited upon us or rather me on New Year's Eve. Regular readers will already be aware, and many no doubt upset, that my book had been very severely treated by many of my friends in the run up to Christmas, and things did not improve yesterday. Mr. Clipboard had brought with him the copy which he had bought the day before when it had been mightily abused verbally, before been burned, having paper planes made from some of the pages, and providing some low quality humour for the large contingent of under achieving public schoolboys present. He clearly wanted to continue to "enjoy" it in his own twisted way. Public schoolboys, don't you just love them?

After the very pleasant walk, the lovely Maryse, wife of The Wingco, reminded us again that she was an avid reader of my daily column. This was too much for The Wingco and he expressed his distaste by helping Mr. Clipboard further abuse his copy of my book, already bereft of most of the pages. This meant more paper planes.

Anyway, whilst the public schoolboys amused themselves at my expense by using some of the remaining pages as serviettes to mop up spilled beer, I took in the wonderful surroundings, and once the Wingco and his fags had tired of their juvenile humour, I managed to take this picture of a fat man and his friend, which I mentioned earlier. I am not prepared to answer questions as to which is which, or who is who.

Wingco finds a new friend

Master Mariner Mundell telephones to attempt to apologise for the assault on my beard and book. Seemingly he was distressed by my use of the word "bullying" to describe events that occurred, but how else can you describe being held down by four chaps and having your beard forcibly cut off? I say apologise but later in the evening when I suggested in front of witnesses that he had apologized, he back-tracked and called it a "statement of regret". I had to drag the "apology" out of him; in fact I was not certain at first why he had called. Anyway, I told him I accepted his apology and to think no more of it, but of course that is totally disingenuous,

I shall be constantly on the look out for an opportunity exact revenge of the most destructive kind.

For only the second time in a month, poor weather returned today and had the effect of postponing the golf until today. Mr. Clipboard has organised it and we are to report to St Donat Golf Course for lunch at no later than 12.30, the tee time is 1.58 we are due to have completed 9 holes by approximately 3.56 , leaving some 24 minutes for a beer before returning in time to join him for drinks at precisely 5pm. The Wingco, the worst time keeper in history, will of course take no apparent notice of the schedule, and will no doubt be arriving late comme d'habitude.

He was for instance an hour late for that group walk on New Years Day but luckily we had all factored this in when planning when to arrive. I managed to take this picture of the old village of Gourdon looking down towards the sea at Cannes. Eat your heart out Mr. De Mille.

A view from the hills behind Gourdon down to the sea at Cannes

Today marks the first occasion we will venture out on to the golf course during the festive season. St Donat is, in my opinion, the best value golf facility in the area, and has the added advantage of having a fine restaurant on a sunny terrace overlooking a lake with a huge fountain, which reminds me that last night. On a short restorative early evening visit to The Queens Legs pub in Valbonne, I was faced with another huge fountain, this time of verbal dross emanating from the mouths of Mr. Clipboard, the Wingco and Paul Thornton Allan, my opponents today.

The subject was the golf handicap system, which I consider is abused by these cowboys, whilst I adhere religiously to the spirit of the rules. Again I had to put up with a constantly recurring theme from these three, trying to claim the moral high ground whilst actually in the mire. I suggested that I always win against these less talented golfers and they took exception, based on the handicap system which is a fad designed to allow them to "compete" with me.

As the argument became more heated, I suggested that today we should abandon the handicap system and play man against man. Of course to no one's surprise this was rejected out of hand, which leaves me once again with the spectre of winning, but listening to a lot of upper class bleating about how I had lost.

Post Golf Facts

Let's be straight about it, I won the golf. The public schoolboys who were my companions played their own little game, the highlight of which was that they did not seem to be required to putt, such were the long putts they were giving each other. The best comment of the day emanated from the Wingco who, upon seeing one of my magnificent drives caress some leaves on its way to the centre of the fairway, responded to my comment about the tree shivering in anticipation, by suggesting that it was more likely shivering at the memory of its lost brothers and sisters that had been pulped to provide pages for my book "Summer in the Cote d'Azur".

Later on, we were invited to early evening drinks with Mr. Clipboard. Amongst the guests were Mr. Humphreys, my style guru, who was free, and whose first reaction was to praise me for my daring choice of attire. Hitherto, he felt he was alone amongst his peers who could carry off the wearing of a petrol blue cashmere (effect) sweater, but it seems in his opinion, which is for me omnipotent when it comes to fashion trends, that I pulled it off (not the sweater).

I did discover a very interesting fact from the lovely Sylvie, wife of the brooding and magnificent Hans the Dutchman. Mr. Humphreys has a race horse named after him. How flattering? I am not certain I would view this as quite the honour that Mr. Humphreys thought it was. No, it is not jealousy; it's more the opening up of an endless range of jokes at one's expense from people like me. I admit that Mr. Humphreys is an easy target for humour in many respects; I mean would you rather be named Ferrari or Shergar? Maserati or Mr. Ed? It seems that Mr. Humphreys (the horse) is a flat racer which by implication means he is not good over the jumps; do you see where we could go with this?

Also enjoying the finely marshalled drinks and nibbles was Master Mariner Mundell, who again took exception to the implication that he may have been involved in bullying. When we were unable to agree about whether this implication would stick he threatened more violence. So, no implication of bullying there then. Mr. Clipboard finally condemned his copy of my first book to a funeral pyre on his living room fire, and then took photographs, much to the glee of the other public schoolboys present, who will surely regret their actions, particularly when recent events are referred to in this, my second book.

The best line from the Christmas period came from the BBC's Mrs. Browns Boy's claiming that one of Santa's reindeer was called Richard the brown nose reindeer. It seems he is stationed directly behind Rudolph the red-nosed reindeer but he has trouble stopping.

This seems a suitably apt way to wave goodbye to the Christmas season and with half an eye on regular reader the Reverend Jeff, thank Christ for that. It is all very jolly and great fun for the first few days, the first week even, but the last few days become a marathon and, given the carnage (brought in by eating too much meat?) wrecked on my slender figure, I will need to run several marathons to regain my normal sylph like shape.

Back To Reality

We all know that all the fad diets, the gym, and all the other getting back in to shape routines have at their root the three principles of eating less, drinking less alcohol and exercising more, so I have decided to try to embrace these principles for the next ten days. At least I had until a chance conversation yesterday with the Head of Currencies Direct, France, the lovely Pippa Maile, who told me that giving up alcohol completely for a period of time was dangerous for the liver. It seems that this fine organ adapts to one's lifestyle and sudden changes to one's routine and one's intake can have an adverse effect, thus I have had to reconsider one part of this worthy triumvirate, and reconsider the planned period of temperance. But as the song says "Two out of three ain't bad".

Part of this get thin routine will involve eating loads of vegetables, and avoiding red meat and I am concerned that people may mistake me for that weirdest sect, the nearest to the totally weird anorexics, vegetarians. All right-thinking people know that vegetarianism is fundamentally wrong. Has anyone ever seen a vegetarian that looks well? I well remember a concert promoter in Aylesbury in my youth who was of this ilk but tried to impose a similarly misguided dietary approach on his pet dog, a Jack Russell, but unknown to our famous impresario, on visits to the house after the pubs had shut, and normally with a take away Chinese containing spare-ribs, the little mutt got a quick break from his all vegetable diet…well the poor dog had to have some relief.

The French have little truck with vegetarians; indeed many restaurants locally do not even cater for them, but which diet is recognized as the best in the world, and with the lowest obesity rate in the modern world? France of course and the Mediterranean diet especially.

There was unprecedented wind last night, a great deal of it probably caused by over indulgence in the Christmas diet, at least that was what the Nice Lady Decorator claimed. The mistral blowing outside was as strong as anything I have seen in the seven years I have lived in France. I suspect I may have to rescue some of the garden furniture from the swimming pool this morning.

Of course wind is an important element in flight, and I had some sympathy for some Brits who were due to take off to return to England last evening. I say some, because I have absolutely no sympathy for those people flying back who were responsible for tearing pages out of my book and making paper planes from them during the festive season. In fact I have a picture below of the Wingco in just that despicable act of sacrilege, and although he has remained here in the Cote d'Azur, others are on their way back to the UK in fierce winds. I do hope their flight was uncomfortable.

With Christmas over, the spirit of goodwill to all men seems to have ended rather abruptly, at least as far as that Nice Lady Decorator is concerned. I should have known as soon as the first nag of the day woke me from my slumber. I think I had failed to iron my dressing gown or shut a drawer or something else equally piddling. Just as I was sensing that this would not be an easy day, the clincher arrived. It was the nag about the wrong shape of log.

During the winter, and with a huge supply of wood from the trees we cut and the logs we collect daily on walks around the Valmasque, we tend to keep a fire going through the night using what we call a "night watchman", a big log at night to try to keep it in. It is the agreed duty of the first one up to make that all important first cup of tea first thing in the morning, and to attempt to get the fire up and burning. To this end it is my duty to ensure there are logs in the log basket, but until yesterday, when it fell to that Nice Lady Decorator to prepare the first tea of the day, and thus attend to the fire, I was unaware that logs had to be a particular shape.

It transpires that the log she had selected from the basket was the wrong shape (too long, I think she a phrase I don't hear far too often). Obviously I had fallen down in my duty and needed a good telling off as the room had filled with smoke and it was my entire fault. It came to my lips and I almost blurted out that there are some 500 logs outside, perhaps she could choose one where the tree had produced, or rather I had prepared, a log that did not displease her. I took this picture of the fire last night. I think these are the right shape but cannot be certain. I googled "correct shaped logs" but nothing definitive came up, so I will no doubt be getting more examples of her anger until I can ascertain what shape of log pleases her.

The wrong shape of log, apparently

For some unaccountable reason the reference to logs reminds me of a time in my teenage years when I once lived at the house of the Reverend Jeff's family. His mother was a staunch Baptist and often had the vicar around for tea. The Reverend Jeff had rather unkindly deposited a log of a quite different kind, a sort of semi-circular deposit, in the toilet just before the vicars' visit, much to the chagrin of his mother, who spent some time flushing the loo and beating the offending item with a stick to try to flush it away, before the weight of imagined church disapproval descended upon her.

Before I set off to the golf course yesterday, to work, I enquired of that Nice Lady Decorator as to what activity she had in mind for the day. She said she had quite a few jobs to do including identifying which birds were visiting the now sorely depleted and slightly less than luxuriant pomegranate tree, which is now doubling as a bird sanctuary.

Now call me old-fashioned but I do not see how looking at birds could be construed as work. If that is the case then I have spent a great deal more of my life working than I had previously thought. When I arrived home she excitedly revealed that amongst the feathered visitors to her bird sanctuary was a long-tailed tit. It gets worse; as she went on to give me the bird over my writing of my daily column. She suggested that with a slight tweak of the spelling of the name of her ornithologist discovery, one could easily describe the style of writing I employ. So now I have been blessed with another epithet, apparently I am now a "long taled tit".

Talking of old fruits; I see there was a comment from the Reverend Jeff implying that I may have been the perpetrator of the semi-circular turd that would not flush, which was causing his mother such anguish prior to an expected visit by the vicar. I am afraid I had to poo-poo that suggestion. It is important toilet my readers know that is untrue.

As expected, there has been just too much to write about to include a full report of my singles golf match at the Grande Bastide yesterday. Suffice to say it was cut due to lack of space.

Wild time? I thought she asked, and for a fleeting moment I forgot my advancing years and said, certainly, where and when? It was something of a surprise as we were not alone and it was not the first Saturday in the month but, what the heck I thought, don't look a gift horse in the mouth. No, "Wild Thyme" she said with that look that can pierce a hole in steel. I know she loves me and I love her but the look that Nice Lady Decorator keeps in her armoury for special occasions, actually not just for special occasions, but for any time I have muttered something which does not find favour, is frightening to behold. So, no more than four or five times a day then, on a good day. She was referring, of course, to the abundance of that herb on the hillside where we were taking in the view.

We were walking up a very steep track above Gurdon, exhausting but ultimately providing a sensational panorama from Nice across to St Tropez. After a deserved beer, it was back home to change, ready for the first social occasion for some days, with Master Mariner Mundell at one of their many residences, this one in the heights of Opio or Plascassier.

To be able to have lunch outside is a treat whatever time of year it is, but to be able to do it in January is a special bonus, and so it was that nearly 20 grateful ex-pats sat outside, and enjoyed an eclectic mix of roasted meats, lasagna, quiche, a bean stew and 2 cheeseboards. This was a triumph for variety over planning, which as I assume was undertaken by the Master Mariner himself, and was errr…creative to say the least.

When one is asked to bring a dish to a party, the normal thing is to liaise with the host to ensure all food bases are covered and a balanced meal results. Clearly this element of the planning went a little awry, but a splendid afternoon, and a lovely melee of food was enjoyed by all.

I was hampered somewhat as my BlackBerry, normally my faithful old note taker, decided to run out of power just as lunch commenced. With my memory being what it is, many people have escaped (unless memory returns or someone snitches) with faux pas that I would normally gleefully record, ready for regurgitated the next morning in my daily column.

What I do remember is Blind Lemon Milsted's beautiful Scandinavian goddess of a wife Ingeborg fatally undermining his determination not to purchase a copy of my book, by buying one and then coming to my table to ask me to sign it. I contend that it was entirely coincidental that I was seated next to him when it happened, but I swear he does not believe me. Anyway, I can report that she is thrilled with her purchase, and he has a newly grumpy countenance which does not suit him.

The wonderfully 1960's icon Anthony "Dock of the" Bay was one of the many attendees along with his beautiful (and very considerably younger) wife Amanda. I made the mistake of complimenting this compelling old smoothie on his wearing of a cravat, but was corrected in no uncertain terms. It was not a cravat but a silk scarf. As a council house boy who may never understand the distinction, I shall be careful not to comment about one or the other in future.

There is still a lot of abuse and hostility floating about concerning the recent demise of my splendid beard, at that lunch at the end of last year at the Auberge St Donat, overrun by public schoolboys. My Australian mate Bruce (yes that is his real name, I have not had to caricature him at all), suggests in the comments section that what my beard really needed was just need a bit of bikini wax, rather than the ritual destruction administered by the Master Mariner and his coterie of thugs, and it is a good point well made, and fundamentally ignored by the public school bullies who have still to be interviewed by the police for this common assault. Actually, I suppose they would argue that it could not possibly be a common assault, as they all went to public school, which as mere mortals know is not common at all. Common is where common people live. I myself was born in London between Wandsworth Common and Clapham Common, but I don't know where I am going with this.

The Wheels Of Commerce Begin To Grind Again

I had a meeting in the afternoon in Valbonne with Gerald Gomis, who is now working with award-winning local estate agents Blue Square, who have offices in the old village. He kindly offered to make me a cup of tea, which was somewhat of a departure for the French, and I jokingly asked him if knew how to make it. He assured me that he did and promptly added the teabag to the freshly brewed coffee he was making for himself.

It was a bold effort, and, to his credit, as soon as he had done it, he put his head in his hands and said "Oh no, this will be in the blog". I assured him that I would not be this cruel, and promised not to mention it, so please ignore this last sentence; it was just your imagination.

Lunch with some of the usual suspects, Master Mariner Mundell, the Wingco and Dancing Greg Harris, took place at the Auberge St Donat and followed a very pleasant game of tennis with the same personnel in the continuing warm winter sunshine.

As the MOGS have been so dominant in recent months, it was

decided to split up the weaker players, but as much as I tried to remove the gathering certainty as to who was the weakest player, I am afraid to say that young Greg ended up on the losing side.

The loser at lunch however was once again the Master, who continued to defend his recent involvement in bullying. His claim was that, as I had on a previous occasion managed to thwart the bully boys in late October by claiming that I wanted to keep my beard, at least until the book launch, I had, by default, given an implied licence to allow it to be hacked off at a later stage.

This is clear nonsense; it is like a failed rapist claiming that as he had been fought off and not reported, the victim was implying she was game for a shag at a later stage. He should be ashamed of himself. He also had the audacity to suggest he saved me from injury by holding me in a tight head-lock whilst Mr. Clipboard became Mr. Clipboard and performed the "annoying facial hair" surgery. He suggested that I should be grateful and seemed sincere. I have seldom witnessed a clearer case of self-delusion, but as he is a Currencies Direct customer of course I forgive him.

Absent today was Anthony "Dock of the" Bay, who had joined in with the general abuse of my book at the end of last year. When I mentioned to the others that Anthony now has this splendid new epithet for this book, one of the public schoolboys dredged up an "amusing" take on the old Percy Sledge classic; "Sitting on the dick of the boy". Once a public schoolboy always a public schoolboy it seems. Old habits die hard (if you get my drift).

The France Show

So, to London, away from the sunshine, and into the arms of the deep English midwinter. The idea, of course, is to bring a little sunshine into the winter lives of my countrymen, this time by way of attending The France Show, armed with copies of my book, which I will gladly give to people, along with my signature and dedication of their choice, in return for the measly sum of £10. Three days of intense media pressure awaits me so I must be strong. My suitcase is full of books, and if that Nice Lady Decorator gets her way, the suitcase will be empty, and will require replenishment with clothes for our return on Sunday. It is probably the first time we have been in agreement about the hopes for the number of sales I want to achieve. I am not sure whether to be pleased or not. So rushed off my feet was I, that I cannot recall if it was 3 or 4 copies I sold, my feeling was that it was 4.

It is the kind of show that attracts a large number of what I call one per-centers, dreamers who dream about living in France, others that have lived there, some that love French culture and food but have no intentions of ever living there, and the odd eccentric. My picture today is of an odd eccentric.

Let me start with the eccentric. I met a chap called Mark, was the highlight, mainly because he had been able to spend several years cultivating a splendid beard and moustache. Regular readers will already be aware of the inherent dangers of trying to nurture a moustache of this luxuriance and magnificence when one lives on the Cote d'Azur.

Another great character, and old friend, who holidays regularly in

Cannes, Gordon Cato, was visiting, I think with the sole purpose of buying a copy of my book. Over a glass of wine in the champagne bar at the exhibition, he expounded an interesting theory about regulating ones drinking. He is a man with a prodigious appetite for wine of any colour. He was advised some years ago to take one day off from alcohol per week. His theory was that as he didn't drink a drop until he was aged thirteen, he had a lot of days in credit. Now that this advice, to avoid alcohol, has been recently raised from one to two days a week, his plans are in disarray and a recalculation is necessary. This is the man who, a number of years ago asked his doctor what the maximum number of units was recommended for a man to consume and was told 28. "That's fine" he said, "I couldn't drink that in a day". The doctor meant per week. I like a man who knows his own limits.

My daughter, Charlie, aka Sprog 2 came to meet me yesterday, convinced that I had hired Earls Court and staged The France Show just to promote my book, and was a little disappointed by the scene that confronted her when she arrived. She had expected that her father would be the major attraction, and be feted by huge crowds and be the centre of attention, and had even brought her video camera in order to record the whole day for posterity. This was something of a shock to her, and indeed a shock to me that she could be quite so naïve.

Later at the Indian restaurant, she continued this theme of blond dizziness by asking Manuel, the far from Spanish waiter, the entirely reasonable question (had it not been an Indian restaurant) "do you have Nan bread" A somewhat bemused Manuel answered in the affirmative. I cannot think of an Indian restaurant that does not serve Nan.

Earlier during the afternoon I finally gave way to the incessant requests for a TV interview and granted one to the organisers of The France Show. At first I thought it was a good move, to allow the pre-eminent TV crew exclusive access to my good self, but having interviewed me extensively for almost 30 seconds, they moved on to that Nice Lady Decorator for several minutes for her reactions to the show itself, which was ultimately, to my chagrin,

115

the piece they used in the film.

Lights, camera,....shopping

As I had predicted, that Nice Lady Decorator has been engaging in retail therapy of the most intensive nature. This means that all our cases are now crammed full of new purchases and there will be precious little room for any unsold copies. I have been bleating to her about this rather unfair scenario, and what was I supposed to do with the bulky unsold merchandise, but the only helpful suggestion she has made so far was to suggest that the table upon which was balancing a plethora of, mostly empty, wine bottles, could use a book to stuff under one of the legs in order to make it a little less wobbly. Such are the challenges for a successful author in my little world.

Yesterday I rather naively mentioned the word "dash" in the context of a trip to Gatwick. Well, getting to Gatwick from London was the usual horrible packed, sweaty trip but at least the train was on time. The "dash" bit fell apart when we got to the airport. Because it was a Sunday I presume that was the reason only five security aisles were open, whilst at least the same number were closed. Has it dawned on the imbeciles who run the airport that the numbers of people traveling at the weekends may be the same, or perhaps more than a normal weekday? What is the point of having shiny new facilities then not manning them? Is there a shortage of willing recruits looking for jobs?

The comparison to a well-run airport, Nice, could not be starker. When traveling in to London on Thursday from France's second busiest airport, there was no waiting, either at passport control or security. You may wonder where this is going (back to France, of course). I am escaping back to the land of good wine and the vine.

Whilst working in London at the weekend, I received several encouraging and helpful comments and tips about what to do with any unsold items. Tony "I invented the internet" Coombs was the most inventive, sending me exact details and a map of a recycling centre near Gatwick, the implication being that perhaps sales were not going at the pace I had thought, and that I may have a problem with excess baggage on the return journey. It seems closer to the truth that I have excess baggage in the supportive friends department. All I can say is that I know where you live and with your history of incoherence after a sniff of wine, retribution will come eventually, actually probably rather quickly but I don't mind how long it takes.

Escape From London

That Nice Lady Decorator's 4 x 4 was loaned out last week and unfortunately sustained a puncture. She said to me "what are you going to do about that spare tyre?" I said not to worry I would pick it up today. She said "not that spare tyre, the one hanging around your waist". Actions is very definitely required, so more exercise and less food and drink is on the cards, at least until Wednesday when I have my normal tennis match followed by lunch at Auberge St Donat.

I have never been afraid to use long words but this is a bit scary; hippomonstrosesquippedaliophobia, whilst at first look seemed to express a phobia of giant four-legged hippo's (is there any other sort?), is apparently the fear of long words. It has been said by some of my public schoolboy bullying friends that I have a poor understanding of long words but that is intercontinental. I know exactly how to spell bullying.

I heard a story yesterday on Riviera Radio about what seemed to be a serious drugs bust with tragic consequences. It seems that a chap was brandishing a shot-gun and threatening his neighbours over in the Var.

He was distressed because he thought they were stealing his pot plants and was threatening to shoot them (the neighbours, not the pot plants). The police were called, and, when he pointed the gun at them, the police shot him dead. My first thought was that those that live by the gun die by the gun, and that maybe the ganja he was cultivating was of a particularly "high" quality, and he was understandably appalled by the prospect of having his stash raided by the local inhabitants. It crossed my mind that given his apparent involvement with the drugs world perhaps he expected to die, but it turns out that he was seventy-five years old, and the pot plants in question were lavender plants. Summary justice French style.

Sunset over Valbonne, but who left that light on?

A mild day yesterday ended in a spectacular sunset and it was mild enough to sit in the newly repaired Pav in early evening for a calming glass of wine, from where I took this picture. A great sunset like this implies a few clouds in the area, so perhaps some hope for the local ski resorts?

It is not often that the Nice Lady Decorator and I are in complete agreement, but it happened yesterday. The bathroom scales are charged with the unenviable task of monitoring the weight reduction process in which we are both involved at present. Eating almost nothing and increasing our daily exercise over the past 3 days has seen a considerable improvement in our respective shapes, but we both expected support and confirmation from the weighing machine in the bathroom. It has refused to cooperate, and clearly deranged, it is doggedly sticking to some readings from last week.

This is obviously a problem with the machinery, which is battery powered and has an electronic readout. I have tried talking to it, cuddling it, even stamping on it, but it refuses to cooperate, so there is nothing else for it, new batteries will be inserted (very roughly if I get my way) tomorrow, after which, if it fails to cooperate, then more drastic action must be contemplated.

Given the terrible disaster playing out just along the Italian coast, where the Costa Concordia has sunk with much loss of life, and my son's interest in models, I rang the up market toy shop in Valbonne and asked if they had any construction kits of the ship. The shop assistant said he had one left, so I asked him to put in on one side for me.

I am not to blame for that joke; it is the clear responsibility of my chief researcher Peter Lynn. Earlier in the week he had already sent me some very tasteless jokes on the same theme that were very funny but far too controversial for this column.

So to Wayne and Lucy's the Red Radish Secret Supper, so secret, that everybody with whom I came into contact knew about it. Wayne Brown with another marketing masterstroke, It was a fun evening, however the fun turned to horror for me when I discovered that a copy of my book had been stolen, and placed in the smallest room in the house, accompanied by a rough hand-written sign inviting users of the facilities to use the pages for....well, I hesitate to say exactly for what private activity, but I think you may smell a rat so to speak. I took a picture of it in situ as evidence should the police wish to press charges for this crime.

Earlier in the day I was dragged from my ~~kennel~~ office to be a lumberjack. "Just a few branches" she said, but within minutes the longest triple-section ladder in the world was out and I found myself teetering on the top most rung with a bow saw in my hand. I am not saying it was high but I could see the coast of Africa. In an attempt to get something rewarding from the experience, I did my utmost to get the enormous bough through which I had been commanded to saw to land on the heinous hound Banjo, but I suspect he realised he was in danger. Just as the monstrous oak was beginning to go, I called him over, but he remained obstinately out of range; A triumph for poor training. What on earth that Nice Lady Decorator sees in that crappy cretinous cocker I shall never understand.

Midem Approaces

MIDEM, the annual music business convention, starts in Cannes next weekend. I shall no doubt be entertained to dinner eventually at my expense by my legal representative, Nigel Davies from Davenport Lyons. He has an alter ego after a few drinks when he turns into mythical northern Jewish lawyer Al Yiddley, who hails from the very Jewish area called Allwoodley near Leeds. I am invited to dinner on Saturday, so I shall take my biggest credit card. It seems that Joss Stone will be at this annual music biz junket this year and will be talking at some event. I think I would prefer her singing.

"It's a pity those birds cannot hang on to those greasy balls" said that Nice Lady Decorator yesterday afternoon as we toiled in the garden trying to bring it some order. Always a master of the double entendre, I did a double-take and made a comment of which I am not proud but she had the good grace (or base sense of humour?) to laugh. She was of course referring to the special balls of bird food she has been fastidiously hanging on our pomegranate tree. It seems that certain species of bird are unable to get sufficient purchase on these spherical bird attractors in order to feed, but I have yet to work out how the balls being greasy had anything to do with it, or precisely how it impeded them. She is excited by the range of bird-life she has attracted to the garden, at the last count running now to over twenty species that she has already identified, of which I found the whimbrel the most interesting, if only it had been so easy to attract birds when I was younger. I too, could have been very good at ensuring my balls were greasy if it ensured it increased my success rate with women, indeed there are several girls.....but that was a long time ago and I do not want to go into that now.

Today's plan is to jump on the train from Mouans Sartoux and go for lunch on the beach at Juan les Pins. It is something that must be done. 6 weeks of almost exclusively sunny weather requires a considered response by us ex-pats, and having considered the possibilities very carefully, I think lunch on the beach is the right thing to do. I need to get into training for MIDEM. It was 17 degrees yesterday afternoon – if you are reading this in the UK, why are you still there?

It is that or another infernal walk up a mountain; in fact this picture was taken just before the New Year on just such a walk and depicts a view from the top of the hills behind the beautiful village of Gurdon, looking down into the valley above the village.

The donkey track above Gourdon

I am arraigned in the comments section for the quality of the photographs that appear in this column. This is rather unfair as I consider myself to be a writer, indeed a successful writer, rather than a photographer. My preference is for atmospheric shots, or, if I am honest, pictures of embarrassing digressions, or better still humiliating examples of private excess. Quality is not my photographic watchword, shocking is. The fact that some photos I have published are shocking in whatever context, actually quite pleases me. I have mined a very deep seam of fascination with local intrigue and excesses, or so it seems. Just to illustrate this point, I publish today a picture taken over the Christmas period for which I have no explanation.

Nope, I have no idea either and I don't even want to speculate.

Yesterday I was assigned to deliver the gorgeously athletic Lisa Thornton Allan to the airport. She regaled me with details of an event that took place the night before to which I do not appear to have been invited. Mr. Humphreys (he was free, as was dinner for the guests from what I hear) was apparently having a birthday celebration at La Jarrerie, a fabulous but expensive restaurant on the way up to Bar sur Loup, bandit country, up on the northern edges of civilisation, a village that is beautiful but rather basic, a bit like Yorkshire which, although being up north retains a savage beauty.

What astounds me is that I was not invited. I shall doubtless receive a written apology in due course. Perhaps it is a question of style? Mr. Humphreys, when free, as regular readers will know, is my style guru, my inspiration for sartorial elegance, so perhaps my recent clothing choices have been found wanting? I am at a loss here, I now have a petrol blue cashmere (effect) sweater, a lime green made to measure golfing suit (to match the silver golf shoes picked out with lime green trim in almost the same shade), I have some Kenyan multi-coloured patchwork house slacks, but all these garments purchased and worn under the careful tutelage of Mr. Humphreys have clearly not been sufficient for me to reach top table status, or indeed any table. However, I will not be down-hearted and, as the annual sales have started, I shall be going into Cannes today for some personal retail therapy and search for some clothing of which he would approve. I wonder if there is a transvestite factory outlet anywhere nearby?

More Work

An evening of networking is upon me at Internations local meeting at Juan les Pins. Work can be so irksome but arriving at the sublime Juan les Pins at sunset, a little early for the event, was the perfect antidote as my picture below I hope depicts. Fifteen years ago I would have instead been aboard a commuter train from London, standing up, cold, tired and soaked through from having been rained on. Maybe the Reverend Jeff is right, there is a God.

"I just need you to move a few boxes for me" was the request from Mr. Clipboard (or Mr. Clipboard as he has become known after the enforced removal of my beard in that restaurant "accident" at the end of last year). I felt it was an unreasonable request, not easily declined, and once I had agreed was told, in typical Clipboard style, to line up in an orderly fashion at 07 30 with The Wingco to report for duty, properly equipped for boxes, loading of. I am sure some of boxes contained spare clipboards.

What I had not bargained for was an entire morning of acting as an unpaid removal man. As the range and scale of tasks became clear, I demanded that, at the very least, lunch should be offered in payment for my services, a demand that became ever more strident as my car was not the only vehicle being used in the removal process, there was a huge van as well, which was also loaded to capacity, before being driven to Plascassier to unload.

On my way to work at Juan les Pins last night

Mutinous is a good word to describe our mood when we arrived at our destination, because the contents of my car and a lorry the size of Valbonne had to be man-handled up 49 steps to his house, what he called a "minor detail" when challenged. Under immense pressure from and the Wingco and I, he gave in rather too quickly when we demanded lunch at Lou Fassum nearby as payment. The prospect of lunch at this stunning Michelin star restaurant, with views down to the sea, had the effect of keeping the troops (myself and the Wingco) quiet, well, apart from a lot of cursing and moaning, throughout the longest step class in history, as we lugged all those spare clipboards, or whatever was in the containers, up the longest staircase in Christendom. When finally it was done and the military task had been fulfilled to his satisfaction, the smirking Mr. Clipboard drove us down to Lou Fassum for lunch. It was closed for refurbishment. He must have known which is why he agreed with such alacrity to our demands. Too exhausted to argue too much, we instead adjourned to the Auberge de Provence, where myself and the Wingco made a memorable effort to extract as much value from a free lunch as possible. Fois Gras with a glass of sauterne, fillet steak, coupe colonel, (the only part of which the military element of the character of Mr. Clipboard found favour), the best wine in the house (a cheeky little Bordeaux that was really rather too young to be out on its own) washed down with the most expensive, indeed the only cognac on the menu.

MIDEM will commence tomorrow and I shall be entertained to dinner this evening by the alter ego of my lawyer whose name in costume is Al Yiddley, the Jewish lawyer from Yorkshire. When in London he is a partner in Davenport Lyons, one of the leading London litigation lawyers who will be extracting monies from me in the coming year in a High Court action but when in Cannes, and fuelled by the alcoholic delights of the Cote d'Azur comes over all Jewish and Yorkshire. We will start, as is the tradition, at The Carlton for a glass of champagne or two and head to the old town of Cannes, probably into Le Suquet for dinner, a full report tomorrow, probably.

He will no doubt be staying in a suite at The Carlton or The Martinez probably with its own Jacuzzi. I think it sums up the client lawyer relationship where the client pays the lawyer all his money and leads the life of a comparative pauper as a result, whilst the lawyer lives in the lap of luxury, feeding on the customer, literally. The word parasite comes to mind.

I say I will be entertained to dinner, but what I probably mean is that I will be entertained at dinner. Nominally, he will pay the bill but these things have a nasty habit of turning up in disguise as "a disbursement" on my bill, effectively recharging me for the dinner which one can be forgiven for thinking is a nice gesture for a client.

Before that, I have an insignificant birthday to celebrate. My polite enquiry to Mr. Coombs, shown below, in summer pose; "Will you have something a little stronger" issued one minute after midday was, I now realise, a statement exhibiting a particularly poor piece of situation management. Initially I thought one bottle of fizz would prove sufficient for him and his wife, the lovely fiery redhead Pat, for them to feel that they fully celebrated my birthday. Even the second bottle between four of us seemed to be a scenario that I could drag back from the brink, but when I was forced by that

Nice Lady Decorator to open the third bottle, and with the Rioja flowing as well, I began to realise I had a problem.

His gift of some Cohiba Cuban cigars clouded my judgement and I stupidly allowed them to undermine my proposed evening activity by allowing myself the indulgence of entertaining them It started with me asking if he was working on anything worthwhile. "Internet 2 "was his answer, although he was not big on detail, in fact he refused to supply any more details about what Internet 2 could bestow upon us than the internet we all know and love.

The fun started when we began to discuss the swimming pool he had promised his lovely wife he would install in the garden of their house near Grasse. So far, over a period of thirteen years, there seems that there have been any number of "reasons" invented by our intrepid inventor which have conspired to allow him to renege on this promise. Can you imagine having a house on the Cote d'Azur with a large garden and sweeping views across the valley, and up to the hills, having a large terraced space ideally suited to the installation of a swimming pool, making a promise to your wife and young children that you would build one, and then finding every excuse under the sun not to give the go ahead for its construction. Disgraceful. The art of extracting as much fun as possible from these situations is akin to opening oysters. These tricky little blighters are best opened by sliding a knife into the heart of their being and then forcing them wide open with a series of twisting motions. Let me tell you that in situations such as these, I am an artist. So a great deal of fun was had at the expense of our inventor, but I have promised not to mention it again, much in the same vein as his promise to have a swimming pool.

And so to Cannes for dinner. Because of the earlier impromptu luncheon I was perhaps not at my best for dinner, or at least, if I was, then I do not recall the full details. I do recall that we had a drink at The Carlton bar which cost me a little under fifty euros, and then went for dinner at nearby Pastis, a restaurant just behind the Dior shop on the Croisette for a ruinously expensive meal, so expensive that I felt compelled to pay half the bill, which in itself was more than one would normally want to pay for dinner anywhere. My lawyers alter ego, Al Yiddley was in awesome form and very amusing, but I am ashamed to say I recall little of the content, except for one phrase; "Mushy peadophile" which he used, and I have been racking my brains to imagine any context at all in which it could be used without risking arrest. It will no doubt feature in The mutterings of Al Yiddley website I intend to launch.

To say I was not at my best today following dinner out with Al Yiddley in Cannes the night before, following being attacked by the Coombs, would be like saying Bin Laden had been a bit naughty. I had forgotten that Al, when informed that La Chunga, the bar across from the Martinez in Cannes, was a known haunt for ladies of the night, had insisting on going there after a fine dinner and three bottles of a very good but vastly overpriced St Emilion Grand Cru, and once again it seemed to be my round. He was desperate to go and dance with the pretty vacant-eyed beauties and was a bit indignant when none of them wanted to know. Apparently a fiver and a fish, chips and mushy pea dinner are not quite sufficient for any of them to contemplate incentive for doing the business he had in mind... I have heard it said that good judgment is the result of a bad experience, but the bad experience is usually down to poor judgment.

The last time I was there, I was seated close a lady who was, well how can I describe her; she was no stranger to a kebab. Her ability to eat what looked like her own bodyweight in fois gras has left an indelible mark on my memory, one that I hope to be able to lay to rest today. Mrs. Creosote lives.

It got worse. By the time I left Valbonne for the last day of MIDEM in Cannes, the rain (ushered in by all those Brits arriving from wet and windy England and bringing their filthy weather with them) had turned to wet snow and the puddles on the lawn were beginning to ice over. This is the Cote d'Azur for Christ's sake, this is not what I signed up for, and this was not in the brochure. If there was a god and he did not have a call centre in India (or probably Jerusalem, come to think of it) I would have made a complaint in the strongest possible terms. Imagine, if that was the case, what would the number be? 0845 godisgood, or for complaints: 0845 godiswrong? But I digress.

It is not that I dislike snow, I like it when it is in its correct place, and indeed, will be seeking it out later in the week and next week with a jaunt up to Limone, just across the Italian border for a bit of skiing. What I am complaining about is that I am not dressed for and don't expect this kind of thing in the jewel of the French Riviera. My velvet smoking jacket, silk cravat and black and white spats are not suited to this kind of weather (neither is the music biz for that matter). I want my money back.

Still, I am a trooper, hardly ever complaining, so I was looking forward to my beach luncheon with typical bulldog spirit, half thinking that the restaurant might be deserted, but then I thought, these are music business professionals who are made of sterner material. They may be languishing in Cannes but were not going to let a bit of wind, rain and the possibility of snow deny them the opportunity to raid the expense accounts, so I expected Geoland to be buzzing, that and steaming, or at least that is what I imagined it would look like, clouds of water vapour rising from the assembled music industry entrepreneurs, the movers and shakers of the digital content world but natural events overtook me.

The first sign of trouble was the picture I received on my phone from that Nice Lady Decorator, showing snow settling in Valbonne. In the next breath I heard a delegate complaining that all buses had been cancelled due to snow being expected, and that the trains were next. It was a very quick decision, but the options were to go to lunch on the beach and then get marooned in Cannes along with loads of drunken MIDEM delegates, drowning their sorrows, complaining that they were unable to get home, or take an early train back home and have lunch locally in the snow. This was a picture from my garden yesterday afternoon as I arrived back, just in time.

There's no business like snow business

Snow In Valbonne

Whereas I love lunch on the beach any time of year, the Auberge Provencal in Valbonne Square is an idyllic place to have lunch when a winter wonderland surrounds you. Having just managed to get home through the snow and breathing a sigh of relief, what better plan could there be but to head out again to the Auberge Provencal for lunch? Well, I had a number of different opinions, most of which involved hunkering down in the snowstorm and not venturing outside, however in the spirit of democracy, and with that Nice Lady Decorator having the casting vote (dare I say the only vote?) I went with the democracy, at least as the way she sees it.

Once every 30 years said the locals. Snow is a rarity so close to the coast but it seems that I left Cannes on Tuesday just in time to be certain of getting home, before the plethora of abandoned cars helped block the roads. The fact that two years ago I was marooned at Gatwick when Nice Airport was closed during the last local snow storm, and took three days to secure another flight home, seems merely to feed the frenzy over global warming. Let's be straight about this. At present the earth is going through a slight warming, due almost entirely to the activity of the sun which even this week has had the effect of producing the northern lights as far south as Yorkshire. I know that is much farther north than most civilized people wish to venture, but that is a different discussion. A few percentage points less carbon created by man can in no way significantly affect the warming of earth as much as sun spots or other solar activity, and whilst it is a worthy cause, the amount of hot air produced by politicians in support of this unsustainable argument does little to help. Indeed the emission of methane by animals over the world far exceeds the amount of carbon produced by man (with special emphasis on the hot air spouted by the believers) and excreted into the atmosphere.

I have a picture today of the effects of global warming in the Cote d'Azur. It was taken just before we set off on foot to Valbonne village in a party that included Pete Bennett from Blue Water Yachting, Slash and Burn Thornton Allan and their respective wives, the cycling phenomenon Julie (just about to set off on a charity bike ride in Kenya), and the steely eyed Lisa. The plan was to walk into the village for a coffee at the Cafe des Arcades.

Global warming in retreat?

I suppose I was to blame. Demob happy after several days hard slog at MIDEM, I called for a cognac to accompany my coffee. Not to be outdone, and with the dawning realisation that with many roads shut, schools closed, buses not running, offices closed and the added bonus of sipping coffee in pleasant sunshine glinting on the snow, that little would be achieved on the work front, the chaps in the party joined me in imbibing large cognacs to keep out the cold. I use the plural advisedly because a communal taste for more than one coffee with cognac swept the male contingent and before I knew what was happening, coffee had turned into lunch. How the pre-lunch bill could reach close to 90 euros is still a fact with which I am wrestling.

Lunch was taken, wine was drunk and several of our impromptu luncheon posse returned with us at the behest of that nice Lady Decorator to take an afternoon cap (as opposed to a night-cap) in the Pav.

Subsequent events are a little hazy but I do remember having a conversation with my accountant about the late filing of my UK tax return, and I am certain that I issued detailed instructions as to how to deal with a number of issues raised. It's just that at this moment I cannot exactly recall the nature of those instructions.

Today I shall be dealing with outstanding paperwork (indeed any paperwork with which I am involved is always dealt with in an outstanding manner) when I hope to be able to retrace my steps and unravel the instructions handed down to my accountant yesterday. Success may mitigate my tax liability, so what more incentive could a man need?

After he retired, Sir Winston Churchill took a cruise aboard an Italian cruise liner. When questioned about his choice of carrier by some journalists, he explained that he had made his choice based on great food, wonderful service and if there was an emergency on board, there would be none of this women and children first nonsense. Never a truer word was spoken in jest. How prescient, given events recently, with the Costa Concordia running aground and with the captain one of the first to safety. It seems from one report I saw, that he had steered too close to the coast so he could wave to some relatives.

Talking of mighty vessels taking improbable courses, I hear today that one female amongst yesterday's brigade of happy souls in the "cognac and coffee followed by lunch party" in Valbonne Square seemed temporarily to have lost control over her coordination. It seems that on her way home, she popped into a friend's house to collect children, even some of her own, and was in such a state that the friend had to button her coat for her before she stumbled into the evening. Regular readers will know that my cardinal rule is never to reveal the identity of the perpetrator of these kinds of embarrassing events, but I believe that Paul Thornton Allan shares my knowledge of the miscreant's identity and perhaps it is not too illuminating to reveal that he has close, some may even say marital, links to and with the subject in question.

Today, as long as it dawns as forecast, i.e. to be bright and sunny, we shall jump in the car and head up to the snow fields nearby. A quick aerial photograph may suggest that skiing could be on offer in Valbonne itself, but we have a plan to battle up to Greoliere Les

Neiges, about an hour's drive away, for a mornings skiing, before a trip to Limone Piemont just over the Italian border next week.

Wisely I had earlier turned down the opportunity to play golf with the Landlubbers, an off shoot of the REGS golf society this weekend. I say wisely because I was being exhorted by Dave "Gruff" Goddard to play on the basis that the weather forecast was good for the weekend. It seems 20 cms of snow sitting on the golf course may have justified my refusal, and may not have figured in his planning.

Last night was predicted to be coldest night for years on the sunny Cote d'Azur with as low as minus 6 degrees Celsius being talked about. Given that there is no real lagging on pipes in this area because it is not normally needed, we may have some work for the hordes of Polish plumbers who had overrun Britain a few years ago. I predict a nasty spate of burst pipes once this cold snap is over. I have heard a Zen teaching which suggests that experience is something you get just after you need it. With global warming perhaps now is the time for builders automatically to lag pipes.

Going To A Ski Resort To Escape The Snow

There really is nothing better in winter in the sunshine other than to be in a pretty ski resort, do some un-taxing skiing and then have lunch in the sunshine. My explanation to Currencies Direct that I was heading up into the mountains to search for new customers was dismissed with the contempt it richly deserved.

It was not frenetic skiing by any means and with dinner last night scheduled at the big man's house, with Peachy Butterfield and his delectable wife Susie, it was clearly imperative that we returned from Greoliere Les Neiges in time for a siesta in advance of last evening's hostilities, which were far more interesting than yesterday's hostilities.

Just as I was slipping into the bed sheets after a skiing and lunch, having cheerily removed my smoking jacket and cravat, that Nice Lady Decorator said to me what I heard as "what I really need is a good screwing". That was when the trouble started. It seemed that rather than referring to winter sports of the bedroom variety she was referring to her reading light, supplied by a screw-in bulb which had fused. At that moment I felt much the same, but whereas her problem was easily resolved by the insertion of a new one, my problem was solved by....I am not sure where I am going with this, suffice to say that one of my jobs today will be to go to the supermarket and stock up on screw-in light bulbs.

So to dinner last night with the voyeur of viognier, the crown prince of prosecco, the Cheshire cheese of Chardonnay, Peachy himself, newly returned from Christmas in the UK and desperately in need to some south of France fun and frivolity.

Greoliere under a metre of new snow

The evening did not start well. I am at best ambivalent about cement mixers, but Peachy and that Nice Lady Decorator were quickly engrossed in a discussion about the relative merits of petrol driven or electrical powered devices. All I knew was that having spent a good part of my career and a chunk of this week at MIDEM involved in the organization of music mixing and re mixing, I felt that work time was over and preferred talking about wine or indeed sex, but more of that later (talk I mean).

Later on it emerged that Peachy, in search of a new career direction, particularly one that allows him to remain in the south of

France somewhat more than now, is the case, has come up with a master plan. He is going to sell curtains. For a moment I considered using an old joke about a salesman traveling in ladies underwear which I have chosen to avoid, but given the bright colours he always wears I did not have the heart to say to him that if he took it on, he would be travelling in curtains.

If you live down here you will have noticed a distinct lack of curtains in most houses. This is due in main to the local propensity for shutters, negating the need for this outdated English obsession. I pointed this out to Le Peche Enorme, but he was not down-hearted, far from it, in fact he asked me for the number of Mr. Humphreys, firstly no doubt to see if he was free, secondly to ask his advice about colours in general and curtains in particular. Regular readers will know that Mr. Humphrey's has a track record of wearing bright colours and garments that often look to me like curtains, so to me the connection was obvious. Anyway, it seems that shortly we shall all be able to purchase top quality curtain material locally. I told him not to give up his day job if he ever got one.

I had forgotten the excellent magnum of Wrexham Rioja which I had found quite by chance in Super U in Plascassier. At least that is what the label said after I had spent three minutes with a computer and a printer before setting off for dinner with Peachy Butterfield on Friday night. So pleased was he, that he wanted to show his appreciation by coming around yesterday lunchtime for a small tincture as he called it.

Earlier, I had been doing my best to impersonate a lumberjack in the Valmasque forest where a number of branches, mainly pine, have broken off under the weight of the unaccustomed snowfall recently. There is something primeval and satisfying along the hunter-gatherer theme about going out and collecting wood for the fire. I had to stop Mr. Paul "Slash and Burn" Thornton Allan from embracing this concept rather too enthusiastically, he was all for taking his chain saw and cutting down an acre of two of protected national park, something that may have upset the authorities.

The Revered Jeff made a comment about my piece yesterday about Peachy Butterfield becoming a curtain salesman and suggesting that this could lead to a number of curtain puns. This "rings" true I would rather draw a veil over this suggestion; a blind man can see it will be curtains for him if he continues to go off the rails, we are poles apart here.

Ok, that's done. So we left the Cafe des Arcades, just in time to miss the first ten minutes of the rugby. By this time it is fair to say that we may have outstayed our welcome, and whether we were any more welcome chez "Slash and Burn" Thornton Allan is debatable as we had collected some human flotsam during the afternoon, including The Wingco, Master Mariner Mundell and Nick "I am not 60 yet" Davies, who as his nickname with which I have supplied him suggests is in age denial. I sense the aroma of a bus pass here. A splendid evening followed with hordes of rugby fans spending loads of time in the kitchen avoiding the rugby, eating shepherd's pie and consuming yet more wine.

Many people's blushes were spared as the battery in my BlackBerry, which doubles as my faithful reporter's notebook, upon which I like to make notes to remind me of embarrassing interludes or funny stories had died. Some recall of events was triggered this morning, when I discovered the two gentlemen to whom I have alluded above, asleep in my house. One was in the spare room, one on the sofa, at least that it was they wanted me to believe, but quite how that item of clothing owned by that gentleman on the sofa arrived in the spare bedroom is not something I want to go into but I will say these former public schoolboys just cannot leave it alone.

Chapter 6

Limone Skiing

The trip to Limone, a pretty ski resort village just across the Italian border, for a few days is due to start on Tuesday, with the attendant risks of eating and drinking that is likely to entail, and having had three very unrestrained days, plus a creeping insidious hangover, I decided to have a quiet day yesterday despite it being a Sunday, which as the Reverend Jeff knows is a special day normally reserved exclusively for fun and entertainment.

I had expected more of a backlash from my public schoolboy friends, to the allusion I made in my daily column, about some items of clothing belonging to one being discovered in the bedroom of the other on Saturday night, when both were staying with us (in separate bedrooms according to them). Perhaps they have not yet looked at yesterday's episode? I am sure that when they do they may be slightly agitated, perhaps even uncomfortable? If I see them today it will be interesting to see which of them has trouble sitting down.

I turned down lunch. Just take a few moments to contemplate the significance of this statement. I am living in the beautiful south of France, on the edge of Provence amongst the hordes of idle rich ex-pats who live in Valbonne, am a renowned luncher and I had turned down lunch. I was not ill or hung over or suicidal, at least at first, but I was however subject to a three-line whip issued by chief whipper-snapper herself that Nice Lady Decorator.

Actually some of the public schoolboys who invited me to lunch are themselves no strangers to a three-line whip but in their little private sordid world it has a very different significance. Thus I did not go out for lunch and did not get drunk with Master Mariner Mundell, Peachy Butterfield, the Wingco or the Naked Politician, despite the fact that they had collectively decided that today was my official birthday and wished to celebrate it with me.

The reason for the whip (or the hand brake as the Naked Politician describes it) was of course that I had a number of jobs to do. Exactly what they were was never revealed to me by that Nice Lady Decorator. That, and we were expecting people for dinner.

My feeling is that in the absence of lunch it was important to stay reasonably sober before that trip to the Italian Alps and this was achieved by drinking several bottles of Gigondas, several bottles of Rioja, a bottle of Limoncello and a bottle of Biscotti Baileys (Jude O Sullivan, eat your heart out) by way of preparation for the hard time that will surely confront us in the coming days. Because our guests, Mr. and Mrs. Clipboard, did not arrive until around 10pm this seemed to me to be a good effort. Thus by the time we retired for the evening at about 2 30 am, this, early enough to be fully ready for the trip up to the Italian Alps this morning, we knew we would all be in top form for the big drive.

One of the discussions during the evening revolved around flatulence and Ashley, otherwise known as Mrs. Clipboard who revealed that on a recent visit to a 2 star Michelin chef's establishment in Wimbledon someone with whom she is intimately acquainted had succumbed in a most gaseous fashion to a seafood dish which involved artichokes.

Vegetables do not usually loom very large in my life and now I know the reason why. They are a menace and I try to avoid them. Regular readers will know that on the subject of vegetarians, I stand just a little to the right of Jeremy Clarkson who is a little to the right of Attila the Hun. I will claim however to be open-minded about this sordid and dangerous cult. Whatever they do in the privacy of their homes is fine by me.

Talking of public schoolboys with knowledge of the kind of activities that can impede sitting comfortably, Mr. Clipboard (pictured below), together with his lovely spouse Ashley are our guests overnight before we set off tomorrow. We shall be joined for this annual jaunt by "Slash and Burn" and his beautiful powerful Amazonian wife Lisa.

We shall be staying at Aracador, a chalet restaurant at Limone, reached only on skis, or by snow mobile when the ski lifts are not operating. It is a wonderful place and very popular, but with just 4 guest rooms. What is impressive is that they were prepared to have us back after last year. Bad behaviour by, it has to be pointed out, the female contingent last year, when the unattended bar was mysteriously liberated of several bottles of Sambuca late one night, when dinner should really have finished long ago (a fact reflected by the chef/landlord dozing off in a chair whilst waiting for us all to go upstairs), may have precluded a return. The poor chap gave up at 1am and with no security on the bar, temptation proved too much for the one or more of the three girls at the scene, of which one may have been that Nice Lady Decorator.

The trip will not all be fun, frivolity, theft and skiing, there is a serious scientific side to the trip as we are conducting a survey of where to get the best Bombardino (espresso, accompanied by a local brandy and Advocaat and topped with lashings of whipped cream) on the slopes.

Limone Piemont is a pretty village ski resort on the western edge of Italy; just over 2 hours' drive from Valbonne. On the way I was asked if I was excited about the prospect of selling my house in the UK, which has been on the market for seven years, and further asked if it had been firmed up. I responded by saying that it was very exciting but I preferred to keep private how this excitement manifested itself in my personal being.

So we arrived at Limone just in time for the sunshine to disappear and be replaced by a ferocious snow storm, so there was little option but not to ski and to have lunch instead and see if it would clear. I think it was over the third cognac that the realisation became certainty that the snowstorm was developing into a sensational blizzard.

After a few more cognac's the natural shyness of the public schoolboys, with who I was lunching, began to recede. For some reason the discussions had turned to the relative merits of the poor (literally) comprehensive school and grammar school children. When I suggested that there may be some differentiation between these two intellectually diverse groups (the Reverend Jeff will immediately recognise his status in this context, having himself attended a comprehensive school as a result of failing his 11 plus) the public schoolboys guffawed and declared that as far as they were concerned all were oiks.

During lunch I was intrigued by the fireplace at the Ange Blanc at the base of the Limonetto ski slope, our venue for lunch, which was open on both sides. At one stage Mr. Clipboard suggested that I crawl through the fire so that he could take a photo. He had the clear intention of re-enacting a scene from Tom Browns school days when a "fag" was roasted over a fire for insubordination. As I was obviously cast to play the part of the fag I decided against an acting career.

I had a picture of this potential fire storm ready for today's missive and it may yet rise to the top for publication. In days to come but it was superseded by this photo which I took of the TV in the bar.

I think they were saying 36-24-38

Let me explain; we were finishing lunch when my attention was drawn to the TV screen, which was showing a programme which turned out to be the Lingerie Superbowl in America. I jest not. A number of scantily clad ladies were playing American Football and I managed to take several pictures of the action, of which this is the only one I can reproduce. There is so much material here that it would be too easy a target. The Lingerie Superbowl. I will leave you with that.

After brief siesta it was time for dinner at Aracador. I have a vague recollection of events that involved several men ending up naked on the brightly lit terrace in the 50 mile an hour blizzard at midnight. Any suggestion that one of these people was me is denied and suggestions to the contrary will result in proceedings issued by my lawyers Sue, Stoppit and Lye. Furthermore, should pictures emerge of this alleged event they will clearly have been fabricated.

I need answers; please study the picture below and answer 2 questions; 1/ who is the public schoolboy in the picture? And 2/ what is he doing apparently naked in a blizzard?

This poor behaviour exhibited by some of the public schoolboy idle rich on Tuesday evening has been the source of much hilarity for most of the day yesterday and last night. It was a quieter night than the night before which can only be a good thing. So, no nudity, blizzards, sledges, dodgy photos or debagging were in evidence. It seems the rather juvenile pranksters amongst them ran out of steam. Perhaps that was in part due to the proprietor of the hotel in which we are staying revealing that he has closed circuit television cameras located all around the exterior of his property, and was thus aware of all the shenanigans that had taken place the night before. Perhaps either the guilt about events or the emerging realisation that the TV tapes might incriminate them had some effect? Suffice to say I think a cash-for-tape exchange will take place this morning and that will be an end to it.

Another question; Why?

Let me finish my report on yesterday's activities with a comment made by Mr. Clipboard in relation to the two french girls who were sharing a double room in the hotel where we are staying. Apparently there is an expression "plate-lickers". This was a description that sent them, and to be fair me, to bed.

A sublime morning yesterday of skiing under blue skies and in copious amounts of fresh snow, was topped only by a splendid lunch on a sunny terrace of a restaurant, talking about life in general. It came to a premature end just as the cloud which will bring more snow today arrived.

As is usual over a glass of wine at lunch the stories begin to unfold and yesterday was no exception. The intellectually inspiring steely eyed beautiful ice maiden, who is Lisa Thornton Allan, reminded me of a story she told against herself recently. It seems that she was recommended by a friend to read "Death In Venice", and struggling through it, told the friend she found it very confusing, long winded and unconnected. It seems the book she was actually reading was "Death in Venice and other short stories" and she thought it was all one novel. It may be the blond hair that causes problems of this nature.

Then it happened, the public schoolboy obsession of the "dark side" of sexual relations reared its ugly head. Not content with a string of innuendo aimed at the two ladies sharing a double room at our hotel, a theme which has continued to both intrigue and amuse him over the past three days, ever since he discovered this cozy relationship, together with an on-going morbid fascination for all things lesbian or homosexual, Mr. Clipboard was at it again. It was an innocent expression that in any other context, and if uttered by anyone else ,would have had no significance, but in the ears of Mr. Clipboard "Can I push your stall (stool) in?" was loaded with a double meaning of the most sordid kind. Whilst it is true that I did not receive the benefit of an education of quite the same stature as he, I do learn from him every day, and often wished I did not.

I allowed him to do this, push my stall in that is, and then kept a very watchful eye. Previous experience over the past few days has left me forewarned as to the depths of depravity to which he can descend in an instant.

I don't know how we got to on to the subject of Egypt but given one member (there we go again) of the sordid company I have kept over the past few days whilst skiing , and the constant sexual innuendo pervading every conversation, his expression "taking me up the Nile" made me feel a tad uncomfortable.

Back To Vabonne Fully Clothed

Mr. Humphreys (who obviously has some time free) confessed to the congregation at church at Café Latin on Friday, after our return from Limone, that he was about to start a welding and metal work course. For a man who wears purple and mauve at least as well as any woman, and has avoided obvious gainful employment for so long, this seemed a rather extreme new career direction upon which to embark. Personally I am a little suspicious of the exact nature of the allure presented by attending such a class, which will no doubt be crammed full of a number of strong, hulking, well-built, perspiring, testosterone-charged males, whilst he will doubtless be attired in a nice fetching pastel coloured overalls, but then who am I to judge? When confronted about just that question he alluded to the film Flashdance, which I must admit has not been at the top of my "must see" list, where one of the major figures was apparently a dancing welder. I invite you to draw your own conclusions.

One can see from this how easy it is to fake photographs

Now, to my picture above. It was taken earlier in the week in Limone. The skidoo to the hotel can take just three passengers so, as there were six people in total in the party I volunteered to be one of the last to leave, a bit like the captain of a ship, although we were in Italy where the modern way seems to be that the captain tends to leave first, but I digress. Captain Clipboard was first aboard in the advance party, and kindly changed into this costume and hid in my bathroom to surprise me when I arrived. I think you will know how much this pleased me.

Following my piece in my column about innuendo in Italy, the Reverend Jeff suggests in the comments section of this column that the Italian word for sex must be innuendo. It is the type of stupid, inane juvenile pun of which I would have been proud; I don't know how I missed it.

Another Italian word that I came across in Private Eye this week is "Schettino". It means roller skate, so it should come as no surprise that the captain of the Concordia, the cruise liner that "fell over" recently was called Captain Schettino. That's Captain roller-skate to you and me; you could not make it up. I have always thought that roller skates are dangerous but I suspect that after the court case, our dear brave captain won't even be allowed to be in charge of one skate let alone of a pair of them.

After several days hard skiing last week, that Nice Lady Decorator got home safely and then on Friday promptly slipped on some ice, fell and hurt her ankle, thus I was the unlucky lackey upon who fell the responsibility to be her slave in the absence of her ability to walk.

So drudgery became the watchword of my life yesterday. I am not sure if any of you are old enough to remember Allo Allo? , the TV series with the semi-invalid mother that lived upstairs and rang a bell when she wanted anything? Well, you get my drift. She has crutches for Christ's sake, and is she making the most of it. I "cooked" dinner under serious and continual abuse (she called it advice) and was left in no doubt as to my shortcomings in the kitchen department. In fact it seems that I have suddenly developed faults in every area of my persona. I am as certain as I can be that this sudden sea change can in no way be attributed to her injury, as that would be a very selfish stance to adopt, but I am beginning to think my certainty needs revisiting.

To say that she is a poor patient is a bit like saying Steven Hawking is mildly disabled. That Nice Lady Decorator, usually bubbly, bright, busy, amusing and beautiful is......still all those things, but when injured most of these qualities are hidden. Her ability to delegate by way of orders delivered in a staccato style stream is well known to those close to her, but her own enforced inactivity seemed to lend a new sense of urgency to the usual torrent of orders issued. I know of slaves that have had less to do than I did yesterday.

When dealing with the injury, the French health system lived up to its high quality reputation, within 2 hours we had driven to the Tzank hospital in Mougins, seen a doctor, had an x-ray, had a diagnosis (sprained) received a prescription and driven home, and half an hour of that was traveling to and fro. It was a fantastic service. The doctor warned her that she must do no sport for ten days, but clearly that applied just to skiing and walking and had no effect on the kind of sports that I like to call bedroom Olympics, which I may have previously referred to as sport. It means however that the return skiing trip to Limone this coming week will involve more sitting than skiing.

Today though, whilst I was undertaking the slavish duties that have befallen me after that nice Lady Decorator be fallen over (olde English or old Buckinghamshire slang) I happened upon this spectacle. I was on my way to sports shop Decathlon in an abortive attempt to get the family (minus that nice Lady Decorator's) skis waxed in time for a trip to the ski slopes, when I encountered a sportsman of a different kind, riding a bike with his dog on the back.

I have heard of taking the dog for a walk but never taking one for a cycle. Indeed dog walking is part of my daily exercise and I have often been amused at the chap who parks in the same place each day in the Valmasque, where I often walk and who stays in his car and smokes cigarettes, listens to his radio, and reads his paper whilst his dog remains in the car desperate to get out for a walk. I am certain he goes home after an hour telling his wife he has walked the dog. Anyway, this chap on the bike is also denying his dog a walk, but at least he is getting some exercise himself.

It gave me an idea about how I could take that appalling hound Banjo, the cantankerous cocker owned by that Nice Lady Decorator, out for a walk. My idea involves a long lead and my

Mercedes with sports mode selected. I could go into details but the RSPCA may read this so I will stop there.

Dog keeping an eye on owner

Who needs a rhetorical question? So said the email from my friend and fellow author Bill Colegrave. He is of course a proper author having written about his discovery of the source of the mythical Oxus River, one of the most sought after expeditionary goals in Victorian times. Whenever we meet he tends to take the metaphorical high ground, not least because of his educational background (Oxford or Cambridge, I can never remember which) but because the subject of his book was higher above sea level than my subject, Valbonne.

Delinquent Dog

So doggy walking duties befell me, and once that Nice Lady Decorator had spotted the rope and the Mercedes, there was nothing else for it but to walk them. It was on this walk around the Valmasque that I took this picture looking towards the ridge at Greoliere Les Neiges which, as you can see, still retains most of the metre of snow that fell there last week. From that particular ridge, one can sometimes see the island of Corsica looking back overhead of this shot on a clear day.

Greoliere Les Neiges viewed from the Valmasque Forest close to Sophia Antipolis

A clear day is unusual not because of the air quality but due to the bonfires the French insist on lighting as soon as the sun comes out which is most days. How much extra carbon dioxide is going into the atmosphere because of this local obsession?

Do you sometimes wake in the morning and decide which hat to wear? Obviously the chap in my picture today who I photographed at the Col de Tende tunnel on the way to Limone yesterday faced this dilemma and in the end could not decide which hat to wear, so he chose to wear both of them.

We got to our hotel in Limone, called Hotel Limone (damned inventive, these Italians) where that nice Lady Decorator reminded us that the last time we stayed in the town itself as opposed to Aracador where we resided last week, we had stayed in the Hotel Touring (now sadly closed), also known as Hotel Diesel because of the smell that emanated from the basement. Sprog 2, the female one was aged about thirteen at the time and was awoken at 2am by the headboard in the bedroom next door crashing rhythmically into the adjacent wall for some time before hearing the exclamation "magnifico" through the wall. My explanation that the Italians are passionate about football failed fully to convince her that the sounds and exclamations she heard were that kind of sport.

Which hat? I know, I will wear both

Apres ski was commenced at the slightly unprepossessing Hotel Petite Meuble, which the French speakers amongst you may translate as Hotel of little furniture, and sometimes the literal translation is best. Less furniture would have been better than what was there, and no furniture at all would have been better still. Anyway, the Bombardino's, being a peculiar local liqueur coffee which we discovered a couple of years ago when skiing in Italy were of top quality, so a couple of these were required in order to set us up for the evening meal.

Normal ski etiquette to me involves a couple of runs in late morning interspersed with a few Bombardino stops, followed by a long leisurely lunch and then a mad ski down the mountain in the near darkness for some apres ski entertainment usually in the form of a refreshing ale.

Skiing with teenagers opened the possibilities of skiing properly in the afternoon and I must say I don't like it. That Nice Lady Decorator spent the day relaxing and lounging about the hotel in the village due to her unfortunate engagement with some ice at home and sent me on the slopes so that I could be "looked after" by my offspring, Sprog 1 and Sprog 2. They repaid her by dragging me to parts of this expansive snow domain covering three valleys I had never even dreamed could exist.

So I finally got down the mountain at 4.30pm when it was nearly dark. Every fibre of my being aches, my thighs feel like they have been ravaged by forest fires, I can only feel my arms in terms of where the pain is, my knee joints are welded together and my backside feels like it may have attracted the serious attention of some well-endowed public school types, but otherwise I am fine.

Lunch was a joke, twenty minutes of grab pasta and leave, no time to sample the local viticulture produce, no time to take in the view and indulge in conversation from which I often cull information for this daily column, no, instead I got what I think they called "my money's worth", although why one would pay to have one's body put through a ringer is anyone guess.

Before I was being subjected to this most violent personal physical abuse, I spotted a chap using a novel method to clear snow from his terrace, shovel it in to the street and hope a passing snow plough will deal with it. What luck he had as my picture shows!

The snow is rubbish

Limone is such a better skiing experience than Isola 2000, the closest of the bigger ski resorts locally. Whilst the skiing is good at Isola, the monstrous carbuncle that is the main building in the village, purpose-built in the worst of the 1960's style, is the most unedifying resort I have ever encountered. By contrast, Limone is a real village with history and with tiny streets, the centre of which is mostly restricted to pedestrians, and offering some alpine charm and several very decent restaurants, some nice bars and just a nicer après-ski experience than Isola, and has the added advantage of not having that torturous long-winding switchback approach by car. It takes 15 minutes longer to get there from Valbonne, but the rewards in terms of a bigger ski area and prices of food and drink some 30-40% lower means for me there is no question that Limone offers a better option.

The open and quiet ski slopes of Limone

So we headed down the hill and stopped at that Nice Lady Decorator's favourite Italian grocery store to pick up the usual supply of parmesan, olive oil and wine at prices you would not believe when you live in the south of France. For instance I picked up some 2 litre bottles of Barbera d'Alba 2004 for under 8 euros a bottle. I bought all the 3 they had in stock. With a visit to Peachy Butterfield's in prospect this evening I also found a 5 litre bottle of Italian table wine which should take care of the quantity one must take when dining there, the quality should also be somewhat superior to the Macclesfield Merlot or whatever concoction with which he is planning to surprise us this evening.

Peachied

Peachied. It's a new verb which describes perfectly what happens to any poor souls who are invited to dine chez Peachy Butterfield and glorious wife Suzanne. It is a gargantuan evening on just about every level, the man mountain himself is the centre of attention due to what he is wearing, what he is saying, what he is doing what he is eating and not least what he is drinking. To call Peachy quite big would be like calling the total eurozone bail-out quite big. Once Greece defaults and leaves the euro which in my opinion is inevitable, welcome back the drachma, the Portuguese escudo, maybe the Italian lire and maybe even whatever it was the Spanish used for money, but I digress.

It is a gigantic problem, and so is Peachy. The first problem is the starting time of 5pm....5pm for dinner? I know it gets dark early in the frozen north where he was born but for Christ's sake (it's Sunday so that is just to rile the Reverend Jeff) it's still light at 6pm. So why so early? Probably an attempt to extend the drinking time? In order to give him more time in which to take onboard supplies? Perhaps it was in deference to his house guests, The Ratcliffe's of whom I have the highest regard now they have bought a copy of my book, and who are also from the tundra-strewn north of England where they call having dinner "having us tea". All I know is that it was too early but I made sure we were on time at tea time. I did not want to miss out.

Talking of big, funny and tasteless, I found a hotel with a sign which seems to capture these three traits. It was in the ski resort of Limone where I took today's photograph. What were they thinking?

A post-Peachy hangover was, as expected, to the fore, and I would have liked a Bloody Mary yesterday lunchtime to ease the pain but the night before last that Nice Lady Decorator once again drew attention to a tiny bit of extra weight she claims I am carrying. She alluded to what could be achieved by using the example of a dear friend who has lost a lot of weight due to a cancer scare and subsequent chemotherapy. There is only one conclusion one can draw. The clear implication was that she wanted me to lose weight and if that meant being diagnosed with cancer, so be it.

It is a slightly tenuous link, but talk of weight-loss implies dieting and that brings me to an expression "salad dodgers" which was used

152

at dinner by Peachy on Saturday night. I had not heard that phrase before but it seems I may have been typecast. He is a confirmed salad dodger himself and I am very content in mid-summer to consider a salad as long as there is a copious amount of salad cream to smother the taste, but salads in winter? Not a concept any right thinking red-blooded male can consider.

A hotel for fat bottomed girls or Peachy from behind?

You will note that I have said salad cream and here let me be straight I am talking about Heinz Salad cream and not that very poor impersonation of the classic creation called mayonnaise. There is a great difference. And tomatoes? Spawn of the devil.

Talk Is Cheap, I Am Cheaper

I have been invited to speak at a meeting of Premier Mardi, a networking group. My ego could not resist the invitation from the co-founder of this group the beautiful Karen Hockney, a far more accomplished journalist than I shall ever be.

Imagine my predicament: an ageing Lothario with a massive and mostly misplaced self-belief, who spends much of his time imagining that all girls find him fatally attractive, being asked by a beautiful girl to speak to a gathering of other attractive girls, to the exclusion of men? What was I to do? I considered the offer for a nanosecond and accepted immediately after managing to get my tongue back in my mouth.

Eat your heart out David Bailey

Casting around for a picture this morning I discovered this shot I took at Breil sur Roya on the French/Italian border on the way back from Limone. Moody huh? Apart from that duck in the middle of the river...

Another tenuous link; I admit I may have been a little moody myself yesterday. A hangover, no hair of the dog, a cup of tea last night instead of a glass of wine, I have every right to be moody. This state of affairs is planned to continue until Wednesday midday when lunch with any number of suspect characters at the Auberge St Donat will probably see me breaking the alcoholic fast upon which I am now embarked, if it still in place by then.

Hop-along-decorator is still getting me to do loads of the jobs she was clearly born to do as her sprained ankle seems to be taking a suspiciously long time to get better. Anyone suggesting that she may be milking the situation would be entirely correct. I know it was x-rayed but I want a second opinion.

The winter wonderland of Valbonne a few weeks ago

This means that dog-walking duties in the wonderful Valmasque forest have fallen to me exclusively. With two dogs and two adults (well nearly adults, stay with me) normally striding out together, naturally I take responsibility for that fine old English Springer, Max the family dog, kind, honest, obedient, tolerant and good-looking whilst that Nice Lady Decorator wrestles with the disobedient, cantankerous, sneaky, smelly, neurotic kleptomaniac, overweight 37 kilo (!), intolerant Cocker Spaniel Banjo, whom she foisted upon this household against my proven-daily better judgement. No wonder then I need that Nice Lady Decorator back on her feet.

The warm sunny weather we are now experiencing is somewhat different from just a few weeks ago when I took this picture from my bedroom window. I have had enough snow now, roll on the warmer weather.

A story has reached me about events leading up to and after the performance of "Barefoot In the Park" at the Pres des Arts in Valbonne last week by the South Of France English Theatre. If anyone noticed fire engines and flashing blue lights in Valbonne village during a lunch-time last week, I think I know the name of the culprit. In the chaos of the preparations for the first night performance, following a fire at their rehearsal studios and a broken-down van transporting the set, an hour before the doors opened the director noticed that there was no door handle on the main door of the set, so the carpenter was sent to find a door handle from somewhere. With no hardware shop nearby and no time to source a new one he took one off the door of the tiny windowless toilet (not one of the bedroom doors you note) in the flat they are renting in the village. This was at worst a little inconvenient but no more until a member of the cast, alone in the flat and dashing naked into the toilet the day after the second performance, found the door shutting on her, locking her in whilst mid-ablution so to speak. Three hours later after her cries for help had been heard by a neighbour who had alerted the pompiers, she was released, still naked and now perspiring into the arms of the startled firemen who had rescued her. I am told although understandably traumatised, she will be sufficiently recovered for the next performance in Cannes tonight.

The problem with having a few days off from the social melee that is the cocoon of the idle rich in Valbonne, is that nothing happens and therefore I have nothing to write about. I could always make it up and that would be in keeping with what some people believe, however I contend that nothing is invented although the expression "terminological inexactitude" springs to mind. Another way of saying it was voiced by a diplomat in a spy case in court in Australia a decade or more ago; when accused of lying under oath he denied it but did admit to being "economical with the truth".

This is uncharted territory. Three days without a drink and I am beginning to get hallucinations. For instance I saw this picture on Wayne Brown's Facebook page a few days ago and my first thought was that the red snappers were a trifle overdone. Turns out they are shoes designed to help a girl through an evening aboard an Italian Cruise liner. I have been accused of being flippant in the past but never flipperent.

These are more like slappers than slippers

Talking of girls' shoes, if any of you are unlucky enough to be cognisant of Peachy Butterfield's Facebook page you will know that this is one of his fetishes, that and travelling in ladies curtains which I believe he is about to commence. I shall be taking this up at lunch with him today.

Talking of children, I played tennis this morning with the Naked Politician, he having been allowed out of sight of the hand brake, as he refers to his beautiful wife, Dawn, to play and then have lunch at the Auberge St Donat. Modesty forbids me to revel in the scale of my victory last time out, against a man who has had scores, even hundreds of tennis lessons, has lost 10 kilos and is at least 15 years younger than me, but I can reveal that in two sets he did win one game but only at the expense of an injury to his hand sustained in a diving save, to secure that one small victory. I need not tell you that after 3 days without a drink I am expecting a mighty fine lunch and have blocked out the afternoon for err.... consultation and quiet study, although with my hammock broken and having instructed the removal of one of the trees which used to support it, I am slightly concerned as to where this quiet contemplation will take place.

More Tennis Triumphs

The last time we were pitted against each other was actually last year. He was full of enthusiasm and hope having had some 40 tennis lessons; he fully expected to give a MOG (Moustachioed Old Git) who has never had a tennis lesson in his life, a serious political run around on the tennis court.

However, yesterday, although he revealed a 300% increase in his achievement against my good self, a figure of which he should be proud, he had to drown his sorrows over lunch at Auberge St Donat in Plascassier having once again come second in a tennis singles match.

I cannot reveal the full scale of his defeat as I would like to be invited aboard his boat at some stage in the forthcoming cruising season (can I say that?), but if I say that in two sets the first time we played he was lucky to win one game you may be able to work out his level of under achievement against an untrained, fat (in the eyes of That Nice Lady Decorator) chap nearing his seventh decade.

I hate (read love) to use the word thrashing, but I cannot think of another verb that fits the situation. Anyway, enough of that. Lunch at Auberge St Donat was as usual a triumph, so successful that we adjourned back to the web, our outside bar, for a few post prandial digestives. Wonderful warm sunny weather helped (me) to underline the reason why we live here in the south of France and Valbonne in particular.

Last night then into Valbonne to talk to the assembled beauties who were gathered at the Premier Mardi networking event at the now defunct La Pomme Rouge. That Nice Lady Decorator also came along to keep a close eye on me and Master Mariner Mundell arrived to be my roadie and book sales manager for the evening. So persuasive was he that 10 more books were sold. Just how persuasive (read irritating) he became was illustrated by one particularly lovely participant who paid him 10 euros to stop bothering her. I was a little embarrassed but a sale is a sale. One of the co-founders of the group, the lovely Fiona Macleod has been involved in art sales at the highest levels even dealing with the sale of Picassos so I thought today's picture should be a nod towards the art world.

It's art Jim, but not as we know it

Tennis With Dennis

More tennis! I played with Amanda Bay. That is the phrase I told her husband, Anthony I was going to use. The Master Mariner, who was Anthony's partner, seemed oblivious to the fact that one of his opponents was a waif-like beauty who had not played for a year, and repeatedly and rather unsportingly thrashed the ball past her at every opportunity. Perhaps he was upset by her very accurate description of his looking just like "Dennis The Menace" from the children's comic The Beano? with his hooped red and black tennis shirt, dark trousers, dark socks and unruly hair? Well, on the back half of his head anyway. It was an uncanny resemblance.

Lunch was once again taken afterwards, as is the tradition, at the Auberge St Donat where some debate took place as to what value I could possibly bring to last night's event. My contention that wit, charm, personality and a rudimentary understanding of writing a blog was more than enough was dismissed in a chorus of guffaws accentuated by the very late arrival of the Wingco for a glass of wine. It gave him another opportunity to describe this daily column is his customary manner: "ghastly" but with several more h's, phonetically more like "ghhhhhastly" in the way only a public schoolboy from an upper class family can master.

A new days dawns but I contend that it was not my fault that the Nice Lady Decorator twisted ankle a couple of weeks ago although I got the blame. It was not my fault that as a result she had to sit out skiing with the Sprogs in Limone although I got the blame. It was not my fault that the stairs from the parking area in Valbonne are fenced off due to some building works which meant having to scramble down a bank and she tweaked her bad ankle as a result although I got the blame, and guess who was to blame for having to postpone our dinner engagement as a result?

Before that disaster befell her and before the full blame was assessed, distributed and apportioned once again to me we had decided that the weather was too good not to lunch in Valbonne Square where we happened across the Naked Politician and Peachy Butterfield, filled with similar intent. I made some notes about the conversation – but could not quite understand what I had written-. The phrase "champagne belly button boy" was one part that was easily decipherable. Once again I have details of indiscretions that I wish I did not. Clearly I cannot reveal details here especially as it may in some way be connected to the Naked Politician and he must never be linked to anything so questionable.

Another story emanated from lunch about a different lunch these two reprobates had once taken at the very swanky Columbe d'Or in St Paul De Vence, a famous establishment packed full of original paintings by the likes of Matisse and Picasso who had paid their keep with their work when struggling young artists. The man mountain was apparently not feeling his best but I feel his expression "I nearly puked on a Picasso" was a little tasteless.

As I sat in the Square a member of the public approached our table in search of a signed copy of my book, which of course I was delighted to sell her. It was in no way staged as was suggested by all and sundry despite doubt's raised by me having a spare copy with me, but is a clear illustration of the esteem in which I am now held in our beautiful village. I have always loved the expression "delusions of grandeur" so it was perhaps inevitable that discussions turned to what would happen if this column were ever turned into a film. Clearly Brad Pitt would have to play me although it is fair to say that he was not a unanimous choice, however we were all agreed to who should play Peachy; Russell Grant of course! Not least because as Peachy said "he's a little bit fat and a little bit gay".

Winter Lunch On The Beach

Juan les Pins is an apt name as it turns out. That Nice Lady Decorator, determined not to miss out on another social event after twisting her ankle and having to cancel a dinner engagement on Friday, decided that dosed up on Dolipran pain killers she was steady enough on her "pins" to get to a birthday lunch on the beach yesterday. Of course in reality it meant one thing; I would have to carry her most of the way. Actually that is a bit of an exaggeration but she was certainly no dancing queen as I had to adopt a crutch replacement position, of which more later.

La Petite Plage in Juan les Pins is one of my favourite beach restaurants. It is quite intimate, slightly funky and the food, especially the fish, is excellent. The sea is just a few feet away and it has occurred to me that the lack of any serious tide in the Mediterranean means that on the beaches the buildings can be that much closer to the waterline than most places in the world. It is a testament to my photographic abilities that my photo I took at the time entirely fails to capture that intimacy.

Ok that's enough boring stuff, on with the gossip and innuendo that are the hallmarks of this column. At the beach in the same establishment by complete coincidence we bumped Paul "Slash and Burn" Thornton Allan and his steely eyed and stunning wife Lisa, with whom we are going to Cuba next month. Paul received his epithet after his willingness, no, that is too weak, his excited determination mechanically to machete his way through the Valmasque forest with his chain saw after the recent snow had brought many branches down.

Anyway they joined us and our friends the Cato's, Pauline whose birthday it was and her partner Gordon, on holiday from England and, talking of crutches, I think it was after the arrival of the ninth bottle of rose (well there were six of us) that the really stupid and tasteless ideas began to evolve. Why it was decided that when we leave for Havana with the Thornton Allan's we should invent and adopt alter egos for the trip, and why that was so funny at the time is a mystery. Also mysterious is why Slash and Burn should invent for himself, how can I say this and it remain tasteful? Answer; I cannot. He decided he would pretend to be a "designer gynecologist". Let me allow some moments of quiet contemplation before we sew this subject up for good. We had all started to consider exactly what form his mythical activities might take place in his new little world, all of it too graphic for my perception of what is acceptable to publish in this column. Then I began to think of what I could invent for myself and before I knew it I happened to say something about having a lot of fingers in a lot of pies, and there this ends, now. I think you will know who coined the phrase "designer vagina". In no way was the idea for the title of this book born that day.

For my epithet, I appear to have been given the choice between being known as Boycie after the character in "Only Fools And Horses" or a lazy lay-about atheist whose family have not worked for generations due to being publishers of the Gideon Bible (catch phrase "Thank The Lord")

To Be Peachied Again

Talking of alcohol, at the lunch at ours recently Peachy Butterfield took a particular shine to that 5 litre bottle of table wine I bought in Italy as a joke to point up his requirement for quantity not quality, declaring it good and then proceeding to demolish two-thirds of it himself over the course of the afternoon. This took a great deal of pressure off my stocks of the 2004 St Estephe Grand Cru.

Earlier during my normal morning constitutional around the

Valmasque (where I saw sights that would make Slash and Burn salivate) on the edge of the forest I spotted a house with a satellite dish protected by an umbrella.

No, I cannot explain it either

Now what is the owner thinking? I assume satellite dishes are designed to live outside? Is this some kind of parental guidance as to what is actually received? Maybe he has a fixation about the Weather Channel? It is a mystery I doubt I shall ever solve.

As usual when I walk I am accompanied by two dogs (although not by that because of her ankle) Max, the lovely old but now profoundly deaf springer spaniel and Banjo, who I wish was profoundly dead. Banjo is a mutant by any measure and with a character and aroma for which the word mutant does not do full justice. Unsuspecting people pat and stroke him until they realise that they need to wash their hands in order to avoid funny looks and people giving them space due to the stench. He is of course not my dog but is owned and fawned over by that Nice Lady Decorator but with her injured ankle it falls to me to be responsible for him and his actions when out walking. I must have done something very evil in a previous life to have this foisted upon me.

He was on top form yesterday, trying to bite a tiny little dog a twentieth of his size, defecating in the middle of the path (although reserving a particular noxious example to deposit it on my lawn later) , barking at plastic bags and generally being a nuisance. His new foul habit is to eject a glob of doggy saliva into the laps of anyone stupid enough to let him near. His one redeeming feature is at least he does provide some column inches for this daily tome.

On Valentine's Day recently that sent me out to get that Nice Lady Decorator something sexy for her. For some reason she was not impressed when I came home drunk. All right that did not really happen but it's a good joke.

I had reason this morning to visit our local doctor Dr Patrick Ireland at his office (it is not grand enough to be called a surgery) on the Forum roundabout in Valbonne. He took my blood pressure and seemed quite pleased. I suggested that it was good because of my lifestyle, what with all the tennis, walking, logging and fasting. He gave me one of those sideways glances, fixed me firmly with one of his best doctorial looks and said "I have on occasion been unlucky enough to read your blog; keep taking those blood pressure tablets I have prescribed, you need them"

Talking of high blood pressure, several people have contacted me complaining about my comments yesterday about that Nice Lady Decorator dog, Banjo. One even wanted to administer doggy justice to me and at one stage duelling swords were mentioned. Could this be described as a case of a duelling Banjo over a defecating Banjo? He did it again today, barking at the man who is digging some drains for us, to the extent that the operator was afraid to leave his cab. Perhaps he has some unexplained deep-seated need to be unpleasant wherever excretions are involved. Banjo, I mean, not the digger driver.

When at Limone recently we were asked to fill in a survey about the hotel in which we were staying and were presented with a small red handbag for our troubles. Because of the alarming colour I had decided to present it to Peachy Butterfield who wears colours that would make my style guru Mr. Humphreys cringe (if he was free). I took it to the Valbonnaise last night and by coincidence it matched what he was wearing and his iPhone perfectly as my picture shows.

Peachy looking a bit red in the face

He was in top form, holding court about his visit last year to Chateau Petrus and telling all that, as he stood between the vines of the finest vineyard in the world and the neighbouring vines some 6 feet away, he could not understand why the crushed fruit, as he called it, on his left could fetch £25,000 per case whilst the vines on his right could fetch just £250 per case.

So up in the big bird in the sky today headed for the delights of Gatwick and Parents Evening at Ashbourne College in Kensington, with the reward that only a pint of London Pride, the finest beer known to man, can bestow, to follow.

Many of the chaps I play golf with at the Riviera Ex-Pat Golf Society are involved in the world of yachting and some are yacht captains and thus sophisticated chaps. One lives very close to me and I took this picture outside his house. I cannot name names here but in a completely unrelated subject Jez Dean, (who lives near me) has led me to believe that he is the captain of a very large private yacht. I shall be discussing this picture with him when I next see him.

A few rather rude comments were received yesterday about the attire of Peachy Butterfield in yesterday's column picture. He prides himself on (in his opinion) being able to wear bright colours even to the extent of flirting with his gay side. In fact he revealed that he once asked one of his friends, a gay chicken farmer from the frozen north of England whom he referred to as Oven Ready Eddie (must be ready frozen) if the pink shirt he was wearing might make him look a little gay and was told with utter certainty that no gay guy would be seen dead in anything Peachy was wearing.

So this is what a 50-metre yacht looks like?

And so to London (after a delay at Nice airport due to Air Traffic Contempt) to Sprog 2 parents evening. I am so glad to see the money spent on education is producing results. It is the quality of these results that is the problem. And here is the conundrum, that Nice Lady decorator's fearsome examination of Sprog 2's activities and any criticism of any backsliding is fatally undermined by said Sprogs knowledge of too much detail of her mother's schooling. Her father's achievements are a shining beacon of industriousness, her mother's less so. That is all I am saying.

France's School Of English

France's School Of English, now there is a concept to make the Wingco weep. Knowing a lot of public schoolboy types as I do, and not having received the privileged education that they have and furthermore having to put up with a great deal of abuse for the writing in this column, I was understandably delighted to see that my particular style of writing appears to have been recognised. I was also unaware until I was able to take this photo that I appear to have attracted some high-powered sponsors in the shape of Starbucks and Colonel Saunders himself whose Kentucky Fried Chicken outlets will now never again receive a cruel word in this daily look at life in the Cote d'Azur.

Literary perfection recognised?

Whilst in London I tried on some salmon red trousers but without my style guru Mr. Humphreys to hand (obviously not free to guide me through the vagaries of haute couture in London,) I found my determination not to languish in denim and chino wilt as I looked in the mirror. That and they were truly horrible. Then I changed my mind and bought them anyway.

I also have some business in curtains. As I may have mentioned some time ago, man mountain Peachy Butterfield is now representing a curtain manufacturer and I have agreed to allow him to debut in Cafe Latin by taking over the pulpit to preach about the benefits of curtains, an alien concept down here of course as we all have shutters. However, I don't like to see a grown man whimper so I have agreed to introduce him to Mr. Humphries if he is free.

My style guru was free and was sporting a very daring, perhaps slightly retro, even 60's hippy great-coat style with military overtones as my picture below attempts to capture. What may not have been immediately evident is that the stylist himself has used his new metal working skills (he has just started his welding course of which more at a later date) to add buttons to this military uniform. Not liking the buttons on the coat when he first bought it he searched for buttons he liked, but they were going to cost 4 euros each, more than the coat cost him. Outraged by the price, he felt certain that he could find something for a euro a piece and that was when the brain wave hit him. Why not actually use one euro coins and drill holes in them and use them for buttons! It is the kind of forward thinking, thinking outside the box that I have come to expect from a sheet metal worker in touch with his female side.

But it does not stop there, oh no, once he had embraced the concept he sought out euro coins from all over the eurozone which he has sewn on in order of perceived value starting with Germany at the top and Greece and Portugal at the lowest point. It was not immediately clear in which position he had placed a French or an Italian coin, but as he later went on to say he was looking for coins to go on three-quarters of the way down the back around the anus area and he did not mention where he had put the Irish coin so I am afraid I jumped to unworthy conclusions.

Style guru on the cheap

Chapter 7

More Doggy Capers

One of the extra benefits of being away for a couple of weeks is that I shall have to spend no time at all with the heinous hound, the apple of that Nice Lady Decorator's eye, Banjo, the smelly mutt. His motto should be "I will lick my balls then later cleanse my tongue by licking you," an expression that I have "researched" from one of my friend's Facebook pages. Recently in Valbonne village I took a picture of some dogs that must clearly be as badly behaved as Banjo to merit such treatment which I show today.

Dogging in Valbonne?

I don't know why my comments about the cocked-up cocker spaniel's licking habits reminded me but I have been sent some pictures of the Cuban virgins who reputedly roll cigars on their inner thighs and all I can say is I understand why they are virgins.

Representations have been made by several people working together to ease my daily burden of writing this column whilst I am on holiday, by undertaking to take over its creation, but such have been the slanted biased abusive nature of the submissions so far that I have been forced to abandon consideration of this generous but dangerous offer. Dangerous because too many people have found unjustified reasons to want to "get their own back" for material that has appeared here from time to time, such is the honesty and integrity for which I would hate this column to be renowned.

Our Man In Havana, Nearly

Our trip to Cuba nearly got off to a bad start. "Slash and Burn" Thornton Allan was almost arrested at Nice Airport after security was called. The problem was the skateboard, not his you understand, at least that was what he claimed, although with his sense of style and clothing and grizzly bear hair he could perhaps be mistaken for a skateboarder, but there are not many chaps with bus passes adept at the "hospital flip" or "dark side" as I believe those with skateboards call those jumps.

His son, who always takes his skateboard aboard flights with Easyjet, indeed has done so at least a dozen times, was suddenly told it had to go in the hold at a cost of 30 euros. To say that Slash and Burn was a little unhappy was as understated as saying the Wingco's moustache is a little bristly.

By the time I was airside some twenty minutes later, I could still hear him having what he later called his "little chat" with 5 security guards. A little later on in the executive lounge and after he had paid the 30 euros and we were trying to calm him down with a large cognac, we discussed other examples of heavy-handed airport security. I was only half listening as I was writing this because it was too good to miss, but I half heard the expression "crying his

170

eyes out when his cosmetics were taken away" and I thought it was referring to Slash and Burn himself, an honest enough mistake considering his habit of carrying a rather gay looking man bag most of the time.

Aboard the plane we discussed the various ploys we had heard about or engaged in to try to keep a seat clear in the middle seat a set of three. With a flight often nearly full and with the configuration of most Easyjet flights being three seats on either side of the aisle, a great deal of ingenuity has been employed by many a resident of the Cote d'Azur to avoid anyone sitting in the middle seat. Obviously if there are two of you traveling it is imperative to take up the window and aisle seats leaving a seat in the middle for all ones books, coats and in the case of that Nice Lady Decorator, Sudoku puzzles. I have heard it said that a bigger puzzle is why she puts up with me but I digress.

Regular readers will know of the success enjoyed by my friends the Philpot's, who carry Jehovah's Witness literature which they place between them, but some ideas I had not previously considered were suggested. Coughing without a hand over one's mouth the second someone looks at the spare seat apparently works, but timing is everything. Spitting was also proffered as an idea but that does have unfortunate consequences, where does one spit for instance? A burqa accompanied by mumbling or rhythmic chanting whilst reading the Koran would work for me, but in those circumstances nowhere on the plane would work for me. Worst of all would be a snotty nosed kid full of e numbers, a bottle of coke and a big box of Malteasers. That would probably be the ultimate deterrent.

So the joys of Gatwick followed by lunch (at my expense grrrr...) with Mr. Clipboard and lovely wife Ashley. I thought Burger King looked nice but we were dragged to The Onslow Arms, which seemed to me to apply to the character in "Keeping Up Appearances". It was however very good; an ideal venue for one of Hyacinth Buckets's candlelight dinners perhaps?

Mr. Branston and his Virgin Atlantic was thus charged with transporting us from drizzly and grizzly Gatwick to the joys of

Havana, at least I hope they will be joys (or…) I am writing this from the departure lounge with a Bloody Mary before leaving, but by the time this is published I shall hope to have consumed an elegant sufficiency of Mohitos and smoked a big cigar in Cuba.

Yesterday at lunch with Mr. Clipboard, a renowned carnivore, he revealed that he was worried that he was partially bulimic. Partially, he said, because although he binge eats he forgets the being sick part.

The preflight entertainment was provided in the executive lounge by "Slash and Burn" leaving his iPhone on charge on speaker phone. The hushed serenity was shattered by the loud ring tone refrain "Excuse me sir, someone is trying to contact you telephonically, shall I tell him to f*ck off?" I cannot be sure what was funnier, his headlong dash to intercept the embarrassing, loud and abusive monologue or the raised eyebrow reaction of several blue rinses in the lounge.

For the next ten days there will be a complete lack of political correctness in many senses. The bit I am looking forward to is the lack of a ban on smoking. It seems that one can smoke a fat cigar almost anywhere, even over dinner which is a civilised way to live one's life.

Hemingway was very fond of Havana and spent much of his drinking life there. His most famous book was "The Old Man And the Sea" not "Man at C & A" as at least one of our party thought was the title. I read the book, all 99 pages on the plane and it's about a man and a fish which does not end well. If this is great literature then surely soon I will be feted by one and all.

The flight was wonderful on one level, there were no children. Where it fell down spectacularly was three hours out, or put it another way, 6 hours to go and they had run out of red wine. Disappointed, I said I would accept white wine, but no, they had run out of all wine, so we were faced with the prospect of 6 hours without a drink, Mr. Branson you have got this wrong. We were thus forced into buying a couple of bottles of champagne from the on board shop to keep us all from massive dehydration.

I had to intercept Slash And Burn, still a bit punchy from his altercation with a handful of security guards at Nice airport the day before, from risking arrest by "discussing" this shortfall with the cabin crew, by diverting his anger into calling Sir Richard Branson (with whom he is slightly acquainted) to demonstrate with him. He was finally "headed off at the pass" as I think our American cousins call it by a combination of my reasoning and one look from his steely eyed goddess of a wife Lisa.

The opened-topped 1950's style car, as recommended by the exquisite Dawn Howard was indeed the perfect way in which to become acquainted with Havana on the first full day of being in Cuba. So yesterday, we boarded the ancient, battered, worn-out but still charming (a bit like me?) open-topped red Chevy, a government owned taxi with, as our driver told us, with 2 million kilometres on the clock to explore the city, and what a city. The 50's film set here is a living thing. The plethora of fascinating, and in many cases, utterly decrepit vehicles are everywhere, a symptom of the American embargo which has been in force for nearly 50 years. The whole place is so much better kept than many other 3rd world destinations I have visited, and apart from being famous for cigars, it is where both the mohito and the daiquiri were invented and Ernest Hemingway seems to have been involved in both. It seemed important to me to sample some of both at the seat of their invention so we started with a mohito in Bodegito Del Medio after a visit to a flea Market left me feeling unaccountably thirsty. Our driver was very informative, even pointing out what he called a hotel with free food, drink and beds, and supplying a free if rather rough massage. He was referring to the police station.

The luscious Lisa who is with us on this trip to Cuba, has the added advantage of being blonde with all the advantages and occasionally disadvantages with which that particular colouring can be associated. From a male perspective I have always loved blondes (and brunettes and red heads and, well, all pretty women) but the insight that a blonde can bring to a conversation is fascinating. She is a very well-educated woman but her claim that she thought our aeroplane operated by the very disappointing Virgin Atlantic had travelled at an average of 2000 miles per hour to get us to Havana revealed some discrepancies with the completeness of that education. I pointed out that if that were the case, and Gatwick to Havana being a little less than 5000 miles, by her calculations we should have made the trip in about 2 & 1/2 hours. Perhaps a blond was driving and got lost for 7 hours?

We had been recommended to go to lunch at a fisherman's cottage restaurant called Santy, but when we got there it was under reconstruction so we refused their kind offer to have lunch in a windowless room and our driver took us to the good but overpriced Vistamar which as its name suggests has a view of the sea. Discussing the revolution with our driver, as soon as any question about how the local populace feel about Fidel or Raul Castro, the guys running the country, one senses a shutters-down blank reaction. Suddenly his English is patchy and he does not understand the question, and you begin to realise that freedom of speech here, taken for granted where we live, is not the norm. He does drive the most wonderful car though, so what better way to go to the seaside than in this open-topped beauty.

The 1956 Chevy Bel Air convertible, our taxi to the beach

Taste Of Culture In Cuba

The world of ballet has pretty much passed me by. Rap music I like, but the concept of men in tights has always troubled me, so it was with alarm bordering on panic when Mrs. Blond "Slash and Burn" suggested that a nice cultural diversion might be to go to the Cuban National Ballet. Looking back I think it was my initial guffaw that sent me on the slippery slope. Those steely blue grey eyes fixed me with "that" look and I was informed that she had purchased 4 tickets (from our holiday kitty) and I was to present myself washed and scrubbed, and in best bib and tucker at 7.30 sharp in the hotel ready for a visit to the ballet across the road, in what is admittedly one of the most wonderful building exteriors there has ever been, it is just that I did not want to see the interior and certainly not to see a load of "ballet balls" as Slash and Burn later mumbled later.

I looked at him for some support but was stunned to see that he had already succumbed to the steely gaze and heaven knows what he had been promised in return, but he agreed. We should see some culture whilst in Havana. I suggested that perhaps I would sit this one out, spend a quiet evening contemplating the meaning of life over a couple of beers, I tried pleading, whimpering, tears, I even had to try the last resort, the so called "war wound" defence where that limp caused by a piece of shrapnel was playing up, but nothing worked. I was going to the ballet and that was that, decision made. That Nice Lady Decorator was no help, she actually wanted to go. Even the brainwave, where I suggested that with her still dodgy ankle she should not wear heels, meaning that I would volunteer to stay behind with her, failed.

And so it came to pass that I, council house boy from south London who has made a career out of rubbishing unworthy art, from Van Gogh to modern art and most of what lies between, was dragged kicking and screaming into a scenario unvisited in my worst nightmare, ballet in Spanish. I guess it could have been worse, opera in Italian maybe? Actually as it transpired it was worse than even I could have imagined. Let me set the scene; some very average dancers directed by a chap with the surname Castro, (that might be a clue) weave a ridiculous web of nonsense which is loosely based on The Phantom of the Opera but with vestiges of River Dance, taking in flamenco influences on the way, in Spanish. In other words, a silly mask, lots of silly dancing coupled with lots of stamping and hitting sticks on the ground, in short at utter farce of catastrophic proportions, well worth £30 of anyone's money. The only I can say in it's favour is that for me the second half was better than the first as I managed to shorten it somewhat, finally getting off to sleep early in the second act.

But I did get my money's worth. I had prepared a number of one-liners ready to amuse myself, pointing out the true horror of what had been seen, but to see the rest of the party in total agreement, the knowledge that it had been accepted that I was right was very rewarding.

After that visit the night before last to the Cuban version of Strictly Come Dancing in the shape of the Cuban Ballet, which exuded less culture than a week old yoghurt, a less cerebral day was planned for yesterday, although it still involved eating and drinking; a day at the beach. Perhaps we have been spoilt by the beaches and beach restaurants of the south of France. Juan les Pins and Cannes offer the most wonderful beach experiences, so I know what I expected from what was billed as "the most swanky beach club experience in Havana", the Mirimar Beach Club. Whilst the beach itself was very attractive a very ugly jetty stacked with building materials and old rusting containers on one side of the beach robbed it of much of its scenic beauty and a very ugly "Dive Centre" on the other side seemed to sum it up.

My conclusion was that this particular beach offering was somewhere between Centre Parks and Butlins was perhaps a bit harsh. If you want one tip for eating in Cuba, don't order chicken. I fancied some creole flavouring and the only option was chicken. Some of our party has reason before on this lovely island to be disappointed by this choice, so from my perspective the chicken population can rest a little easier in their coops.

I am not certain whether or not it was the chicken, or the

realisation that at least one of our party came to the conclusion that he had booked his connecting flight back to Nice from London for the day before we arrive back from Cuba, but some people got a little irritated over lunch, to the point at one stage of threatening to throw a bread roll, however good humour was restored when I pointed out that this was about to turn into our very own Cuban missile crisis.

The day before, we were down near the harbour having a daiquiri. The stirrer looked like it was made of hickory and it occurred to me that this was a clear case of hickory daiquiri dock. I do like it when I make myself laugh.

Cigar Heaven Awaits

Today we are supposed to be getting up early to visit the Partagas Cigar Factory. I can see it from my hotel window but it seems their production takes place somewhere else and the tour starts at the ridiculously early hour of 9am. If the subject were anything else but cigars then I suspect my alarm clock may not go off. If that were to happen could it be described as "close, but no cigar"?

What is a major reason for coming to Cuba? The flora and fauna maybe? The beaches? Or could it be for the country's only real export and for which it is justly renowned throughout the world, the production of the best cigars on the planet. When something important is involved, you go to the best. The single major reason for coming to Cuba is to experience the world of the cigar. What then is the point of walking out of a bar in Havana, the smoking capital of the world saying loudly that it is like being in the middle of a forest fire and holding your nose because of cigar smoke? Answer; no point at all. The English, don't you just love them? Perhaps their tour guide had omitted to warn them that smoking cigars anywhere on the island is a right?

We think we have a free society where we live in France or the UK, but we are not free. The health and safety brigade has ensured that my freedom to enjoy a good cigar in a restaurant has been eroded and thus it is wonderful to come to somewhere so unhindered by health and safety red tape and enjoy that freedom. Before all you sanctimonious non-smokers start, look up the country with the longest life expectancy. Do not be surprised to find that is cigar heaven itself, Cuba.

In celebration of the national identity, yesterday we visited that Partagas Cigar factory in Havana. It was a fascinating tour giving an insight into exactly how labour intensive is the production process, the Cohiba brand being the best quality. What I did not know until I got here is that all Cuban cigars are made in the same factories. From the lowly panatelas to the Cohiba Esplandido, all emanate from the same tobacco stock, through a careful selection process. I have a picture today of the barman at Bodeguita Del Mcdio explaining some of the finer points.

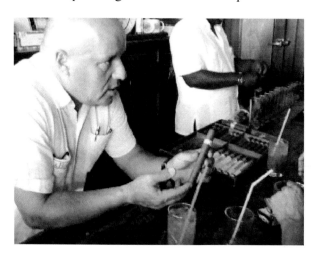

Note the cigars for sale and the line of mojitos being set up

No one believed me when I told them that a very discerning chap I met at The France Show at Earls Court in January told me he had bought 2 copies of my book "Summer in the Cote d'Azur," but his identity has been revealed as David Baumann. He commented on this column yesterday, even if it was to point out an error. However, as he also described my book as "the funniest book I have ever read" you will understand that I have the greatest respect for his words and in my eyes he can do no wrong.

I had no idea that the very pleasant brandy I was drinking as a nightcap at 3 am this morning was £15 a glass but I stopped drinking it after the third one. The reason was that the Nice Lady Decorator discovered the price when she went to sign the tab. Imagine how much worse today's hangover would have been had I not been sobered up by that look earlier this morning.

It was the Reverend Jeff who first suggested that I would, at some stage, be guilty of using the pun Havana a good time. I told him I would not consider it and I will not use it as it is beneath me as a successful writer.

I know us writers should stick together but I was feeling a little delicate due to rather too much indulgence in the renowned products of Cuba to risk the bumpy taxi ride over to Hemingway's house. It is a pity because it seems it was left exactly as it was when he died and gives an insight into his life, and I would have liked have discovered a few tips for when I die (if I die) and how I should leave my house for future generations of admirers of my work to discover.

A symptom often associated with excessive eating and drinking is snoring. I have never snored myself despite that Nice Lady Decorator's contention that I do but Slash And Burn seems to have form in this area, and was described yesterday as sounding like a warthog caught on a barbed wire fence emitting sounds one would more normally associate with a David Attenborough programme. I thought that was a bit harsh until I heard the recording.

We visited the old Partagas factory, from which production has been switched whist the building is refurbished, and from where we were precluded from taking photographs. They had obviously forgotten to tell this Cuban virgin about the move as she was the only person at work in the old factory. The maximum number of cigars one can bring out of the country is 50, so with me taking over that Nice Lady Decorator's entitlement (there was no discussion, I just did not tell her), I hope to have sufficient for my needs until the end of the month.

Finally, they have left. Slash and Burn and the beautifully miscalculating one, Lisa finally did the decent thing and left on the

Virgin flight yesterday evening. However, before that they decided they wanted one last long lunch, so we adjourned to Los Marinos, a charming seafood restaurant built on a jetty extending into the river. At the restaurant was another Cuban musical ensemble, charming again but playing the same set of songs they all play. If I hear "Perhaps, Perhaps, Perhaps" again in my life it will be too soon. Almost without exception after you have enjoyed the Cuban musical experience you are asked if you would like to buy their CD. With every fibre of my being screaming "no" I can still see that Nice Lady Decorator reaching for her purse on so many occasions to buy a CD that I believe we shall have an excess baggage issue on the return trip. Yesterday's sales ploy however reached new levels of sophistication. The singer said "very good CD, 15 songs, all different". Obviously a bargain as most of the CDs she had already bought was probably of the same song.

Discussion inevitably turned to the events of the last few days and I was reminded of a story told by Slash and Burn himself about an old girlfriend. It seems that she was quite pretty, a model, and as a result Slash and Burn was prepared to put up with a few eccentricities. One of these was her love of all animals and creatures. She apparently rescued an injured sparrow and nursed it back to health and became so attached to it she used to have it perch on her shoulder where it's rather loose bowels were given complete freedom of err...movement. Not unreasonably she called it called "Hoppy" (although "Crappy" may have been more accurate) and not unnaturally she became so attached to this rescued orphan that it became almost a child to her, to the extent that she would send thank you or birthday cards apparently signed by Hoppy. What I cannot explain however, some years after the relationship had come to what I would have thought was an inevitable conclusion, is why Slash and Burn had in his possession a touching card saying "To Daddy love from Hoppy". A Father's Day card from a sparrow is a hard act to follow. I even considered giving him the bird, indeed so doubtful is this behaviour I think he should be up before the beak.

Whilst into the land of the pun, I feel it is necessary to reveal that before we leave we plan going on to cane the Havana Club distillery where they make rum. I shall make no jokes about it being a rum do as that would be well beneath the standards my readers have come expect from this daily look at the lives of the idle rich currently on tour away from Valbonne.

Taking the pun to a higher level, we were discussing the Catholic faith in terms of ice cream (don't ask why, it just seemed the right thing to do at the time). I think Popeastachio was my favourite but I did also like Vaticone and Pontifigranite.

Dairies are an important running narrative on one's day-to-day activities. That Nice Lady Decorator has taken to keeping one recently, especially when we are away from home, perhaps inspired by "The Motorcycle Diaries" written by Che Guevara about his exploits before he turned into the world's most popular revolutionary. I ventured the opinion that this column, my daily font of knowledge and wisdom, was on a par with these Motorcycle thingies, a persuasive daily insight into the issues surrounding a trip to a foreign country, but I regret to inform you that unlike many of my readers she does not seem to share this opinion. When I suggested as much she put her head in her hands and began moaning slightly and shaking her head and I got the feeling she did not entirely agree. I may be wrong; perhaps she thought this daily "diary" was superior but cannot be certain.

First target yesterday on our nearly completed trip to Cuba was Batista's Palace, now the Museum Of The Revolution; the opulent offices occupied by that the brutal dictator whom Fidel Castro deposed. It has been made into a shrine for the revolution complete with bullet holes in the marble where an earlier overthrow attempt by the students of Cuba failed, Batista escaping out of a back door, which I suppose could also be a euphemism for homosexuality if one was to be so vulgar, but certainly not in this column.

Regular followers of this missive will know my feelings about the Health And Safety brigade who are destroying the fabric of life in UK, so will know that I was delighted to see here in Havana no fences, railings or warnings of any sort to pedestrians or motorists nearby because even a moron could work out either by sound, vision, vibration or smell that there was a steam train nearby.

Smoke masks were not compulsory as some of us like the smell of smoke, either from a classic old steam engine or a good cigar. It remains an inconvenient fact for the HSE loonies that no one has ever been injured by this train.

I especially like that unsecured metal plate just by the track. Health and Safety eat your heart out.

Buena Vista Social Club

Yesterday to Casablanca, the small fortified castle and lighthouse area across the river mouth reached, according to our tour guide and leader, that Nice Lady Decorator, by a taxi to the port, cost 5 CUC (convertible Cuban Currency), a ferry crossing in a dangerously antiquated ferry (cost 2 CUC) used almost exclusively by the locals, an exhausting walk up a winding road and some 300 steps in 30 degree heat, a horse and cart ride (cost 3 CUC) and took about an hour and a quarter. The return trip in a taxi, through the tunnel I discovered after our intrepid and convoluted expedition out there and which had apparently escaped the notice of that Nice Lady Decorator and which cost 5 CUC, took just eleven minutes. Still, we did experience a little of real Cuban life. After a splendid lunch involving more wonderful and wonderfully cheap lobster on the roof terrace of Hotel Ambos Mundos, that Nice Lady Decorator

Informed me that we were to visit a shrine to Hemingway. It crossed my mind that "Hemingway" might be a good name for a sewing machine factory and was stupid enough to mention this to that Nice Lady Decorator who is a huge Hemingway fan and was treated me to that glazed angry look that silences me immediately. She told me that the Hotel room, 511, was dedicated as a shrine to the writer who stayed there regularly whenever he was in Havana and where he wrote "For whom the bell tolls". He always took the same room because of the view. What can I tell you? It was a basic room with a typewriter. Worth 4 CUC of anyone's money.

After this cultural delight, a couple of mohito's at the Bodega Del Medio (upstairs is my favourite place in Havana) we set out for the highlight of the visit to Cuba, an opportunity to see The Buena Vista Social Club perform at a large restaurant bar called Cafe Taverna in the centre of down town Havana. For the uninitiated Buena Vista was a regular gathering of Cuban musicians catapulted to fame by musical collusion with Ry Cooder which turned them into international stars through a number of concerts including Carnegie Hall and spawned an Academy Award-winning- film of the same name. However, it nearly didn't happen at all. The sign outside, seemingly the only advertising existing warned us we needed to book tickets and we were thus refused entrance. I had accepted that we were going to be denied the opportunity to see an iconic band perform at an intimate venue in their home town but they had not reckoned on that Nice Lady Decorator. All the rock 'n roll heritage which she has built up over the years when she was seemingly able to gain entrance to any gig anywhere by adopting a series of ploys (including one impersonating a journalist whom she knew was on the guest list for a Dr Feelgood concert and who was later denied entry as a result) came into play. It was the third time she tried and found a chink in the armour, securing seats in an unused terrace at the back giving us some of the best seats in the house.

I do not know how she did it or what it cost and I do not want to know. It was hard to identify exactly who was who but given the age of some of the band all the living originals must have been there. It was an electric experience, witnessing a piece of music history live as it were, and given the ages of some of them, live is the operative word. Some twenty great performers ran through their repertoire with the rumba, a musical style reinvigorated throughout the world by this group, obviously to the fore

The legendary Buena Vista Social Club live at Cafe Taverna in Havana

Continuing the Hemingway theme at the Ambos Mundos hotel in Havana on Thursday I spotted a starter on the restaurant menu called The Old Man And The Sea soup as my picture today attests. Given the Hemingway connection I can sort of guess what aspect of the sea might be included in the ingredients, marlin or shark perhaps? But it was the old man bit that captured my imagination. What part of the old man might be mixed in with the fish, some nail clippings?, some earwax? maybe some nasal hair? Or maybe the Old Man means something far more sinister? Maybe it describes the implement with which the soup has been stirred? As that Nice Lady Decorator remarked, if that were the case at least that could contribute to the fishy taste, although how she would know this is not something I wish to go into here in this column.

Yesterday on our last full day in Havana we embarked on a tour of the Havana Club distillery where we learned about the rum-making process. The Reverend Jeff will no doubt expect me to make some idiotic remark about it being a rum do, but my style is now at so superior a level I did not even consider the possibility. I did however agree with the chap behind me when it was suggested that we walk through a door made from a giant rum barrel, originally used in the maturing process, when he said "I am mature enough already". I think that now sums up my writing style.

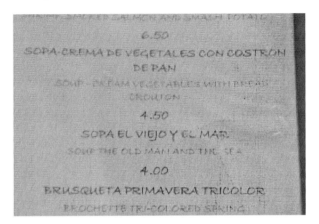

Interesting menu choice?

That Nice Lady Decorator, now nearly recovered from her sprained ankle, spent most of the tour complaining that her feet hurt, and when, even after the free tot of rum and an extra mohito had been downed she was still complaining, she noticed that she had her new leather sandals on the wrong feet. She will deny it of course but facts are facts.

After lunch taken again at Bodega Del Medio comprising braised pork shin with black beans, fried plantains and sweet potatoes, I settled down to enjoy a nice fat Cuban. I know that many of my public schoolboy friends who are regular readers of this daily report may place a different interpretation on this statement but they will know in their hearts that as I did not attend public school I was referring to a nice cigar. I cannot speak for them for certain but I fear the worst.

Last night we succumbed to pressure and decided we would visit the Hotel Nazionale as it was reputed to have a very special cocktail lounge and be a wonderful place for a sundowner at sunset. The fact that we left it until after dark probably did not help but the desperately poor service and ignorant waiters were too much for that Nice Lady Decorator so we left quickly. For me it was the busloads of tourists returning from their day trips and the number of people with tattoos and wearing scuzzy sleeveless t-shirts or football shirts with socks and big trainers that did it. I may go back today just to check.

Virgin Disgrace

What is the point of putting on your website that one can check in at 12.30 at Havana airport when in fact you cannot until 4pm? The omens for another spectacularly ordinary flight with the appalling Virgin Atlantic back to London Gatwick were good. The plan then was to jettison bags early and then pop out for a sneaky last lunch but these were dashed by this useless piece of information. Dickie Pickles, the bearded wonder and titular head of Virgin will be getting the sharp end of my pen in the coming days. His airline has now forever damaged the Virgin brand in my mind. It was not just the misinformation, they had run out of wine 2 hours into the 9 hour outward trip thus making a mockery of their claim to serve drinks throughout the trip and the in-flight entertainment was limited - of poor quality both artistically and technologically with constant fuzzy lines and black outs on the very few things worth watching. They claim to have won the award for the best in-flight entertainment. If that is the case then I want a steward's enquiry.

The trip back was little better, so with once again no stewardess in sight I stirred myself to go the galley to secure a drink. Finding no one at the first one, I went to the second one where the curtain was drawn. Asking for a glass of wine was clearly an affront to the rude member of staff who tersely asked me to give her a couple of minutes as she was doing some kind of calculation. A full five minutes elapsed and she had still not emerged but luckily some other hapless helper eventually arrived. Disgraceful service from people trained to offer a service. Had she been in my employ then she would now be looking at her P45.

Then that Nice Lady Decorator got in on the act. The idea was to try to sleep on the plane. She even had a sleeping pill to aid her, but someone must have tainted it with some Columbian marching powder or something similar as she was like a jack-in-the-box, drinking a litre of water and waking me up four times to go to the loo. So, an utterly sleepless, mainly dry, miserable experience. I shall never complain about Easyjet again. Virgin Atlantic is officially the worst airline with whom I have flown, worse on this trip than Ryanair.

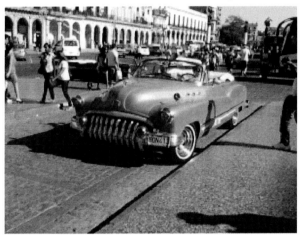

My picture above is of my personal favourite vehicle in Havana. The sheer number of great old cars, many used as taxis on the road each day is something wondrous to behold. At least 25 per cent of the cars on the road must be old American models from the 1950's or earlier, many in a desperate condition and doing a great deal to enhance Cuba's carbon footprint, but as a spectacle and a testament to the American embargo (incidentally being flouted by a number of Americans who can gain entrance via Cancun in Mexico) it is hard to better. Cuba I love, Virgin Atlantic I hate.

Our final lunch was taken on the roof terrace of the Ambos Mundos Hotel in Havana. It was a very agreeable luncheon spot with great views across to the old fort at Casablanca and across the city to the harbour and the other way along the coast towards the centre of the city. This was where that Nice Lady Decorator spent 8 CUC to see a hotel room with a typewriter, their dedication to

Ernest Hemingway.

Warm Sun To Wet Barn

So from the delights of Cuba it has been our misfortune to have to spend most of yesterday emptying a barn in which we have stored loads of valuable personal possessions belonging to that nice Lady Decorator, together with some of my gold and platinum discs. Unfortunately, after the cold weather a few weeks ago it seems a pipe must have burst and has been running for the last month soaking most stuff in the building. So it was great fun to wade through water with your loved one, a bit like we were doing in Cuba a few days ago, however this experience was somewhat less edifying. At least afterwards I thought I would be able to stroll up to The Chequers in Weston Turville for a pint but, as if to administer the final slap in the face reminder that we were back in the cold of England, the pub was shut, it shuts on Mondays. Having no warm clothes and no car, and with the frost beginning to form, we had no choice but to return home and drink all the wine we had, light a fire and huddle around it.

Later we were invited to fridge magnet salesman extraordinaire Paul North for some roadkill surprise, so life is really grim....I found a really good likeness of him in the Lost Gardens of Heligon last year, even down to the colour of his hair.

I will need to move some furniture etc. back to Valbonne and need a furniture removal company. I have seen an advert in some local magazines for a company called Tooth Removals. I mentioned this to that Nice Lady Decorator and she wanted to know why I needed a dentist to transport furniture. Maybe they are based in Denton? I look a bit down in the mouth because I won't be back in Valbonne until next week.

I thought I had done all the dentist jokes until I heard from Slash And Burn that he has a Chinese dentist and he had an appointment there yesterday at tooth-hurty, and I am not joking,

Last night we went to what used to be one of the best pubs in Buckinghamshire, The Chequers in Weston Turville, which has all its character removed by the new owners and is not even a shadow of its former self. It did, however, serve a very decent pint of Timothy Taylor Landlord, which is the second best beer in the world behind Fullers London Pride. A discussion ensued about interesting names given to beers and I think my favourite was one I spotted in Cornwall last year where I found a pint of Ginger Tosser. The beer was awful though, so bad I found the need to call up a couple of my red-headed friends and tell them about it, they were so pleased to hear from me.

Today I shall be spending another day with that Nice Lady Decorator in hoarding mode, trying to reduce the amount of stuff she wants to keep. Actually she has been very good but I need to keep a close eye on her. Let me give you an example; yesterday, she was successful in persuading me she should keep the wooden toadstools I made for a joke 10 years ago. Do you see what I am getting at?

She had bought some mushroom spores or mushroom compost as I had complained that mushrooms bought from supermarkets had no taste and I could not find field mushrooms anywhere. So I could not resist whittling a few "magic" mushrooms and planting them in the same spot about a week later (I know I needed to get a proper job, too much time on my hands then).

It's amazing! Magic mushrooms have grown again!

The Village Gate is a pub that used to be called The Marquis Of Granby. It is just outside Weston Turville and is where many of the villagers who have deserted The Chequers go to eat and drink. This seems a strange name for a pub, and I am not sure whether I would be content with being a regular here as one may consider oneself one of the Village People. Does it mean I have to wear a Red Indian headpiece or get a porno moustache?

Talking of porno moustaches, after my recent restaurant "accident" in which my luxuriant long beard was hacked off by some jealous public schoolboys one lunchtime at the Auberge St Donat in Plascassier, I have been nurturing a splendid handlebar moustache which is curling nicely a la Salvador Dali. I do hope it is not an impediment this evening when I am amongst the Village People at the Village Gate. I also fervently hope that it gets up the noses (not literally you understand) of the many public schoolboy acquaintances I have accumulated when I return to France next week. There are of course no public schoolboys left in

Buckinghamshire.

So having attended the Village People pub, and enjoyed the delights of battered fish and chips with the unwelcome addition of green pea puree of mushy peas made into a much smaller serving by liquidising the horrible green concoction to within an inch of its life, we adjourned to our English house to drink a quite agreeable 2005 Rioja, the bottle of which was covered in chicken wire, a sign, according to that Nice Lady Decorator that the wine was of superior quality, although superior to what was never fully explained.

I suppose I should be glad the pub is not called The Village Bike, otherwise my sabre sharp sense of humour would have been wheeled out and had a field day. This bespoke column could have ended up as a true tour de force with a chain of comments about my handlebar moustache. Ok, I am now tyred of the bike jokes. I have realised that I like writing but it's the paperwork I don't like.

Once again I was set up to be one of the Village People. Yes, I was required to meet the great and the good of Weston Turville and it says much about the village that the best they could come up with was fridge magnet salesman Paul North. Too say that he is a touch unsophisticated is like saying John Terry is a little indiscreet. The farmer's boy from Quarrendon is cleverer than he pretends but not as bright as he thinks.

Let's start from the beginning. Another depressing day was spent discovering relics from my rock and roll past damp and disorganised after a flood. I think the neighbours were a little disconcerted by the 30 or so gold discs drying against the wall and in fact I think I am in need of drying out as well. A decision was made to go to the Village Gate pub to meet some Village People at 7.00 sharp, a collection of old friends, none of whom deigned to appear much before 8.30 by which time the London Pride had stepped in and made its mark. My picture today is a suggestion of what might have been an appropriate car in which to visit the village people.

It was then that one of the biggest of the Village People, Paul North, cast a large shadow over the door. A former butcher, his wit could never be described as subtle, although there is subtle humour in his job which as I said earlier is a fridge magnet salesman. Let me give you an idea of his light humorous touch. He thought it was funny to throw my golf shoes down the garden late last night in the dark although why is still a mystery but I was able to retrieve them this morning ready for an impromptu round of golf with him this afternoon at the dull and uninteresting Weston Turville golf course. He will doubtless still be claiming his girl's handicap of 28, and if he wins will almost certainly take the wagered bank-note and stick it on his head in that childish fashion that so suits him. Of course if I win then it is a noble gesture and celebration of success and not at all tacky.

A suitable car to go to see The Village People?

The prospect of returning to my beloved France and especially Valbonne is looming into view and frankly I cannot wait. Before that though, there is the small matter of golf this afternoon and then drinks at ours before heading to The Raj Indian restaurant in Wendover. Amongst the people attending will be Peter and the fabulously attractive and blonde Janie Savin. Janie will be well known to readers who have followed this blog from the beginning for it was she that spent the week when staying with us in France last summer watering my plastic fake banana palm, and getting her reward at the end of the week when I secured a bunch of bananas to hang on the tree. Also, she cannot say the word Riviera. To her it is always Riverarea, as in Riverarea Radio. This is of course far too tempting a target for me and so I like to have fun inveigling the word Riviera into as many sentences as possible. She is always pleased by this, often to the extent of threatening me physical bodily harm. Some women are so unpredictable.

Golf In Jeopardy

It was over breakfast when I mentioned in passing my intention to take time off from house clearing in order to play golf with Mr. Fridge Magnet Magnate aka Paul North. The look came immediately. You know that look you get when you have been startled by headlights? No that was not her, that was me when she had considered my idea and as a result I had received the laser beam stare and torrent of invective which usually means I have either done something wrong, am considering doing anything wrong or look like I am about to do anything wrong, or in this case because I had stupidly made a decision all on my own. To be fair, with the clearance of our UK house as it has been sold after only 7 years on the market (really quite brisk) uppermost in her mind and her continuing to work like a Trojan from dawn to dusk (after dusk it's to the pub obviously), I should have seen it coming. Possibly the biggest mistake came when I jocularly suggested that perhaps I would be better off out of her hair. This did not go down well, so golf was postponed. Mr. Fridge Magnet Magnate can keep his £10 and his girl's handicap for another day.

When one is awarded a silver, gold or platinum record as I have been fortunate enough to have done in the course of my music business career, one does like to display them, especially if one is an insufferable show-off like me. However the kind of display featured in my picture today was not quite what I had in mind. The flooded barn had damaged a number of them and so they were left out in the unseasonable sunshine to dry off before the process of repairing or scrapping them is undertaken.

Those who have said in the past that the music I have represented was a bit wet get their reward.

I am invited to attend an evening of Cuban music in Sophia Antipolis shortly after I return to France but have declined saying that if I heard "Guantanamera" one more time in the near future I was going to kill someone, which was probably a little ill-judged as that is where they are still keeping all those Al Qaeda suspects, in Guantanamera Bay.

What looks as if it will be another astonishingly good day today in terms of weather for March in England will be beautifully counterpointed by an astonishingly bad day of my being a removal man and revisiting one of my earliest jobs when I was a dustman during my A level summer holidays. As Winston Churchill might have said: "never, in the history of human nest building have so many items been collected for so long by so few." And so, as you read this I shall be knee-deep in Lady Decorator detritus. Please pray for me.

It was as she was unscrewing the screws holding up one of the corner cupboards on the wall of our house in UK whilst I was holding it to prevent it falling that she said "I could have done with something with a longer handle". My retort, which was that she had married me so she had to put up with the results', was met with that dismissive snort I have come to covet.

So after a busy morning wading through the accumulated detritus of our lives, Mr. Clipboard showed up to have a nose around. Inevitably, after he had cast his eyes over my belongings and selected some of the best pieces in order to adorn his new abode, we adjourned to the pub, The Chequers in Weston Turville, which is much nicer outside than inside but to which I am warming as at least the staff are pleasant and the beer is good.

Inevitably, at least inevitably in my opinion, discussion turned to the success or otherwise of my book "Summer in the Cote d'Azur". Mrs. Clipboard who, along with Mr. Clipboard was visiting us in Buckinghamshire, mentioned that her brother is the famous historian and fellow writer Andrew Roberts (mentioned by our Prime Minister Mr. Cameron during his public pronouncements with President Obama recently) who is nearly as famous as I.

She had told me some weeks earlier that she would ask him to review my modest offering in his column for The Sunday Times, but it appears, and this may be an understatement, that he was slightly reluctant to do so. Jealously can be so destructive don't you think? I do feel us writers should stick together and support each other. I was saying just the same to my mate Ernest Hemingway to whom I was speaking in a bar in Havana until I realised it was a bronze cast.

On Friday evening at the excellent Raj Indian restaurant in Wendover, Slash and Burn, who is our house guest whilst we are in England, was praising the tarka dal served to him saying it was best he had ever tasted. When I remonstrated with him that he was cruel and heartless and that I did not think a curry was a very pleasant ending for an otter he declined to agree saying that if anything it should be a little hotter. A clear case of Tarka The Otter.

Slash and Burn also claimed during an early evening pint yesterday, in surprisingly warm sunshine, to have made some 250 flights last year which sounds excessive to me and I must admit I lost the thread of the conversation. I heard mention of DVT as a result of this "high" life but as anyone with any knowledge of technology will know this will soon be replaced entirely by Blu-

Ray.

Anyway, the local populace was enjoying the weather, summer has come early to England but soon it will be over and then winter will beckon. Sadly I will be sharing this fate with them much more than I would like this year due to Mr. Sarkozy and the idiosyncrasies of the French tax system which has involved my becoming a UK tax resident again.

Just two more days now and I will be returning to France and although the last few days have produced a rather rich vein of blog fodder, I feel that Valbonne provides the richest and most continuingly reliable seam to mine. I shall soon be donning a miner's helmet and begin to dig.

The plan was to go to the Bell in Aston Clinton. We went and it was better but still underwhelming. This is the pub which was a famous restaurant and, I think, a hotel, the haunt of pop stars and film stars in the 60's and 70's. In my youth I recall a story about Mick Jagger being refused entry because he refused to remove the mink hat he was wearing. It was one of the places at which to be seen until the late 1990's when the owner died, I think being run over in a tragic accident outside the pub which was on the original route of the A41. It was then taken over by one of those horrid pub chains intent on making each of their establishments indistinguishable from another, a homogeneous disaster, removing all sense of honest history and character and instead applying an appalling sanitised fake horse brass style, anathema to anyone with a true love or understanding of old original English pubs.

The Last Knockings Of Weston Turville

After a long day spent impersonating "white van man" pretending to be a removal man and saying things like "all right guv" and "over there me old china" it seemed somehow right and proper that we had been invited to neighbours Mr. Paul Fridge Magnet Magnate North, who has often featured in this column in the early days as a figure of fun, for a parting drink. He has a rough rustic charm which is endearing in a limited and mind-narrowing way. Who can forget his many pronouncements about "Johnny Foreigner", Arsenal Football Club or when talking about his golf slice and his contention that all golf courses should comprise 18 dog leg rights, or indeed his conviction that all wine is crap and his hatred of all things French, or indeed foreign. They are forever a stain on my memory. However, with passing of the years I had hoped that a smidgen of maturity may have emerged, a slight relaxation in his resemblance to a latter day Alf Garnet and I think it is true to say there has been limited progress as the picture I show today, taken in his garden seems to reveal.

It is of course a couple of garden gnomes, the collection of which is an endearing English habit for the lower classes and one that despite my humble upbringing I never quite understood, far less embraced. What I think is interesting here is that they seem to be dressed in Arsenal livery. Perhaps it is some kind of oblique comment on the way the team is playing at the moment? Suffice to say that on the graph of social improvement Mr. North has made rather slow progress. His school report, had he ever attended such an institution, could read "not good enough, see me afterwards".

The one on the right is clearly training to be a policeman or a cricket umpire

I left France with that Nice Lady Decorator on March 6th and will return for the Easter period to welcome back my two expensive Sprogs who even at this moment I can feel plotting to extract as much money from me as possible. It is a bit like being stalked. Whilst I shall be pleased to see them both I am thinking of sewing up my pockets before they arrive.

The pleasures that await me however are enough to compensate: lunch at the Auberge St Donat, sitting with a glass of rose in Valbonne Square in the sunshine, golf, tennis, walking in the Valmasque and the return of my style guru from New York. Mr. Humphreys who is not currently free but has instead been free-wheeling (Mr. Fridge Magnet thinks this refers to a three-wheeler) his way around the East coast of America and has been causing quite a stir in the Big Apple with his "unique" style. I am anxiously awaiting his sartorial reaction to exposure to Manhattan. I do hope that he is home by Friday for "church" in Cafe Latin to witness the results.

Before we left and on my way to the tip in my final role as white van man, the driver from hell, me, the guv, was listening to the delights of 3 Counties Radio, an audio offering from the BBC in Buckinghamshire. Once again I was piloting a large white van full of rubbish and "quality items for storage" before flying back to France last night. As is required by law when in charge of such a machine, my language had degenerated into East End Wayne Brown speak which in normal circumstances I find utterly incomprehensible. It is amazing what powers you inherit when hiring a big white van. One can cut up other motorists with impunity, well, one does not notice the opprobrium directed at one as a result, previously unknown swear words appear and expel from one's mouth without warning, one's driving abilities are reduced to Neanderthal level, one's middle finger takes on a life of its own and seems to be permanently erect, and the ability to park badly in inappropriate places is honed to perfection. That reminds me, I must make a note to pay that parking ticket tomorrow.

Anyway, it was on the BBC, on the radio whilst I was driving about swearing, with my middle finger pointing to the sky that I heard on the news a story about some poor girl, for some unexplained reason, being taken up the Ridgeway. The Ridgeway of course is a famous ancient track, now a footpath and bridleway that runs through the countryside of Buckinghamshire, Hertfordshire and Bedfordshire, much loved by walkers or ramblers. Personally I have never been taken up the Ridgeway but hope it will come to pass at some stage.

We arrived a Heathrow terminal 5 at lunchtime whereupon that Nice Lady Decorator told me she was going to treat me to a no expenses spared slap-up lunch at the caviar and seafood bar in recognition of my white van heroics. No expense spared that is, until I asked for a third glass of Sancerre.

As we boarded the plane we bumped into Valbonne resident Captain Custard as we have come to know my occasional tennis foe, BA captain John Coward, who was famously in the pilot's seat when that Boeing 777 pancaked at Heathrow a few years back. He said he was on his way home, but I must admit I breathed a sigh of relief when our plane actually reached the runway at Nice Airport.

Chapter 8

Back To The Sunshine

Tennis doubles can be so exacting, even on a beautiful sunny and warm spring evening at the rather deserted Vignale Tennis Club. The problems, if they arise, always lie with having to rely on one's partner. Normally I would be entirely content that the colossus at the net, my usual tennis partner, the Wingco, one half of the MOGS, the Moustachioed Old Gits would have been there as an utterly dependable stooge who, with the benefit of my tireless running and mastery of the deep lob (as opposed to the half lob which apparently refers to something completely different) usually enables us to steer to victory.

With the Wingco unavailable, a new partnership needed to be forged. If I had cared to focus the warning signs were there immediately. Our leader and organiser dancing Greg, likes to win almost as much as I, and hates to lose almost as much as I as well. I should have known when there was clear collusion between dancing Greg and Blind Lemon Milsted to play together, so to speak. An incomprehensible partner selection charade then took place to confirm that I was to be left with Nick Goult as my partner for the evening with whom I had not played before. It was a partnership destined to end in a quickie divorce. Nick was previously an unknown quantity to me (and in tennis terms I wished it had stayed that way) but clearly not to the others, and if I am frank, it is not a quantity with any quality. Fine architect he may be but he is as suited to tennis as well as I imagine Twiggy would be suited to weight lifting. His serving was an art form. Perfect little lobs, most of which hit the net ensured that each of his service games was lost, mainly to love and despite my courageous and athletic efforts, the nominal result may have gone against us as a team, whilst personally I triumphed. I have a picture today of another tennis-playing entity whom I suspect may have contributed more on the court than my partner.

Anyone for tennis?

I did not make this point about this victory last night in La Source where we adjourned for a couple of beers afterwards as frankly I had not thought of it then, so had to endure some rather vulgar exhibitions of triumphalism from Dancing Greg and Blind Lemon. How can this be I hear you ask, how can I actually have won personally? Simple, we played two sets losing 6-4, 6-4, but as I was individually responsible for all 8 games we won out of the total of 20 played, on a pro-rata basis I won more games than anyone. I know this will be a bitter pill for my opponents to swallow but life can be harsh, although not that harsh now I am back in the benign embrace of the south of France.

Loose Talk Of Bumming Around

I want that job. I would dearly like to identify her but I promised anonymity to the beautiful wife of a BA captain whom we ran into at Cafe des Arcades in Valbonne on Thursday lunchtime who was on her way to have her beautician, and I quote "work on my arse". I want that job. When I was unemployed in the early 1970's they never had jobs on offer suggesting one could be being paid for manipulating beautiful girls arses, if there had been then I venture to suggest that I would have exclaimed "bottoms up" and made the best of it. I like to have a hand in many things and.....I think I should stop there. There was a friend of mine signed on the dole in Camden when I was growing up, he was registered as a ski instructor and do you know they never did find him a job. Not many ski resorts in North London. Pretty sure he could not ski either. It could be worse, what about having a job walking a pig? I took this picture in central France a couple of years ago. Apparently the pig was called Sarkozy.

I hear a story about a blonde who called her husband in the office to say that the windows at home had frozen. He told her to put hot water on them. She called up 5 minutes later and said the computer doesn't work at all now. Another story that evolved last night was some revelations about the Naked Politician in Las Vegas some time ago. It seems that he lived up to his name, removing his clothes to sprint around a casino before being thrown out. His excuse was that his lederhosen were chafing. No one has yet provided a convincing explanation as to why he was wearing lederhosen in a casino in Vegas.

An interesting idea has been floated by long-term devotee of this column upon which this book is based, Mellissa Graves. She contends that when girls answer a question with the single word "what?" it does not mean they have misheard the answer; they are just giving the man a chance to reconsider what he is saying. This is a sweet and generous concept and one that I shall bear in mind, especially when that nice lady uses the word in a context like this; "what the f**k do you think you are doing?"

Lunch at the Butterfields and Peachy will be anxious to know if I have been successful in my quest to find a 5 litre flagon of wine for 8 euros as was the case the last time we lunched together, but I am afraid I have not, just a magnum of a very good Bordeaux. I know it is far too good for him and I have selected some bottles to take with me to his place but he does like quantity rather than quantity, a fact reflected in his gargantuan waist line. Thus I asked the supermarket for the biggest glass vessel they had and so that is what I shall be taking for him. The Bordeaux will remain my side of the table.

I am not quite certain what is going on in this photo that I took in Havana recently. I am sure that the animal in the basket believes it is a dog but it seems to me to resemble a meercat. Perhaps this chap was seeking the best insurance for his bike? As all insurance companies presumably aim to make a profit, should not the slogan be "compare the mark up.com?"

It is always a big lunch when one is invited to the Butterfields, but quite how big I was destined to find out when Peachy decided to try out a pair of false breasts. Quite why he feels the need to own a pair of quite respectable blow up false breasts which he claims he uses as the ultimate comfort cushion is not beyond me at all, in fact I can well imagine the therapeutic effects that could be secured by owning such an item. Where can I buy one or should it be a pair?

Dog in a manger? Oh no, dog in a basket

Events understandably got slightly out of hand after the early administering of mojitos at lunch but it started earlier than that. The Braderie in Valbonne took place yesterday. It coincided with the antiques market which takes place on the first Sunday of each month throughout the village of Valbonne. After the desultory look around at the vastly overpriced merchandise on the market we ended up having a sneaky beer at the Cafe des Arcades just after the sun had passed the yardarm (somewhere in the world) but that of course led to a glass of rose which was still insufficient to prepare one for the onslaught of lunch. However, Slash and Burn, who was also on the lookout for non-existent bargains was sufficiently disheartened as to order a double espresso, a large pastis and a carafe of rose to accompany one of the many Cohibas he purchased in Havana. It was shortly after this that we made a strategic withdrawal from what was stacking up to be more carnage and headed for lunch.

I espied Chateau Gloria almost before I encountered the many-times-retired Simon Howes who single-handedly allows this vineyard to maintain its frankly ludicrous prices. It is a fantastic wine but we only had 3 bottles (after all, there were 3 of us drinking red) so we had to degenerate into a magnum of St Estephe whilst taking advantage of an overstock of Cuba's finest cigars. I am not sure if Cuba ever had a cigar mountain but a fair dent was made yesterday, in fact in climbing Everest terms I would venture to suggest that we passed base camp one. A plume of cigar smoke trailed through the garden to the distant horizon.

I must draw a discrete veil over proceedings mainly because I have either forgotten them, I have been bribed to forget or the details are far too disturbing even for this daily look at the lives of the idle rich in Valbonne, save to say that the lovely Suzanne must have had the entire Valbonne stock of chickens slaughtered for the meal which for once involved no barbecued road kill, Peachy having been forbidden to get involved.

Actually the expression "out to lunch" could easily be applied to the enormous intellect of the university-educated but fatally-blonde Lisa Thornton Allan. Yesterday she excelled herself again with her knowledge of geography. This time it was her contention that the lovely northern Kent town of Whitstable was on the south coast of England. She was certain because as she said "my mother lives there and I visit regularly and I know it is on the south coast". Beautiful and fit she may be but geographically challenged and suffering from a velocity awareness deficiency certainly. Whitstable is of course on the north Kent coast. She became more than slightly unsettled claiming at one stage "I would be so much more intimidating if I wasn't so stupid" this of course is utterly incorrect, she is even more intimidating when she is being stupid because she has the ability to project her opinions in such a way they have the ring of certainty. For instance, I now firmly believe that passenger airliners can and do travel at 2000 miles per hour, Whitstable is on the south coast of Kent and a camera on a smart phone has 256 pixies.

Earlier in the week in Valbonne in the best and the most expensive fruit shop in the world, the first cherries of the season were on sale, a snip at just 199 euros a kilo so by my reckoning that's about 5 euro each. Cherry pie anyone?

When looking around the garden to see what has survived the winter, it was sad to see the lemon trees have been badly affected by the snow but one perennial survivor is my banana palm. It is able to stay out in all weathers and keeps its fronds all year around, mainly because it is made from the finest plastic and metal known to man. If I had my way (which regular readers will know is an utter pipedream) all the plants in the garden would be plastic, how much less labour intensive would that be? Imagine, at the end of October, a quick five-minute trot around the garden to collect up and bring in all the flowers, stuff them into the washing machine with a bit of Ariel then a quick wash and spin dry, iron and then in the drawer until February and back out again ready for spring and summer, very civilised. No pruning, watering, spraying with insect repellent, no work at all, least of all digging and being mutilated by malevolent plants.

The lovely Lesley Bufton and long-suffering husband Roly have just taken delivery of their new yacht, a splendid looking Fleming. Lesley in particular has come a long way from her humble beginnings as John Hurt's cleaner and they are off to Falmouth this week for sea trials. They have chosen their captain, he is Italian. This piece of information of course led to some merriment at their expense due to a certain Italian captains unfortunate experiences recently. I am not certain of their boat's name but "Costa Packet" was suggested along with "A Bit On The Side" and one or two more tasteless suggestions, "Dead Wood" being one that I can include in this column, renowned for its taste, poise and treatment of gossip. I suppose that the captain of the Costa Concordia will shortly be facing his own sea trial.

Hijacked For A Barbecue

Some days later, after a stiff walk, more exercise was taken to ensure a proper appetite in the form of tennis with the Wingco. He was not convinced that I won but a score of 4-6, 6-2 tells its own story. Nominally it was one set each but on the count back, a method I employ when it suits me, the score was 10-8 to me, a clear victory, lovingly and truthfully reported in this missive. He will not read it of course ("Ghastly" his considered opinion) but many of his friends and even his wife does and many will alert him to my interpretation.

Arriving home at around 4pm I was almost immediately bundled into a car together with several bottles of wine and my traveling cigar humidor for a late afternoon barbecue courtesy of man mountain Peachy Butterfield and voluptuous wife Suzanne. I had noticed a pall of smoke lurking just to the north of Valbonne whilst playing tennis, and had thought it rather dangerous for someone to be having a bonfire whilst the mistral was starting, blowing those thunder clouds away. It turns out that it was sausages. Yes Peachy was incinerating sausages (and probably every animal he could catch or run over in a ten-mile radius) and was ensuring it was all "properly cooked." The barbecue that he was manning could have come direct from Hades. By 6pm he had barbecued everything to a crisp, even I suspect, the lettuce but having missed lunch I was ravenous so tucked in.

I want you to think that the picture below is printed in a loving way with no malicious intent. It appeared on Peachy's Facebook page and the suggestion is that it is he. However if you look closely enough (please avoid doing this with food nearby) you will see two things that suggest otherwise. Firstly the plate he is holding is far too small and secondly had he been consuming anything that he had barbecued there would have been copious amounts of black charcoal and ash covering the much larger plate.

I was beginning to get concerned as I had nothing planned for today's column; a juicy story reached my ears although I simply cannot reveal the name of the family involved. It seems that some years ago the father was involved in some kind of corporate promotion which involved or was using some James Bond images. An Aston Martin was required for a few days and a number plate with the numbers 007 was produced. One day he used the Aston to collect his children, all under 10 at the time from school. Weeks later the children sat their father down and said "it doesn't matter but we know what you do, you are a spy". He asked what on earth had given them that idea. It seems that added to the Aston trip, and the 007 connotation, their discovery in a bedroom draws of a pair of handcuffs was sufficient for them to come that inevitable conclusion.

Dinner aboard a yacht, Peachy style

Lunch in Valbonne Square in the sunshine. For you locals just, consider that statement for a moment, are we not as close to heaven as one who does not believe in such a place can get? Even the Reverend Jeff, who does believe in going to church and living life according to the dictates of the Lord (Voldemart?) has never been exalted to the heights of having lunch in Valbonne Square so adherence to rigid dogma does not always pay dividends. I am certain that lunching in Basingstoke yesterday where the Reverend resides was not as pleasant lunching in Valbonne square.

I love all things French. The French word for school is "ecole", easily mistaken one may think for the word for alcohol, which with typical French cunning is exactly the same word in the local dialect. I accept that when one has a carefully-cultivated plummy accent they may sound the same, and therein lays the problem. One of our friends who shall remain nameless, but for arguments sake we will call Lisa Thornton Allan was on her way home from Mougins School with some of her children recently. She was intercepted by the police at Brittain's roundabout just outside Valbonne and asked if she had taken any alcohol, but she thought that she was asked if she had come from school. "Yes, I have" she said and was promptly breathalysed. Technically, as she had not had a drink (an allegedly rare occurrence by 4pm) this could have been construed as a waste of police time. Recently I heard that she hates whistling or that hearing whistling makes her violent, but armed with that knowledge perhaps I should have so far refrained from whistling the tune to The Bill. A discussion developed about our various experiences when the meaning of words had been confused or misunderstood. It seems that predictive text can throw up all sorts of horrors, especially when one is pressed for time, or in my case cannot find one's reading glasses. For example recently some embarrassment was caused by a texted order for two portions of hummus which became a request for two homosexuals. Any non-salad-dodger ordering such a thing deserves such an unfortunate result.

Earlier in the week after the completion of our long-awaited connection to mains drainage, I had carefully prepared and raked an area at the bottom of the garden and repopulated it with grass seed. Yesterday I discovered a grand larceny, theft on a huge scale, organised crime at its most efficient, although technically I knew where it had all gone, it was still theft and I am sure the Reverend Jeff will have a Commandment that covers that. Ants had fastidiously collected almost every seed from a 30 square metre area and piled them into 4 nests, one of which I photographed as evidence either for a police prosecution if any of the perpetrators survived and can be brought to justice, or in my defence of any charges of mass annihilation (genantocide?) that may be pressed by animal rights groups in the future. This "ant"agonistic behaviour had to be stamped on before it got out of hand, but stamping on my newly-raked area was going to make a real mess so I had to resort to chemical warfare in the shape of Nippon Ant Killer Powder. Now I have had to replace the seed at some cost. Who will pay? I am now officially anti ant. I bet their leader was called Adam or Atom. Some years ago I was able to purchase chocolate-covered edible ants. I may see if I can get some as a warning.

Talking of cooking, which I was not, I was sent out during the week by that Nice Lady Decorator to the English Book Centre in Valbonne to see if I could get a Dinosaur Cook Book. The shop assistant looked at me blankly and after a few seconds said "Do you mean the Dinah Shore cookbook?" which I admit was a bit of a relief, I wondered what she was up to.

Last night we were invited to partake of a curry courtesy of Lisa Thornton Allan, a vegetarian by inclination except for her love of Carpaccio of beef. However, a curry implies cooking so I was resigned to a being presented with a lentil curry, correctly as it turned out. One of the guests was the as entertaining-as-he-is-unreliable (OK, that's a bit harsh, he just "forgot" to reply to some emails I sent him) print guru Simon Asserati, crazy name, crazy guy and occasional user of crazy words. He was endowed with form in this area from birth. The simple addition of an "m" at the start of his surname may have given him a supercharged start to his life but its absence has clearly left its mark. Last night he mangled the English language again, this time with the never-before-heard (by me) word "revolise". What does this mean? As the subject of the conversation in which this exciting new word was used was Cuba, perhaps it was a combination of revolution and revitalise?

Rain Welcome?

I have seldom been happier to see rain. After a sunny start it looked as if my Sunday was going to be ruined by gardening duty. I had "dug" out my gardening attire, tweed suit, cravat, silk gloves, Hunters plus the various garden implements, the uses for some of which I have never fully understood, and as one comment on this column yesterday alluded to: I could take my pick of garden tools with which to "enjoy" my stint in the garden.

The fact that Sunday should be a day of rest seems to have escaped the notice of that Nice Lady Decorator. In truth I was suffering some after burn after over doing the lentil curry chez Slash and Burn Thornton Allan on Saturday evening. I think I now have added insight as to why he is thus called, particular the "burn" bit if this is the kind of food he gets at home. Don't get me wrong, I love a good hot curry but the problem symptoms often materialise the next morning with rather unedifying results.

The coming week is also something that I am not contemplating with a great deal of pleasure. One of my least favourite words has been mentioned, gravel. Readers who have been following this true account of the lives of the idle rich in Valbonne may recall that in the early days of this column, before ahem, becoming a successful author, I spent some time moving some two thirds of the entire French production of gravel to cover various areas of the drive and garden that the Nice Lady Decorator had decreed should be covered in it. I aged several years during this process which took err...several years. It seems however that her granite chip imagination has been fired again as a result of recent drainage works trashing part of the garden and that harbinger of doom, the tape measure, has been brought into play (work for me) with the inevitable consequences. I will be sent to the quarry to collect gravel. I think the Reverend Jeff may have some parable to quote here about some falling on stony ground. I think the only thing that can save me is a continuation of this indifferent weather and a forlorn hope that she will change her mind about what she believes is required and that somehow this will absolve me of any responsibility for hard labour. As I think the awful Supertramp once intoned "you're nothing but a dreamer."

Duck wraps for supper. I would have thought that with all those feathers they would not need wraps. I may duck down tomorrow to avoid just chastisement for a terrible joke, maybe someone will throw duck eggs at me, then the yoke would be on me. Can you tell that nothing much happened yesterday? Usually when I sit down to write this column I have any number of events, comments or gossip to report, but when you don't really leave the house, don't have a drink and don't see anyone, writing is a lot harder.

We talked as we walked this morning about perhaps getting Max a bell to go on his collar so we can find him as he is not hearing our calls, and that made me think that we should also make some sort of provision for that Nice Lady Decorator's disobedient disgrace of a hound, the smelliest and most wet-mouthed (read gobby) dog there has ever been. I got into a bit of trouble when I suggested that perhaps as a special treat we could get him a wild boar costume to wear when we were out walking, particularly in the hunting season. She did seem to realise that it was a joke, as it was not, but it quickly became a joke when I saw the thunder clouds begin to form around her.

So today I fear I shall not be able to delay it any longer. All the usual excuses have been trotted out and dismissed and I can feel the backache starting before I have even lifted a shovel. Ten trailer loads of gravel are what I have estimated as the amount required tocover most of Provence and it all starts tomorrow. Anyone wanting to chip in, get stoned, or enjoy a good stoning with me iswelcome.

I tried grovelling but she was determined that I should gravel rather than grovel. A large area of my garden now resembles the Gobi Desert and still it is not finished. I must venture forth to the quarry again on numerous occasions today for yet more granite gratification.

A Male Model Is Born

The big news, for me anyway, is that my modelling career is about to take off. The lovely Marina Kulik, who is an accomplished artist and runs painting classes in that weird hut with the wooden plane outside near the riding stables in Plascassier, has invited me to be their model next Monday. My choice is on the cover of this book which you hold in your hands at the moment. Marina was very keen for me to bring a number of items with me to the session between 10 and 12 next Monday, which she considered from regular reading this daily collection of gossip and innuendo, summed up my persona. Large cigars, bottles of wine, tennis rackets, more wine, loud shirts, cravat, silk smoking jacket were all understandable, but a walking stick? A mirror? A dog collar? Just what sort of image do I project? One thing I shall not be wearing is the hat-like contraption that is my featured image below spotted at the Antibes Yacht Show last week, made apparently from a plant with a few adornments. I think the spiders are a nice touch. I mentioned earlier in connection with my gravelling that I was stoned, but I would suggest that its creator may have had more than his or her fair share of mind expanding drugs, the basis of course for any modern art in my humble opinion. Marina believes that I should practice posing for my modelling assignment next Monday at her studios in Plascassier. This will involve sitting around with a glass of wine and talking, so when I undertake this practice at any time between now and Monday I hope everyone with whom I am at the time, will realise that it is actually work.

As expected, tennis was a triumph for the moustachioed old gits which comprise my good self and the Wingco last evening. Having cruised to a 6-3 win in the first set against Dancing Greg Harris and Blind Lemon Milsted the MOGS relaxed a little in the second set, obviously contemplating a nice post-victory dinner at Carpaccio in Chateauneuf de Grasse. That I managed to play at all is a testament to my strength and willpower after spending the day shovelling gravel from a pile of gravel that must have been visible to the naked eye from outer space. We had allowed our opponents to build a 5-1 lead before taking charge of the situation and repaired this to 6-6. Had there been a tie break, as is the modern way forward in these situations, then our victory would surely have been confirmed earlier. That our victory was a tad controversial cannot be denied. It was a major topic of discussion over dinner. Nominally under some tennis scoring rules, two sets played and one set won by each team, the score being 6-3, 7-9 the result may have been considered a draw, but regular followers of this column will not be surprised to know that I consider a draw at tennis to be a waste of time so I like to employ a count back. It is a simple enough exercise: one counts the total games one has won compared with one's opponents' and even the mathematically-challenged amongst you (and here I make special mention of the delectable steely-eyed blonde Lisa Thornton Allan) should be able to calculate that the MOGS ran out winners by 12 to 11. You see there is a reason why Mr. Clipboard has been known to refer to me as "the count back c**t. The game was played in sunny but rather windy conditions at the Vignale which played havoc with style and finesse but for Greg especially as he was having trouble with his throw up. Personally I am more likely to have a problem with the throw up after dinner than during tennis but that is the way of the world.

Lunch at Cafe Latin was enlivened by the Bufties (Lesley and Roly Bufton) revealing under pressure from a slight overconsumption of the postprandial bottle of home-made Limoncello that they had chosen a gay skipper for their new boat. This caused some amusement of a rather homophobic nature and a little too juvenile and tasteless to go into detail here, suffice to say that the subjects of rolling, corkscrewing and making camp rather than port could have been the themes.

It was a very generous offer from the lovely Lesley, that in order to satisfy my accountant's requirements that I should spend more time in England than in France and that I could stay on the boat when they tour Corsica in the summer. Sadly she did not seem to be aware that Corsica is indeed a part of France. Can she possibly be related to the similarly geographically challenged Lisa Thornton Allan?

Also at lunch was larger than life Rupert Scott on a brief visit to his house in Plascassier which was previously owned by Edith Piaf and in which she died. He told an interesting story about her death.

Apparently because of her iconic status as a symbol of all things French, the French Government had her body taken to Paris in an ambulance and announced that she had died in the Capital.

Painting An Unlikely Picture

The big painting event organised next Monday is building nicely, nearly at capacity such is the interest in painting me. The prize of the best of the paintings being featured on the cover of this book has proven irresistible. I had thought that the Nice Lady Decorator might have shown some interest as painting must clearly be one of the skills required by a decorator but so far she has resisted the temptation.

So with the sun back in its rightful place and a glorious spring day forecast I suspect an impromptu lunch may occur and judging by the scale of the provisioning that took place yesterday I suspect it will be nearby.

After walking the dogs first thing yesterday, that Nice Lady Decorator made an unpleasant discovery. It appears that a tick had been infested by Banjo, that Nice Lady Decorator's dribbling disobedient disaster dog. Don't get me wrong, I do not like ticks, they are nasty little parasites but even I feel sorry for them if they are having a Banjo infestation. When I suggested as much to that Nice Lady Decorator I was given a thorough ticking off. Anyway Banjo was removed from the tick and another reason for smug satisfaction was denied me.

Tuesday sees us back home in England searching for a new house. I see on the TV that there is already a hose pipe ban in many areas, a fact illustrated beautifully by a Sky News reporter standing in pouring rain bemoaning the lack of water. This could only happen in England. But I will not be downhearted; there are some upsides to being an English resident again. Decent beer and good pubs, cricket in the form of Test matches with South Africa and the West Indies (unless rain stops play during the drought) and of course I shall look forward all the more to my restricted holiday visits to Valbonne. No, it is not all bad, just mostly bad. The suitcase is already all but full of coats, jumpers, woolly hats, ski jackets, long johns and other thermal underwear.

With Sprog 1 returned to the UK to study (for which read drink and smoke and cost a fortune) and Sprog 2 departing tomorrow I will be able to see how much of my hidden stash of wine and beer has remained undiscovered. Very little is my guess. I think the installation of CCTV and electric fences may prove less costly in the long run. I shall miss them, but not by very much. I shall not miss the cat and mouse game where they try to catch me in the presence of that Nice Lady Decorator with some sob story of why they need more money for clothes, cigarettes, deodorant (not the male sprog), toothpaste, food, rent, concert tickets, festival passes, medication, toiletries (again not the male sprog unless it is for condoms) which inevitably leads to WDS, wallet depletion syndrome. If there was a degree in WDS my two would be star pupils.

Bluebell the camper has been stirred from her winter slumber starting first time for the first time this year. I took her for a spin into Valbonne yesterday remembering at the last moment not to enter the large parking area where I once memorably removed the roof rack very quickly under the height barrier, an action that had me in the dog house for some considerable time.

Anyway, back to the impromptu lunch; By the time the last lunchers were persuaded to depart at around 10 30.pm, sometime after that Nice Lady Decorator had "retired hurt" in cricket parlance I counted 30 empty bottles of wine. That this did not take into account in alcohol terms the pre-lunch mohito's and the case of beers bears testament to the ability of Valbonne's idle rich to enjoy a rather windy Saturday outing.

As one might expect, there was no shortage of interesting capers to record with my fully charged BlackBerry, a masterstroke of forward thinking for someone who increasingly needs written reminders of events in order to record them for your delectation and delight in this honest missive.

Sometimes, particularly if nothing happens, this column can be a tad difficult to write but with a cast which included Tony "I invented the internet" Coombs, Irish nationalist John "800 years of repression" O'Sullivan and his spectacularly well-endowed (sorry Lin) wife, and Bailey's aficionado Jude, the Bufties plus Peachy Butterfield and gorgeous wife Suzanne it always had the potential to be a memorable occasion.

But where to start? Perhaps with steely-eyed and geographically-challenged Lisa Thornton Allan, sadly bereft of her husband Slash and Burn who was in Cornwall no doubt slashing and burning as only he can. Clearly missing her spouse she chose a unique, and in terms of this daily tome, a gratifying method of keeping his image alive in her memory. Quite why she kept phone video evidence of him sleeping and naked "sounding like a wart hog stuck on a barbed wire fence" (her graphic description of his snoring) is perhaps understandable. She is a young woman with a considerably older husband and doubtless retains the normal needs for a woman of her tender years, however why she found it necessary to share with all and sundry these explicit and one presumes hitherto private images, first to her "date" for the day, and subsequently to all the revellers present was something I had not expected, and I believe it was not expected by the others who were thus subjected and in some cases traumatised by the contents.

Tony "I invented the internet" Coombs was alarmed to discover when he awoke on Sunday morning after Saturday's epic lunch that he smelled nicely of herbs and had a bruised behind. As his recollection of events on Saturday evening will doubtless be hazy given the state he was in, I believe for one moment he may have feared that he had been the victim of a homosexual advance, but all was well when his lovely wife Pat reminded him that he twice fell into a thyme bush as he staggered towards his lift home, hence the, for him, unnaturally healthy aroma and inappropriate anal bruising. Had he needed medical treatment, might that have been known as a stitch in thyme?

I shall concentrate on social matters or more precisely the fallout from social events when one over consumes alcohol. Bribery is always an option and several at that lunch who should be considering offering me some brown paper bags stuffed with bank notes. Sadly Mr. Coombe's offering was received too late to avoid publication.

Whilst we are on the subject of bad behaviour, Sprog 2 was ejected from Monaco Top Marques car show at the weekend. It appears that the car in question into which she was climbing was off limits to visitors, it having been bought earlier by one of the tennis stars appearing at the Monaco Open Tennis Championships. Had she just sat in it she may have avoided such an ignominious departure but spilling some champagne on the hitherto pristine red and black leather was a slop too far for the organisers. She returns to her studies in England after lunch on the beach in some disgrace, although part of me remains proud of her.

It's all about me. The cover painting competition to feature on the jacket of my next book commenced yesterday at Marina Kulik's painting classes in Plascassier. A record turnout of artists greeted me and for some two hours all the attention was on me, as today's picture taken outside afterwards illustrates.

Ego being inflated nicely

There was some really good work developing and (even better!), 7 more copies of my limited-edition first book were sold, taking the total to 174 now and making me by definition an even more successful author. It was at this point that my ego suffered the almost inevitable blow that comes with its regular over-inflation and my newfound celebrity status took a bit of a knock. As Marina was touring the room advising people on how to improve their work, I heard her tell one aspiring artist "very good caricature" only to hear a response "It was not supposed to be a caricature."

England Expects

We were on the way to Lewes, our home for last night staying at the White Fart Hotel, at least that was what it looked like it was called after a bit of the H of Hart had fallen off (or perhaps removed for a bit of fun?) we revelled in our newfound fortune, being dry in England! The next thing you know England will be suffering from a drought! Ha ha!.

Anyway we had held out until 11am, drinking coffee until that Nice Lady Decorator, who had remained completely teetotal from the day before, elected to break her personal drought with a pint of draft Guinness at the Irish bar in Terminal 1 at Nice airport and I confess that peer pressure here was difficult to resist and I may have joined her in this sad escapade.

It is, I think, a fair description to say that after a few drinks I tend to pontificate. And like his papalness himself, I consider at such times, which are more regular than to justify pride, that whatever I say is the truth, the whole truth and nothing but the truth, so help me God. What I am saying is that in these circumstances I am always right. There is one exception to this of course, even the Pope has sometimes to bow to a higher authority and so in a similar way, do I.

Regular readers of this column will have no doubt as to what form in my life that higher authority takes and may well have in their minds, as I do, a surreal image of an angelic Nice Lady Decorator, omnipotent and all powerful, who in her own mind can do no wrong and is therefore always right. That she is married to Mr. Right and considers herself Mrs. Always Right in no way suggests that I feel any sense of injustice directed towards me. That is the line I wish my lawyers to take.

From Lewes we headed to Chichester in Sussex to book into the Ship Hotel, with half a plan to meet some renegades from Valbonne, Norman and Suzie Philpot to share lunch and complain about English food. It was a good choice of hotel as a ship would have been quite useful in parts of the country today. Norman is nothing if not innovative as my picture today shows. When it is raining the British know just how to deal with it, although it is a shame that this particular innovation was used at the expense of his dog Paddy who had apparently had some testicular anomaly corrected recently. I will however resist the temptation to make a joke about the dog's bollocks as it is beneath the quality output threshold I fail regularly to impose on this column.

When we arrived at The Ship we realised that it was a bit upmarket as actress Prunella Scales (Basil's wife in the classic BBC TV series Fawlty Towers) was lunching there with fellow actor and husband Timothy West. I had half a mind to join them and ask them if they knew the difference between a Bordeaux and a claret but when the offer was not forthcoming we decided to spread our metaphorical wings (or should that be set sail?) and seek less dramatic surroundings. It was however somewhat ironic to be staying in a country hotel and seeing Mrs. Fawlty in residence.

Is this a man of the cloth? He seems to be wearing a dog collar?

220

We made a most unfortunate detour to the coastal resorts of East and West Wittering. Juan les Pins they are not and never will be. To paraphrase Ian Hislop, the editor of Private Eye, if these are desirable seaside resorts then I am a banana. Wittering is what I shall be doing about them from now on. How on earth can anyone expect me, with full knowledge that in a short hop from Valbonne I can park in Cannes or Juan les Pins for free and stroll to a golden sandy and beautiful beach restaurant, and then sit in the sunshine and eat a splendid lunch in comfortable surroundings surrounded by the great and the good, be expected happily to pay £3.50 to park on a piece of crater-strewn waste ground in a gale, lacerated by sand and spume, soaked by horizontal rain with the prospect of lunch in the shape of limp fish and chips in a crap pub without a view of the sea? Jesus, no wonder everyone with half a brain or the tiniest modicum of idea in England aspires to spend their summer seaside holidays anywhere but here. The typical English beach experience yesterday was anathema.

Arundel however, has charm. The castle dominates, there are half a dozen pubs, a dozen or so restaurants and a gentle relaxed style to the place so completely at odds with the Witterings. Our venue for yesterday and this evening is the Swan Hotel, a Fullers-owned pub in desperate need of refurbishment, which is going on as I write. I believe they finished drilling and hammering at 5pm, leaving enough time as it turned out for an uninterrupted siesta before dinner.

Then dinner was taken at La Campaglia. I am not normally at my happiest in Italian restaurants but it looked inviting so I err...surrendered to that Nice Lady Decorator's choice. Her salmon was very good and my home-made cannelloni was excellent but I let her choose the wine. I was distracted by a phone call and before I knew it she had opened the wine list and made her choice. A 2010 Bordelino? I think she thought it was a good choice because it was fresh. I struggled through it but have a headache and a sore throat this morning.

The rain-soaked English house-searching odyssey will commence again this morning. Yesterday, as we viewed a house in Chichester, owned by an old lady who was the proud owner of a Stannah stairlift, I suggested that it would not be very expensive to have it removed but that Nice Lady Decorator commented that it could be left in place as I may shortly be in need of it.

My first reaction was one of hurt. I am in the prime of my life, a magnificent, honed, vital creature but then reality set in. I am just a year a bit away from my seventh decade and I gradually realised that she has a point. But there is an upside. Imagine, after a skinful of wine and beer, arriving back at one's home and having a stairlift to take you up to the top floor for a nightcap? What a splendid invention.

After a torturous set of viewings of many a poor house alongside a couple of nice ones, we asked where best to go for lunch and were recommended to the George and Dragon at Burpham. A lesser writer than my good self when presented with the twin facts of a lunch taken at a wonderful Sussex countryside pub and the village of Burpham may conjure up at least one very poor joke about the exhalation of wind after eating and drinking, but I know my readers would not want me to stoop so low as to indulge those who may be amused at such low humour, thus I shall not mention it.

Exhausted by the viewing process and encouraged by a sudden break in the weather, we walked after lunch to The Black Rabbit, the riverside pub a couple of miles outside Arundel from where I took this picture. The art involved in framing Arundel Castle in the background of both the River Arun and the pub sign should not be overestimated.

The Town House in Arundel, the dinner venue, was also splendid. A Chateaubriand for one is a thoroughly wonderful departure. Normally it is a cut prepared for two and I have long wondered why it could not be sliced in two, in fact one might say I had a bit of a beef about it, but now it can and was enjoyed to the fullest possible extent by that Nice Lady Decorator who would normally require me to be the other steak holding (erk) party. I was thus able to enjoy a far more modest but very tasteful monkfish in a seafood sauce which was as healthy for me as the beef was bad for her. I do love being self-righteous.

Clipboard Lunch

We circled the last roundabout at Arundel about (irritating alliteration?) 11 am yesterday having received instructions from Mr. Clipboard that we were invited to lunch. In his customary regimented fashion we were instructed to be at the house at 1pm sharp, scrubbed and tidy, having previously had a short back and sides and to be ready for inspection.

We arrived breathless with barely 30 seconds to spare to find him looking at his watch with clipboard in one hand and slapping his swagger stick against his jackboots. I don't know exactly why he was doing that and cannot pass any comment as to what gratification he may derive from said slapping, but slapping is a good description. Perhaps it reminded him of something from his school days, but I digress.

Having seemingly passed muster (which until then I thought was in Ireland) we were treated to lunch which seemed to comprise the neatly arranged leftovers from a feast from the officers mess from the night before, to which we had not been invited, but as that included some 1994 St Julien Grand Cru followed by a couple of glasses of 1983 Warre's vintage port ("sip it man, don't glug it") left over from the visit of their important friends who had been invited the night before I think you will understand why I was content to be on report.

One thing that is going to drive me insane living for long periods in England is the diabolically poor mobile phone signal. Even at Mr. and Mrs. Clipbeard's billet less than a mile from the M25, the busiest motorway in Europe, no reliable mobile telephone signal can be found. How can anyone do any work or stay in touch?

Talking of technology, Mr. Clipboard has 3D TV but this wonderful invention appeared to confuse that Nice Lady Decorator. "Why is the TV so out of focus?" "And what are these silly glasses for?" Technological advances have often passed her by with the notable exception of her iPad.

Yesterday, we had just enjoyed a nice lunch at the Old Mill at Elstead, deep in the parched Surrey countryside which was clearly screaming out for some moisture as my picture today captures. It seems that it is so hot and dry in England that people are removing their socks and shoes and walking about the place as if they were in the south of France in summer. Shoes seemingly not required as my picture today of a diner trying to get back to their car, illustrates. The drought in the UK is getting even worse One even has to park one's car near water to keep one's tyres from overheating in temperatures hovering in the high single figures Celsius. I am so glad we are returning to the steamy wetlands of Provence today.

The rain has been relentless and the drought continues. It seems that there must be 6 months of continuous rain in England before the leaky reservoirs are once again replenished and the gardeners can stop worrying about how to water their plants. In the meantime rivers break their banks, millions of acres of farmland are flooded, roads are closed and plants are dying from lack of moisture. What a curious place England will be in which to live again.

The Prodigal Return

Back in Valbonne and straight back into that lovely south of France lifestyle that I adore. Lunch, one of the most delicious words in any language was taken chez Roly and the lovely Lesley Bufton at their palatial abode right next door to their other palatial abode. Most people would be happy with just one but hey, it's a long story which I will not go into here.

A happy throng descended to eat and drink in that typical ex-pat Provencal way. The eating part of lunch was completed at about 5pm but I did not get home until after 10pm. Situation normal, although I do not recall the promised Coupe Colonel, perhaps a good thing as that Nice Lady Decorator hit the proverbial wall early, at 8pm, taking a sort power nap in order recharge those formidable batteries.

With the BlackBerry fully charged and my reading spectacles readily at hand, I was able to record the many details of some of the more amusing events discussed over pre-lunch mohitos, gallons of rose and a rather good 2000 château bottled Cru Bourgeois Haut Medoc.

For example, Slash and Burn got proceedings off to a fine start by revealing that once, after a trip abroad, he was dispatched by his wife, that steely-eyed goddess Lisa (of whom more later) to collect the family's black Labrador dog from the kennels. All was well until Berty the dogs' behaviour had changed notably. The dog went from room to room sniffing, then upstairs where he would not normally venture and then jumped onto the kids' trampoline which was a bouncing departure as Berty was renowned for avoiding the trampoline area, perhaps because he had apparently once been the unwilling star in the Thornton Allan Sprogs re-enactment of the famous Barnes Wallis bouncing bomb story.

Doubts about his treatment at the kennels increased until one of the Thornton Allan Sprogs noticed a curious and astonishing new addition. Berty had apparently grown new testicles during his stay at the kennels. It was I think at this stage Slash and Burn realised that he had collected the wrong dog.

Peachy Butterfield, man of mystery or more precisely man mountain of mystery was very keen to ensure that he did not overeat (although to be honest this did nothing to reduce his intake of the local rose). He stated mysteriously that there was to be no TTT. When questioned as to what this stood for he confessed it was Tummy Touching Table. In his own mind his figure resembles that of the figure in my picture today taken in one of the far-flung corners of our host's garden. But why the garden fork?

Talking of naked, another revealing story was undressed by the piercing blue eyes of Mrs. Slash and Burn, the willowy and beautiful Lisa. I have no idea why she admitted to taking to cleaning the family shower room whilst naked, save for a toothbrush and some red marigolds, or indeed why she should allow an arch blogger such as myself access to this kind of information but it is an image I wish to hold with me until my demise.

A naked forker?

More worryingly Peachy Butterfield spent some time showing pictures he had taken of the naked politician meeting various waitresses whilst wearing lederhosen. I am not sure if I am more uncomfortable about the wearing of those curious Bavarian leather shorts in public, or the fact that Peachy had kept them on his phone and was happily showing them to all and sundry. He describes himself like a duck, swimming around serenely but there is a lot going on underneath. This is a concept into which I am sure my dedicated readership can understand I did not wish to delve too deeply, especially as he had his hands in his pockets as the description unfolded.

Then there was the discussion, the details of which never reached my conscious mind, about the Mail online, or was it the male online? There was also some talk about a kind of desperate housewives TV programme concept but with cleaning ladies, a reaction I think to the steely eyed one's earlier revelations, but details in my memory banks have proven elusive.

So, yesterday we managed it, we did not have a drink, either of us even in the face of the provocation of evening sunshine and a well-stocked bar. Proud or thirsty?

Tennis Can Be Peachy

The cardiac arrest unit at Nice Hospital will be standing by at the Vignale Tennis Club this morning in the full expectation that they will be receiving some customers. I do hope there are no takers.

Let me set the scene. It was at that lunch earlier in the week, when man mountain Peachy Butterfield, just after he had fastened on to his third bottle of rose having tired of the extra strong mohitos our host had thoughtfully prepared earlier, expressed the hitherto unthinkable interest in getting into some whites and taking exercise. The word "exercise" in normal Peachyland speak for anyone that knows him would be opening some Chablis or Sancerre or some other possibly less well-regarded white wine lurking about his person or perhaps more likely White Lightning, the supercharged super cheap sparkling cider that passes for champagne in his homeland up north, as I thought they were the only whites he would understand.

It became clear that he was serious, so after I had stopped laughing I focussed on what he meant; whites for tennis? I know he looks like he was born before Fred Perry, but surely he has seen tennis on the TV? There is every colour on show nowadays except white.

His normal response when any suggestion is made that at his age he should think about some exercise has been to agree then run to the fridge and open another bottle, so it took me some time to recover and to roll up my tongue and stick it back in my mouth.

So today, at 11.00am sharp the three of us, no, Peachy does not count as two although it's a fair point - Roly Bufton is coming out of tennis retirement - and the three of us shall attempt to build up an appetite for lunch afterwards at Auberge St Donat. by playing some tennis. We will be hoping the paramedics and the defibrillators will not be required. I shall play them both on my own and will be triumphant again. The usual rules will apply: if it goes well then a full report will follow, should I face some sort of reverse it will all be glossed over.

You may be aware that I am making the most of it here in France in the coming weeks as by mid-July I must face the prospect of being billeted back in the UK for extended periods. It is not a prospect I am considering with much enthusiasm, but on the plus side we have made an offer on a house next door to a pub with direct access from our garden to the pub garden next door, so drowning ones sorrows appears to be a very real option. That or drowning in the floods during a drought. That would be the ultimate irony, drowning during a drought in England.

As you may know there is an election campaign in full swing over here in France being contested by the hyperactive and hyper ventilating dwarf-like current president M. Sarkozy and the man who would complete the demise of the euro, M. Hollande. As the lovely Julie Faux commented: "Clowns to the left of me, jokers to the right"...

Then to the tennis at the Vignale; it seems that during the planning for this titanic tennis outing, Peachy had expressed the opinion that he had great hand-to-ball control, not hand-to-eye control as I suspect he intended to say. I am a big follower of Freud and I know what he really meant. As expected the match was a triumph for one moustachioed old git. Despite playing against man mountain Peachy Butterfield and Roly "gay skipper" Bufton, not a single game was lost and so some of us, and by that I mean me, adjourned to lunch at the Auberge St Donat with a happy smirk playing about their facial features. Some were forced to accept that their hopes had crashed and burned.

After the sport clash was concluded, we went to the inevitable post-tennis debriefing at the Auberge St Donat for yet another astonishingly good simple meal of fantastic value. However a vast over consumption of wine led to some rather distressing revelations, revealed inadvertently and so much-loved and happily-seized-upon by the author of this book.

For instance, who was it amongst the assembled multitude who released their innermost fantasies when faced with a morning erection, and why on earth should the phrase "hand of god" have entered into this discussion? My own feeling is that this is food for thought but Peachy did not concur, he expressed the opinion that food was for eating and proceeded to give us all a wholesome demonstration.

Lunch however was no picnic. It was there that I secured yet another customer for my book "Summer In The Cote d'Azur" although one sale was secured by dint of Masterful Subterfuge by my self-appointed French sales manager Master Mariner Mundell and the other has yet to be paid for. Why anyone would trust the Master with a 10 euro loan and then accept repayment in the form of a copy of my book is on one level very gratifying but on another level mystifying. I suspect the questionable sales tactics of my sales manager may still cause me problems at some stage but at the moment I am prepared to accept a sale is a sale. One area I need to address is the question of sales commission. I had thought that the Master had been prepared to undertake this onerous task on a voluntary basis. Indeed he had volunteered to undertake this hitherto non-existent position and has subsequently dined out on his sales success at the Premier Mardi event in April where he sold 9 copies and secured another 10 euro (the sales price) from one of the delegates on the understanding that she took a book that the Master would "go away forever."

It seems however that certain traits of the Jewish faith to which he is beholden are hard to suppress. One comment today suggested to me that philanthropy was not as well embedded in his Jewish soul as I had hoped. He does not collect stamps after all and would prefer to collect commission. Sadly from his point of view the business model upon which sales are based precludes such a ridiculous notion as commission.

I had escaped to play tennis only after mixing up a cement mixer full of, well, cement for that Nice Lady Garden designer, her epithet when she is not decorating. When house builder Peachy arrived he had the temerity to suggest that she was a full-on civil engineer, but I have a problem with the civil part of that description.

The weather forecast yesterday was for possible storms so I eschewed the chance to go and play golf with the Landlubbers at the Grande Bastide, as I had previously given my wet weather golf gear to charity in the full knowledge that having moved to France I would never need them again. That full knowledge was not quite as full as I had assumed. With the new capital gains tax rules savaging my plans to live in France, it seems that I may have need of them in the UK unless I give up golf completely, which is still an option.

The combination of living in England for any length of time and advancing years will, I am certain, force me to seek solace in travel so in preparation I have begun to consider the places I need to visit before the metaphorical trap door opens and my soul falls into the fiery abyss. The film Bucket List which stared Morgan Freeman and Jack Nicholson was about things one needs to do before one kicks the bucket. I was discussing my bucket list with Peachy Butterfield over a few after dinner drinks in the web after Thursday's epic tennis victory but he, being younger than me said he had a "fuc*it" list, presumably describing a list of girls (or boys? or both?) with whom he would like to become intimate before his demise. I was thinking of countries I would like to visit he was thinking of can't bring myself to say it.

Earlier, after lunch the lovely Lesley Bufton produced a plastic container and proceeded to spoon the remnants of her uneaten veal and rice main course into her own personal doggy bag. She said she always carried it with her when eating out but I do hope she draws the line at doing the same at private dinner parties or aboard their yacht that is about to be delivered. As I had some of the same dish surplus to my requirements I offered it to her but the offer was politely declined. This led that Nice Lady Decorator to exclaim that Lesley had publicly refused to allow me to put my meat in her lunch box. I can still hear her cackling as I write.

Chapter 8

A Typical Provencal Lunch

Lunch with the Howes, Simon and the lovely Sarah, the saviours of Chateau Gloria was the usual excellent ribald affair.

Gloria in excelsis

After lunch an astonishing thing happened. The cheese had been served and then renowned couch potato Peachy Butterfield returned from the toilet carrying a selection of tennis rackets. One would have thought that the thrashing he had received on the tennis court on Wednesday, combined with the damage inflicted on his corpulent frame as a result of having to run (perhaps that is an overstatement) around for an hour may have put him off sport of any kind for life but no, it appears to have kindled his enthusiasm. That or red-wine-induced bravado came to the fore.

He had spotted the private tennis court of our hosts on an earlier tour of the gardens of this house built by F1 legend Emerson Fittipaldi and to my surprise the entire luncheon party, already stoked up nicely on Veuve Cliquot champagne, Chablis and the aforementioned Gloria took to the tennis court for a number of rather alcoholically-challenged games of tennis.

Peachy did remove his sunglasses for one point, to reveal an non suntanned line above the ear which he said was his blood pressure monitor line, and another luncheon guest local estate agent Cubby Woolf, was a revelation, playing some excellent tennis in his Gucci loafers which, until then, I had though was some king of northern bread, something like Hovis.

I think it was he who began the discussion about hookers. It seems that a little way along the Var towards St Tropez and especially around Lac St Cassien one often sees scantily clad young ladies sitting in chairs on the roadside touting for business. Cubby claims yesterday on a trip down in this direction, for reasons that were never fully explained, certainly to my satisfaction, to have seen an elderly gentleman emerging from the bushes with his Zimmer frame. My suggestion that he was probably just answering the call of nature was not an opinion shared by anyone else present.

As coffee was served it was the token Frenchman amongst us, Robert Angeli who exclaimed that the French Presidential race was about to reach a conclusion and so the party gathered around the TV set to witness the confirmation of the election of M. Hollande as the next French president.

This piece of history was greeted with some despair by all of those present except me. My enthusiasm for his election was in no way based on any political considerations, merely on the extra business that will be generated in the coming months for Currencies Direct as people with euros flee the single currency as soon as they see the damage his policies may wreak on the Eurozone. I predict the doomed euro experiment is about to enter the final phase of its ultimate demise.

Alas today is Monday and despite invoking my age, my bad back, my shrapnel wound, the French election and any other excuse I could muster today, I have to work. Not the higher intellectual work for which I am admirably suited, no, physical hard work. That Nice Lady Decorator turned garden designer has a broad vision of gravelling areas of our garden which had hitherto been able to be dealt with by Terrance the Tractor and his grass mowing capabilities. Her building of a wall now precludes a great swathe of grass from being accessible to Terrance's special abilities. Gravel has been designated and sadly I have been designated the graveller despite a lot of grovelling.

The mass exodus from France has begun. I see from various Facebook comments that the election of a socialist president of France yesterday has sent a shudder of fear through the ex-pat community. Ferraris are apparently queuing up and jamming the slip road out of France to Monaco, fleets of super yachts are upping anchor and slipping their moorings and the euro is beginning to fall out of bed. I only wish I could stay and enjoy watching how this socialist utopia will develop over the next year but the decision is made: France and Valbonne are now merely a holiday destination for me but only as long as there is food to eat and wine to be drunk. I shall be doing my best to make the most of both before they run out and before the working people of France all have retired early and are waiting for state hand-out's.

That Nice Lady Decorator was not very nice about the contents of this column yesterday. "Why can't you be funny every day?" she asked, which I suppose must be a compliment of sorts, after all by implication I must be funny on some days. Actually, now that she has subscribed to my daily column and which incidentally had nearly 500 hits yesterday, a record, especially good for something described as not funny, I have an editorial impediment to free speech in that I can no longer get away with having a bit of fun at her expense. Before that I could take some amusement in the full knowledge that she would probably never read it.

I have also been told by my new self-appointed editor to stop grizzling about gravelling. I fear that her entreaties may fall on stony ground as I intend to chip away at her displeasure and somehow make gravelling funny. I suspect though, in reality she will remain stony-faced. In fact this column is very hard to write when one is stone cold sober. Ok, that's it; I think I have done all the stone jokes.

Our Dear Leader

Tonight, the tempestuous tennis trio (plus one) will once again grace the rundown but still charming Vignale Tennis Club. I want to find out if any of my tennis compatriots are looking forward to the reign of the new Socialist President of France. It seems that our illustrious leader and his former partner Segolene Royale still co-own a house in nearby Mougins. It seems that it was valued at some 200,000 euros, at least for wealth tax purposes a few years ago. This will come as a surprise to residents in the same area with almost identical houses on the same estate, that also boast a private swimming pool, in one of the richest and most expensive communes in France. They would all no doubt be devastated to find that their houses valued at 1.2 million euros have apparently dropped so markedly in value. Any suggestion however that our new socialist ayatollah has stretched tax rules to avoid paying the full extent of what is due is of course a scurrilous accusation and I am certain that come the time he fills in his 2011 tax form shortly, a more realistic valuation will collect him up neatly into his own tax trap.

There seems to be an Orwellian tendency towards some people being more equal than others in the worldwide socialist hierarchy. Perhaps this is a case of "do as I say rather than do as I do"? If one looks at the socialist opponent in the recent London mayoral vote, the scion of Margaret Thatcher, it was the revelation of his byzantine tax avoidance planning that may have tipped the balance against him. If you were to say "Mr. Livingstone, I presume," then you would be not far off the mark. Next shall we look at Mr. Mugabe?

Two days of almost total abstinence was almost inevitably to be followed by a fall from temperance grace and the crumbling of this edifice began last night after another resounding victory on the tennis courts for the MOGs, the Moustachioed Old Gits. The MOGS, a doubles pairing of myself and the Wingco, acquitted ourselves extremely well whilst our opponents, Dancing Greg Harris from Cote d'Azur Villa Rentals and Blind Lemon Milsted, not so well. Some of us are winners in tennis and life, some of them are losers. Details are unimportant to anyone but me but a final set score of 6-1 tells a story that I would dearly like to tell.

Talking of stories, over the victory dinner afterwards at Capriccio up the hill in Pre du Lac, I mentioned that I had recently to attend a funeral for a friend who had been hit by a tennis ball. It was a lovely service.

The Wingco also told the true story of how he spent two weeks in chains in an Indian prison some years ago. On a visit to a rural part of India, I think he called it Arselikhan, to watch some horse race or the like, he decided to leave his passport behind in Delhi not knowing that one should keep one's passport about one's person at all times. You might think that such a minor offence could be quickly dealt with by way of a cable (one must consider, given the Wingco's vast age, how long ago this must have been before modern communication was invented) but it appears that his overblown countenance coupled with loudly expressed statements in his best English accent such as "Do you know who I am?" and "I am English, I demand to see the Ambassador!" or "Where would you be without English manners and culture you halfwit" did not endear him to the local police with the result that he spent a fortnight in chains until this unfortunate oversight could be cleared up.

Dancing Greg is off to Devon for the weekend and we got talking about the quality of some gastro pubs in the southwest of England. I don't like the idea and said I that I for one would never eat at one, a clear case of gastroenteritis.

Mother-in-law is worth her worth her weight in gold, and believe me that is a shed-load of gold. So said one of our luncheon party yesterday who shall remain nameless as we lunched at fashionable restaurant Transat in Antibes. We had adjourned there after another tennis lesson administered by my good self to Roly Bufton, the husband of John Hurt's former cleaner and Peachy Butterfield, who had his mother-in-law in tow - -oops, may have given something away there.

Peachy was in large form and was explaining that he had spent the morning preparing for tennis by reading his son's university dissertation. Given the big fruit's size (le grande peche) one may perhaps have been forgiven for thinking that the word dissertation had something to be with being served with extra desert. He began explaining what he had been doing by using a split infinitive but does anyone out there, apart from my syntax sorcerer Peter Lynn, have any idea of what comprises a split infinitive? Star Trek fans will remember possibly the most high-profile of these: "to boldly go". One must never split the verb. Certainly he did not seem to understand, thus he had no idea why I was smiling when he said (when referring to that dissertation) he was reading it "to grammatically correct it".

One Thing Leeds To Another.

We are apparently to go to Leeds, in Yorkshire, courtesy of Agatha Christie. Let me put this in perspective. The weather forecast for Leeds today is 12 degrees with squally showers and gusty winds. There was no mention of any sunshine, not this month. I know that for up north that is quite balmy, even suggesting that summer is right around the corner but then the softening tundra will unleash a plague of midges. The forecast for Valbonne however is for unbroken sunshine and a maximum temperature of 28 degrees, and no midges.

You may be tempted, as I was as we sat beside the sparkling waters of the Mediterranean in shorts enjoying some exquisite fish which was not surrounded and suffocated with batter and with not a mushy pea in sight, to ask that Nice Lady Decorator what on earth she was thinking of. It took a little time to establish the primary reason: Agatha Christie. It seems that Agatha, when deciding to leave her husband at the "height" of her writing career, disappeared for 11 days, much to the consternation of the British press, and hid at The Olde Swan Hotel in Harrogate, and she wants to go and visit.

Bizarrely, that Nice Lady Decorator holds the opinion that this Agatha woman is a superior writer to my good self, a clear phallacy (erk) as she is obviously female. That should wake up the feminist movement. The woman wrote about a Mousetrap for god's sake, a performance of which I was dragged to sometime last year.

Quite why we need to do this now, during the precious time left to us in France, is a mystery that I don't think even our Agatha would be able to solve. We shall be trapped in England for much of the summer and autumn, but when I suggested that perhaps this little jaunt be delayed until that time, the laser beams that pass for eyes in these circumstances were primed and I was hushed into a state of mere whimpering in the corner.

Perhaps we shall also pop in on Midsomer, the most dangerous place in Britain where many murders take place? The allure of all this Murder Mystery is just that, a mystery to me. Thank god Midsomer does not seem to have a railway otherwise we would probably be treated to "Murder on the Midsomer Express with a Mousetrap."

Dinner was a splendid affair taken in bandit country in the valley just to the south of Bar sur Loup, at the house owned by the only estate agent in Valbonne who insists on playing tennis in his Gucci loafers, Cubby Wolff from Riviera Realty. When one ventures more than a handful of miles north of Valbonne one must not expect to find the same kind of sophistication to be in evidence. One takes a social risk, a bit like going north of Birmingham in England. On the edge of civilisation one can never be certain about whether electricity will be readily available and so it came to pass. After nervously standing outside the electric gates to Cubby's fortified domain which refused to work, keeping an eye out for hungry wildlife, the bush telegraph (OK my mobile phone) alerted Cubby to the plight of his guests marooned outside as the sun was setting and the unseen but clearly sensed local animal and bandit population was stirring. Eventually the gates were opened and sanctuary reached. That our host should be called Cubby Wolf is somehow apt for a man living in such majestic wilderness. Bear Grylls, eat your heart out.

That an estate agent can afford to own Gucci loafers is an affront to anyone selling a house and paying the exorbitant French estate agents' fees, (6% in case there are any English estate agents reading). Personally, if I were ever to employ an estate agent in France I would want him to be driving a dented and ancient Citroen C5 with worn tyres, look down-trodden and not to own either Gucci loafers or a classic Jaguar, or for the matter to own a very pretty house with majestic views swooping over the Loup valley. What's wrong with a dingy apartment? Actually, come to think of it, he does look a bit down-trodden but only in a warm and cuddly kind of way.

In something of a departure, that Nice Lady Decorator scrubbed up nicely and chose a stunning and unique black and white striped outfit together with similarly distressing shoes. Unique, that is until Helen, another guest at dinner arrived wearing an almost identical outfit. A sharp intake of collective breath was followed by a short silence. There was an air of tension and some circling which I thought could be heading for a metaphorical shootout before the champagne, not before time, had its usual calming effect and potential enmity dissolved into friendship, with the codicil that the next time they meet they will discuss outfits before the event.

As the evening drew towards an end, the largish sailing contingent which comprised most of the dinner party who had been feasting, rather aptly, on swordfish, whilst sitting outside on a clear night on a wonderful terrace looking towards the mountain came over all sailorish, licking their fingers and holding them up to the wind and saying things like "we are for a bit of a blow" and "splice the main brace," seemingly oblivious to the reason they were swaying so much was due to the consumption of too much wine.

The Sunday Times yesterday carried a piece about a dog which seemed to be racist. It seems that said dog was completely content and relaxed around children and old people but barked at black people and the discussion was about how to modify its behaviour.

This got me to thinking about how to improve the attitude and behaviour of my least favourite dog in the world, owned by that Nice Lady Decorator who lives with us against my better judgement (the dog that is, not the Decorator). I am not saying that Banjo is racist but he is nonetheless in need of behaviour modification. Take motor cyclists, as he does. He hates them and enjoys illustrating his enmity by barking at and biting them as they splutter along the lane outside our house. The pizza man on the motor bike will no longer deliver because he has lost several chunks from his leg after the last take-away. I will no longer order the bite-size pizza from him as I am so embarrassed.

But the question is how to administer behavioural correction? My first reaction was that a baseball bat might help and that's when the trouble started. It is a mystery that I will never solve as to why that Nice Lady Decorator is so very protective of the glutinously gobby doggy.

Last night then to dinner with Cornish Tsunami, Matt Frost and delightful wife Viv, the lady that first suggested this column could be turned into a book, and is subsequently to blame for the second tome which you hold in your hands. I had all the pages numbered so that's a good start. Matt was talking about his recent visit to the salt mines of Krakow in Poland which sounded both macabre and fascinating in equal measure but I was able to trump him on both levels as we are set to visit Harrogate and Leeds next weekend, macabre and fascinating on a much higher scale.

The lurking horror of this hastily organised trip to England in the rain later this week is exacerbated by the fact that it is not just England; it is up "North". The land of tundra and tempest has but one saving grace, Timothy Taylor Landlord bitter. This beer is the only good thing to come out of Yorkshire except the M1. That it is the second best beer in the world, second only to Fullers London Pride, is not a fact that is acknowledged by that Nice Lady Decorator who is of the opinion that the Taylors offering is superior, but as she once lived amongst the savages the roam north of Coventry, her mind has clearly been tainted. I shall be on the lookout for the archetypal Northerner, a high forehead, eyes too close together, extra digits on hands or feet or both are the tell-tale signs.

After awaking at the crack of dawn, we set out for our normal speed walk around the Valmasque yesterday morning when I happened to say to that Nice Lady Decorator that she was going downhill rather quickly. It was when she turned to look at me as only she can I realised the enormity of the misunderstanding with which I could have been confronted. Of course I meant that she was walking fast downhill with no intent of a double meaning, however it was clear for a time at least she did not believe me.

Perhaps it is the proximity of yet another birthday, her 37th I am told, that is making her touchy. Having had a night off on Monday evening and with a fast-developing crescendo of two birthdays (hers and Peachy's) colliding in the same week, a very last-minute mid-way between birthday's party appears to be happening tonight at very short notice, and what is more it is seemingly taking place at my house. Peachy Butterfield's birthday was last Saturday and fell whilst he was shivering and sheltering from a northern gale in the distant far north of England, in Chester where the sun has just appeared above the horizon for the year. Understandably, he did not want to celebrate it in such inhospitable surroundings and as he is flying back today, tonight was deemed a suitable time for such a prestigious event, especially as we will depart to the bleak north of England on Thursday for the weekend to endure much the same punishment that Peachy has been enduring. This will the ensure, of course, exactly what you want when facing a flight, a massive hangover.

So despite almost no warning at all, a very decent contingent of revellers arrived to take advantage of the early evening sunshine, and then a feast of ribs and meatballs to celebrate the median between the birthdays. Peachy Butterfield arrived from Liverpool, where he must have looked at the very least a bit of a dick in his green Vilebrequin shorts and short sleeved shirt whilst shivering on the tarmac of Liverpool airport.

The first story emerged before the party on the way back from the airport after picking Peachy up. I was cursing the fact that I had to divert for the third visit of the day to the supermarket to ensure we were sufficiently well-stocked with food and wine to be able to survive a sustained attack on mine and my guests' sobriety. My task? To fetch toilet rolls. Peachy, pictured today wearing one of his birthday presents was thus reminded of a story about a plastic surgeon friend of his who was sent to the supermarket by his wife. When he returned home she was stunned to find him in possession of around 50 bread rolls. When questioned he said he had purchased 50 because he thought 100 was too many whatever was the purpose. He had misinterpreted the shopping list which had listed loo rolls.

Who was it last night who claimed to be wearing bottom flossers, seemingly a kind of female underwear requiring very little material? Were they male or female? Once I have consulted my lawyers I will let you know if I can name names.

Agatha Christie And The Frozen North

As I write, it is just after 7am and as predicted I have a horrendous hangover, the last stragglers leaving around 1am. The garden is a mess, the web is a bigger mess and the Pav is a humongous mess but the biggest mess was the kitchen. The evil hound that blights my house (and especially now the kitchen), Banjo, had thoughtfully managed to get past two doors and then redecorated the kitchen with rib bones and the general post-party detritus which was waiting in a plastic bag ready for the garbage run this morning. I would love to kick his arse. Whose idea was it to have a party the night before we leave for misery? As soon as I have finished this there is some very serious clearing up to undertake before confronting something even more unpleasant but, I suppose, also self-imposed, a trip up north. I do hope Jet2 live up to their name and there is not some ancient turboprop propping up Nice airport later this morning.

Any airline flying to Leeds is probably required to serve mushy peas as part of any inflight meal and I have to tell you frankly that if that is the case this morning then vomit will be unavoidable.

So then to the flight to Yorkshire in Geoff Boycott class. We could not afford Michael Parkinson class which would have allegedly entitled us to free tripe and chips as our in-flight meal. It was, err…interesting. I don't like to complain because they allowed dogs on the flight, although this was limited to Yorkshire terriers and whippets, so thank god there is no way the rib-eating kitchen-destroying mutt Banjo would be allowed aboard, and we duly arrived at Leeds Bradford airport in the rain.

With the Olde Swan under some sort of health warning (there was some sort of NHS convention in town) we instead booked into the charming Harrogate Brasserie, where we met up for dinner with very old friends John and Rachel Surtees. At one stage before I trapped her, that Nice Lady Decorator lived with John for a number of years before the relationship broke up and he subsequently married the gorgeous Rachael. Since that time I have fretted that something is out of kilter here. John obviously has "knowledge" of that Nice Lady Decorator but Rachael and I have never shared that same intimacy despite my suggesting that such a liaison would square the circle so to speak. You may be surprised, as I am, that she does not seem concerned about this lop-sided situation and has constantly and fervently rejected such an idea, however when last night she asked if she could try my pork, for one moment...

As I near the midway point of my enforced banishment to the frozen wastelands of northern Britain I have noticed some changes. I have not been this far north for a long time but this northern English enclave of Harrogate, on the outer edges of civilisation is showing signs of progress.

So why is this hamlet called Harrogate? We have had Watergate, Fergygate and any number of other "gates" relating to scandals of different sorts, what happened here? Has Prince Harry visited recently? It was something I began to contemplate over a rather good lunch at The Fleece at Addingham as I watched the rain lash the old mill cottages shivering beside the River Wharfe. The locals seemed pleased, at least it wasn't snow. The fires were lit, piles of fresh peat lay moistly awaiting their turn to smoulder sulkily in the grates and all was well in their own little world.

Last night after drinks at the Harrogate Brasserie we crossed the road to eat at The Elephant Thai restaurant, sited just above "Trotters Bar and Fun Pub". It is based on the classic TV programme "Only Fools and Horses" and anyone suggesting that I in any way remind people of the wide boy character Boycie in that series will be hearing from my lawyers Messrs Grin, Snapit and Sueham. Furthermore anyone who suggests that Nice Lady Decorator bears any resemblance to his on-screen wife Marlene should be in fear of their lives.

So we left the sleepy hamlet of Harrogate behind and headed for the village of Leeds in a vain search for some sunshine. Before we left we had one last look around and once again I was struck by the awe and majesty of "Trotters" bar. It is clearly a high-class establishment, with an up market clientele, that I know would just work in Valbonne. Sadly our busy schedule, my attire and ridiculous moustache, precluded us from entering the establishment due to one simple reason, fear. I am sure that the regulars adorned with tattoos and many resembling tramps and ruffians are all wonderful friendly and accommodating people, but they just didn't look like it so the busy schedule excuse was employed.

Threading our way through the floods which mark the wettest drought I have ever encountered, we eventually arrived in Leeds, another little-known outpost in the north of England and then to an even smaller settlement with the touching and quaint name of Scarcroft where we will be imprisoned for the next two nights. I have in the past mentioned the charming and evocative names for northern towns but Scarcroft does not do it justice. Perhaps it would have been a better name for the Jewish area of Allwoodley, through which we went on our way to Leeds and where my lawyer, sometimes known as Al Yiddley, was born. Would it be too much of a banana skin to mention that few foreskins will be found in this area near Scarcroft? Probably so I will end this here. I will be circumspect from now on.

I have been unable to watch TV and have thus been out of touch with what is happening in the real world so I was naturally shocked by the news that Vidal Sassoon, hairdresser to the stars, had passed away. When I asked for details I was told I needed to watch the highlights.

It seems to have been the longest birthday celebration in history. That Nice Lady Decorator kicked off proceedings with a joint birthday bash last Wednesday but her actual anniversary is today. I cannot reveal her age but she will never be 37 again, at least not until next year. It is astonishing that each year the gap between our ages increases, how can that be? It is a mystery.

So this on-going saga (careful) of a birthday of that Nice Lady Decorator, a continuing and moving feast in more ways than one, moved towards its inevitable conclusion. Perhaps aptly for a Sunday, the final feast, the last supper, which took the form of lunch at The Duke Of Wellington at East Keswick, was the focus point for a gathering of many of the good people of Yorkshire. That they are for the most part uneducated and rusticly-charming people is undeniable and any kind of sophistication eludes them. Salt of the earth that they are, and denied electricity for the most part, one cannot expect much in terms of being worldly-wise but at the same time one cannot help but warm to their home spun charm. Many of them have not ventured more than 10 miles from their place of birth throughout their entire lives, and most are proud of this fact. "If it doesn't come from Yorkshire it's not worth bothering with."

Take fellow diner and Yorkshireman Dave Wurr for example. Few women would, and although I understand no more than one in three of his guttural utterances he is one of my favourite people from whom I like to remove money on the golf course. He is as old as Methuselah and not as good-looking but what sets him apart from many of these country souls is that he has travelled abroad, albeit only to Spain. Clearly it must have been a long time ago because he revealed that once he took a twin tub washing machine to Majorca as hand luggage. I cannot imagine the reaction at the Easyjet check-in were he to attempt such a thing today.

Our hosts, John and Rachael "square the circle" Surtees have done their best to keep a steady stream of alcohol and food coming at us the whole weekend and even organising a tennis match for me to win convincingly yesterday morning. John has now retired from working on The Chuckle Brothers latest output and is now organising his team for the Golden Oldies Cricket Festival in Adelaide in November. Having been selected to play, I have had no choice but to accept, particularly as this will mean at least three weeks away from the dreadful dark and wet experience that will be my lot in England later this year. Winter is not my favourite time. When I asked how many others had been selected, answer came there none. Yes, no others except the self-appointed team captain have achieved the three hurdles required to be eligible; being over 40, have time for a three-week holiday and being stupid enough to want to play cricket at an advanced age.

Walking, tennis and cycling are activities that are high on my agenda in the coming days as I seem to have collected a little more than I would like around my waistband due to an over-exuberant indulgence in English food over the past four days. What is it with English restaurants? Do they not understand the concept of the vegetable? The French understand it perfectly, even to the extent of electing one to run the country. Salad seems to be a word that in English restaurants is followed by the word "garnish", which we all know is an excuse to make a nod towards healthy eating whilst supporting the salad-dodging fraternity. The word garnish should have a literal meaning suggesting "not likely".

Return Of The Writer

In conversation last night with the Wingco after tennis I mentioned that I had begun work on my second book which I was thinking of called "The Valbonne Monologues". He snorted with derision and suggested that it would better called "The Valbonne Monoblogs" which actually has some merit. To put it mildly, he is somewhat underwhelmed by my writing, the word he most uses is "ghastly". It was ironic then that he sent me an email earlier today (despite claiming not to have my email address) "please send copies of any email for proof reading BEFORE publishing. This will avoid any embarrasing (sic) errors of syntax, grammar, punctuation, and indeed, content". You will note, as I did (and as I am sure will regular reader Peter Lynn) that his email contains a spelling error. How gratifying. Having made such an embarrassing blunder, he put forward his defence today, "a sticky keyboard". I can just imagine what he would have said to me had I attempted to hide behind such a shoddy excuse. Regular readers will know that he is part of a coterie of public school types amongst my friends who revel in their imagined educational superiority. He has made it his job to criticise my grammar, syntax, writing style, spelling and content on every possible occasion so with a song in my heart I shall be taking this up with him at lunch today. As he signed this particular email 'the longest member' I was also forced to ask if this had anything to do with the sticky keyboard. As yet I have not received an answer.

My boys luncheon dates, arranged at short notice in the face of a girls lunch gradually disappeared on me, to the extent that I was forced to seek luncheon solace elsewhere. Three phone calls or texts received en route to the Auberge St Donat, all cancelling is a tough one to take on the chin.

But was I down-hearted? Well, yes, so I stole up to the Cafe des Arcades in Valbonne square just to ensure that the girl's lunch was progressing smoothly, but when I was espied by that Nice Lady Decorator and she asked me brusquely "what are you doing here?" I knew it was a mistake.

Ridiculously and without any forethought or planning I decided attack was the best form of defence, I said "I am meeting Peachy for lunch, what are you doing here?" That withering look I know so well was employed and so I had no choice but to call him and say "where are you?"

Well of course he was at home nursing a hangover diligently created the night before with the Naked Politician. What is more he had just stuffed into his mouth a huge carbohydrate-laden baguette in a desperate attempt to make himself feel better. He had made a pact with himself that he was having a recovery day, but after no more than 5 seconds prevarication and mumbled excuses as to why he could not rescue a friend in need, he crumbled and agreed to be picked up and brought out to the Cafe des Arcades to be fawned over by the girlies at lunch. At least that was what I told him was going to happen.

Luckily he is from the north so with skin thick enough to repel bullets he thought he was welcome and so I projected the blame for invading a strictly female only gathering on him. You might think if he had any inkling of the situation that he might have sat quietly at the end of the table and dealt only in platitudes, but that is not the man's style and good on him. My original faux pas of turning up like Billy-No-Mates was forgotten and all blame was directed at him.

I think it started after the second pichet of rose when Peachy announced that his plastic surgeon friend coming to stay in the next week or so. That statement attracted some attention. Ladies of a certain age seem irresistibly drawn to a man who can, so to speak. However his next comment that his suggested penis reduction was a huge success, meaning he can wear shorts again was not received with quite the same enthusiasm.

248

Monaco And Its Yachts

With the Monaco Grand Prix taking place today many yacht owners locally are heading for Monte Carlo, but there is limited space in the harbour necessitating some owners having to park outside in the Mediterranean. This has a down side. There is a danger that if one is parked too far outside the port there may be no TV reception thus it could be a waste of time as one would completely miss the action. This will not stop them however, prompting Peachy Butterfield who will be a guest aboard the Naked Politicians D5 to say that outside the port will be like Tesco on a Saturday, only in the sea.

Last year apparently the Naked Politician and Peachy "enjoyed the Grand Prix" from the Naked one's apartment in Monaco. By "enjoy" I mean they could hear it but not see it. I suspect that in quite a different way, this year may be the same.

To a barbecue last night in Valbonne with John "did you bring any cigars?" and Jude "they have run out of Baileys" O Sullivan. One of the guests was an expert in fragrances and worked in the perfume industry, which of course is well represented in nearby Grasse. His wife was wearing a new perfume called "Come to Me" but Peachy Butterfield who is something of an expert on perfumes said "it doesn't smell like come to me."

The whole evening was a splendid affair outside for the most part although the odd spot of rain from a nearby storm forced me to take shelter lest my Montechristo No 2 was extinguished. Being able to smoke outside in comfortable temperatures at night is one of the wonderful things about Summer in the Cote d'Azur. That sounds like a good idea for a book title, I wonder if anyone has ever thought of that?

With good company, wonderful food, exquisite barbecued lamb and a honey-glazed chicken plus a great deal of a rather good St Emilion Grand Cru lurking nearby, I fear I peaked a little early. On a trip back from the toilet I was overcome by a bout of extreme tiredness and may have had a five-minute power sleep which may have been photographed and uploaded to Facebook.

A more sensible plan, given the arrival of house guests, the

Savins, today for the rest of the week, would have been to tuck up in bed by 9am with a cup of cocoa, but the rare opportunity to smoke some of Johnny O Sullivan's cigars and drink some of his wine was too much of a lure. This morning then to Nice airport, donning my crash helmet and goggles to collect the Savins and if there is not a glass of rose on the go by midday then I'm a Dutchman.

Savaged By The Savins, Again

Golf will be played in this coming week and at some stage a ten euro note will be seen stuck to someone's forehead. If I have lost, which admittedly is a very rare occurrence, then this is a very childish method of celebrating victory and the inevitable wager. However, when I win it seems the most gratifying of actions, thoroughly justified but only in a nice caring sort of a way.

It will be the usual gritty battle between myself and Peter Savin. It is a battle that has been on-going for at least ten years but not all of the battle takes place on the golf course. No, there is a deeply psychological element to it which is acted out on the days and particularly the evening, before the first ball is struck. There is an enormous difference between sportsmanship, where one acts honourably to one's opponent and accepts the result of the contest with openness and honesty, and most of all plays fair, and gamesmanship, which is where winning is everything and almost any tactic can be brought to bear to ensure the win. I would have said that my particular forte is gamesmanship. This year however I have been outthought so far. Normally my tactics are effective if slightly transparent. Supply a great deal of wine, preferably of differing colours, ending up with a heavy red, persuade one's foe to partake generously of all three, bring out the Limoncello and then the brandy at the right moment, abstain oneself from excessive drinking and then book an impossibly early tee time the next morning to take maximum advantage of the resultant hangover.

What I had not factored in is a never-before-seen and steely-eyed determination of my opponent not to over-imbibe. This is a departure, and very disconcerting as a result. Thus I venture out to the Grande Bastide Golf Course early this morning, having conceded a hitherto unexpected psychological disadvantage, so strong indeed that I believe I shall not be able to report the result tomorrow due to lack of space. Regular readers will know the ominous signs of one of my specialties, selective reporting.

With the wine flowing in the Pav last night, that Nice Lady Decorator demanded music. We have one of the first iPods ever made (I think it has valves) which means it is something less than reliable unless you talk to it nicely. If you then add to the mix her distrust of anything vaguely technical, and her patience which reduces exponentially with each glass of wine consumed, and that lunch had turned into dinner and then degenerated into the Pav, you will realise that I did well to prevent said iPod being thrown, together with its docking station, into the swimming pool.

Once I had taken command of the situation and the technology I was directed as to what music to select. Our house guests, the Savins' hearts' lie in the 50's and 60's whilst that Nice Lady Decorator gravitates towards the 70's and later, so eventually I found the Traveling Wilberry's, an album made by George Harrison, Roy Orbison, Jeff Lynn and Bob Dylan, icons from the correct eras with an album made in the 80's which seemed to find favour. All was well until Peter Savin asked if the singer was Bob the Builder, not spotting the immediately identifiable voice of Bob Dylan. That's when the trouble started.

"Its Dylan" she said and his "Wasn't he in the Magic Roundabout?" did not go down well either. I eventually managed to steer the musical direction down a less contentious route and order was restored.

Sometimes there is a certain karma to events. Yesterday that Nice Lady Decorator decided to cook two chickens. I said there was no point; one would be enough for our needs with lunch on the beach today at Juan les Pins with man-mountain Peachy Butterfield scheduled, and a minor disagreement unfolded. Imagine my amazement this morning when I was dispatched to make the early morning tea to find the untouched cooked chicken no longer residing in its tray, and nowhere to be seen, and with horrid hound Banjo smacking his lips and surrounded by chicken bones. Instant karma, (if it had been curried would it have been instant korma?) he will have his arse royally kicked by that Nice Lady Decorator when she sees the mess shortly! How satisfying.

Ok, now to the golf yesterday... Hang on, I have written my customary 600 words and run out of space, maybe tomorrow...

How can lunch starting at 12.30 get so out of hand? It was supposed to be a quiet affair on the beach at one of my favourite restaurants Le Petite Plage at Juan les Pins.

Peachy Butterfield was regaling us with stories, photographs and even videos of trying to get the naked politician back on his boat after he became tired and emotional after a big lunch the day before. Then he got a call, the entire luncheon party were invited aboard D5 in nearby Antibes for afternoon drinks on the poop deck.

Had it stopped there then a great deal less carnage would have ensued but I blame the Buftons who chanced by having arrived in Antibes that very day on their trip bringing their new boat from England. It had taken three weeks and they were desperate for some company so after we left D5 the naked politician headed off for his wedding anniversary dinner in Monaco and the rest of us descended on the web.

I think it was about 9pm when Peachy revealed that his six-pack had turned into a party seven. I had a hidden agenda in that I am due to play golf again today with house guest Peter Savin and he is often prone to a hangover so perhaps it was slightly unfair for me to bring out the 10 year old malt whiskey and the brandy at around 10pm. I need all the help I can get after things did not go according to plan in the golf course on Monday, which sadly I never found enough space to cover in these pages.

The Butterfields will have house guests themselves in the coming week, after we have served our time under similar constraints. Theirs is a leading plastic surgeon and his wife. He is the chairman of the British Association of Plastic Surgeons. The irony of being at the head of BAPS had apparently eluded him until Peachy brought it to his attention.

The lovely Janie Savin, who is blonde and beautiful and was described yesterday as a GILF (a bit like a MILF but a grandmother) by the man with the party 7, has not been watering my fake plastic banana palm on this trip, no, she is way too sensible for that. I cannot recall how we got onto the subject but her blonde genes took over yesterday when discussing Dutch caps and how they were made. The rest of the party knew them to be a valuable contraceptive aid but clearly she had not taken this on board because during a discussion about the manufacturing process Janie wondered aloud why they would need such a process for a mushroom. She has form when it comes to being blonde. I have a picture of her watering my plastic palm tree. She did it for a whole week and I did not have the heart to let on, so on her last day I managed to get a photograph of the moment when she realized it was plastic.

"I can only stay a week and I don't do animals," so said a certain female houseguest, whom I cannot identify (but who was dubbed a GILF by Peachy Butterfield when he met her for the first time this week) when confronted with a brief tour of the wonderful D5, the boat owned by the naked politician. You may think she is pictured above but I could not possibly comment.

This was on Tuesday afternoon after lunch and on the way to the web, a big memorable day, so inevitably yesterday was considerably quieter, certainly in daylight hours as recovery and nursing of hangovers was required.

Over a quiet lunch in the web after golf, of which more later, if the pressure of space permits, certain details of rather poor behaviour by a grandmother who should know better were brought to my attention. As long as the usual ten euro bribe is passed to me in a timely fashion no one need be any the wiser. This is not blackmail, merely reputation integrity insurance.

Dinner was taken at Cafe des Arcades in Valbonne which was another quiet affair apart from the thunder that was rumbling around and the noise of the rain drumming on the awnings. The weather continues to be less settled than normal. I am told it will be better in England which actually would not be impossible given what we have suffered this week. I have even twice this week had to put the top up on the Merc.

I was late for dinner because I had been playing tennis at the Vignale with thunder and lightning lurking around but at that stage just a few spots of rain. This was clearly not conducive to the skills of my partner and fellow moustachioed old git, the Wingco. We won the first set but thereafter my memory became slightly hazy as to what occurred. In my mind I am certain we won but cannot be sure of the exact score.

Today, for the final day of the visit of house guests the Savins, we have half a plan to go to **Lou Fassum** for lunch. This has to be my favourite top end restaurant, but given the prices it is one visited only on special occasions. Peter Savin however is treating us. It is a very special occasion for him as he is celebrating some kind of recent hollow golf victory, one that I cannot recall. Any suggestion that I may have been on the losing side and that this loss was perpetrated deliberately in order to secure a sumptuous lunch at someone else's expense could be seen as a reasonable defence.

Post Savin Recovery

Over a sumptuous meal on the lovely terrace of the Bois Dore it was revealed that a friend of the Buftons once owned a house in Switzerland at a place called Wankdorf. Regular readers of this column will know that information such as this is fuel to the fire of innuendo and gossip for which this column is justly renowned. What a handy place to live I suggested innocently. It has good air and road links so I thought it was handy. Subsequently the lovely Lesley Bufton said "I wasn't going to mention it, but for a long time I had to go there twice a day".

As soon as she had uttered those words in the context of Wankdorf she looked at me and suddenly regretted it. With my BlackBerry in my hand to take notes in order, as it were, to take in hand this piece of information, and in justifiable fear of the consequences she dug that hole of innuendo deeper still; she knew that my reporting antenna was primed and still she said she knew that "she had it coming".

Lunch was charming, as was the waiter who was trying in broken English to explain the cheese option on the Menu Du Marche "pas de goat" he said, and I was mightily glad about that.

If there was one reason to make one less unhappy about having to leave France in about six weeks' time is the news that the recent unseasonable storms have destroyed almost the entire grape crop in the Var over near St Tropez for the next two years. Horizontal hail stones have been blamed and it feels like I may have passed something similar myself after the last few days. So with the prospect of Var rose wine not being available next year and the year after, I shall have to reconsider my antipathy to a return to England. It could have been worse of course, what if a similar catastrophe befell Bordeaux? There would scarcely be any reason for living.

Comments on this column yesterday revolved unsurprisingly around the stories the day before of a house owned by a friend in Wankdorf. It was hard for the less busy amongst my readership to avoid grasping the staff of hope I had given them to enjoy. The Reverend Jeff suggested that I should guide my flock away from erection and towards resurrection. Peter Lynn researched some other tall football stories on the web about being (in) Wankdorf. "How would you feel about playing for the team, Wankdorf?"

Recently departed house guest Janie was determined to sample my dessert and chose an interesting method. Perhaps they did not have spoons in her household when she was growing up, or perhaps she had already eaten all the silver ones.

How to eat a panna cotta

Jubilee Overkill

Just one evening of Jubilee overkill and I have already had enough. Perhaps it was just being sprawled on the sofa feeling wretched but I think I shall be avoiding the TV over the coming four or five days. I feel the same about the Olympics, the hype on the TV is already at fever pitch and beginning to irritate me, almost as much as that ridiculous Belgian detective, the man with a live snail for a moustache, Poirot, another waste of TV production facilities on the same level as Midsomer Murders, both series an utter waste of TV time in my humble opinion, and both beloved by that Nice Lady Decorator who likes to keep at least 40 hours TV of this nature stored on our Sky planner system.

So, off to bed last night with a cocoa and a Resolve, the last-ditch hangover cure, moaning about improbable Belgian detectives and with high hopes that I will feel more sociable in the morning. These were dashed, pebble dashed in fact as was our hallway, pebble dashed by one of the dogs. In my mind there absolutely no doubt as to who is the culprit. Banjo has twice this week broken into the kitchen to steal and eat food. Off with his head.

Last night then, we were invited to dinner with a number of the usual suspects, but with the addition of some charming German friends of our hosts, Roly and Lesley Bufton. Peachy Butterfield popped around during the day to collect the Lucifer Child (his daughter) who had crashed out at ours the night before with Sprog 2 who is home for a long weekend, and we discussed what amusement we might encounter when faced with our new Germanic friends during the evening. We decided that one thing we must not do is ask him his occupation, otherwise he may say "no, just for a few days." Perhaps it would also have been a good idea if we did not mention the war? Discussion about Basil Fawlty and his attitude to Germans followed and whilst we amused ourselves we accepted that our dinner guests might not be similarly entertained, and resolved that Fawlty Towers was off limits.

So we went off to meet the Germans, me adorned in my new dark pink cashmere sweater which so nearly matched the plates. I said before we arrived that I just hope it doesn't go to penalties. This caused me to receive a yellow card from that Nice Lady Referee early on. A red card would probably get me shot. Before we left for the dinner engagement, I went to the fridge for some wine to take and said Handy Hock anyone? As I pointed out on the way home, that line was from Dad's Army so still just onside.

There was one tense moment. Peachy was keen later in the evening to go outside for some reason, perhaps he was a little hot, so to find the patio doors locked was a shock in the short term, but he was released in the end, and was able to escape to freedom. There was also a moment when I mentioned Basel. Peachy thought I had mentioned Basil as in Basil Fawlty, a subject which we had previously agreed was off limits. What he had not understood was that I was talking about the Swiss city of Basel, close to another notable Swiss town, Wankdorf.

A splendid day yesterday aboard Sea Breeze, the wonderful new Fleming boat, owned by Roly and Poly and berthed at Antibes got off to a fascinating start. Regular readers will know that we had two charming German friends of our hosts aboard, both of whom are doctors and neither saur krauts, in fact they were both very jovial.

It seems they had read my comments yesterday relating to Basil Fawlty and Dad's Army so I was a little wary of what would result. They had said that the contents were "very amusing" in a manner I did not find entirely convincing, so when Uli, who is also a research scientist (whom the lovely Lesley Bufton described as "like the horny captain of Das Boot", the film about a German submarine) you will understand that my senses were working overtime. I think it was when he shouted "torpedoes away" as we cruised the channel between the Iles des Lerins and Cannes that I began to become really concerned.

He was referring of course to two fast-moving jet skis, so distant that an "Eagle" eye would have been required to spot the wake. Maybe it was the binoculars, or maybe the forced smile when our hosts gallantly tried to explain the humour the British find in TV series Fawlty Towers, or maybe it was the cold cures I was consuming at regular intervals, washed down with wine, in order to try to ward off a cold I had suddenly developed that magnified my sense of paranoia? In any event I am sure I did not imagine the order to drop depth charges.

I remained on my guard during this sun drenched day with senses heightened and nervously jumping at every rifle-like explosion of the Prosecco corks. Eventually in the afternoon after a fabulous lunch I was lulled to the edge of sleep by the heady combination of fizzy wine, rose and Lemsip.

When I awoke I was not at my best but received precious little sympathy from that Nice Lady sailing person for my predicament. In fact I swear I heard her saying that I was "over achtung".

So as I manfully fight off the worst case of man flu I, or probably any other man in history has ever suffered, I have been languishing on the sofa, having to watch yet more Jubilee nonsense.

This enforced period of "relaxation" has given me time to think over what has been going on during the past few weeks. One thing I had forgotten until today was that last week when our invitation to dine with some Germans was brought forward from 7 30 to 6 30, Peachy Butterfield said it was because they did not want us to arrive fashionably late, between 19.39 and 19.45. This cannot be construed as a mention of the war and if it was then I think we have got away with it.

I am told the drought in England is as bad as ever, but I do not want my readers in England to get the impression that all is good in the garden of the south of France. Oh no, we had some cloud again at times yesterday, keeping the temperature down to a chilly 24 degrees at times, and one of my local readers, the Naked Forker, has revealed that a bird shat on her arm yesterday whilst she drove along yesterday with the window down. You see it is tough down here as well, although I accept that readers in England may not understand the concept of an open window. This kind of deposit is seen as a lucky omen in some circles. It must have been a really good shot. For three years I have driven around all summer (that is from March to November – this for my readers in England) with the top down in the Merc and never once been lucky enough for that to happen to me.

Auberge De La Source

The Auberge De La Source restaurant on the edge of Sophia Antipolis has been revamped and has reopened. I always liked it because you could get alligator and ostrich on the menu when we first moved down here some seven years ago. Its idyllic setting in the woods by a river was also very alluring so that Nice Lady Decorator persuaded me to take her up The Source, as it were, once my tennis match was cancelled.

We managed to secure a couple of drinks but they only open for dinner on Friday and Saturday. The garden area has been delightfully revamped, even to the extent of the siting of some typical modern art pieces. I took this picture of one of them. As you can see it is a flawed piece as I am certain the artist was trying to evoke a sense of fair play, of ensuring that one pays ones debts, but when moulding this worthy creation perhaps more attention should have been spent on the spelling. IOU is just three letters. How is it possible to get them in the wrong order?

This evening an old friend, an incomprehensible Scotsman, is coming to visit. This will almost certainly involve us staggering up to the wonderful Valbonne square, the first port of call for a visiting tourist. I often find the French hard to understand but that is as nothing compared with the Glaswegian drawl with which we will have to contend. Luckily that nice lady interpreter spent some time up north in her youth so she will be able to relay the gist of what he says. Frankly it is all nonsense anyway.

Art in the dyslexic world

My comments about dyslexia and art received a few great comments, of which my favourite was "would a dyslexic, agnostic, insomniac lie awake at night and worry about whether there was a dog?" I promised I would nick it and so I have.

My attention was drawn to an article in the Daily Telegraph which reported a story about two international communities that are making a strategic alliance, or twinning as we call it. Dull, a village in Scotland is tying the knot with Boring, a small community in Oregan. This got me thinking of suitable towns to twin with the charming Swiss town of Wankdorf. The best I could do was to suggest the up market hamlet called Happy in Texas. Happy and Wankdorf, a match made in heaven, and the perfect antidote to Dull and Boring.

Chapter 9

The Incomprehensible Scotsman

So last night the incomprehensible Scotsman eventually arrived from the airport. The twenty-minute drive took him an hour. He was apparently cursing the fact that all the locals were driving on the wrong side of the road and the steering wheel was on the wrong side of the car. At least this is what I heard when I got the translation later. I do not understand more than a tenth of what he says, it was like watching tennis as that Nice Lady Decorator, who understands the lingo, and the incomprehensible Scotsman traded stories. We adjourned to Valbonne square under a slight chill. Although still in shorts, I did take a light sweater in case it cooled too much by midnight.

A late pizza in the square was followed by an adjournment to the Pav to enable him to drink back dinner, which that Nice Lady Decorator had forced him to buy. I left them to it. "Drinking back" is a Scottish concept, where the buyer of dinner attempts to secure effective repayment for the cost of dinner by drinking their own body weight in wine. From what I saw, and the number of bottles littering the Pav this morning, in typical Scots fashion, he got his money's worth.

Before the incomprehensible and geographically-challenged Scotsman departed we loaned him a map for his journey to Albi, over in central southern France, where he is due to attend a wedding on Saturday. Because of his ineptitude exhibited in following very simple instructions, which had needlessly extended the simple trip from Nice airport to Valbonne (normally 20 minutes) into a 90-minute fiasco the night before, we thought it was wise. Albi should be a four-hour drive, but given the form I have witnessed recently he should make it by Tuesday, several days after the wedding. Instructions in English were clearly too much for him.

I am sure he is a charming chap but like that Fat Fighters character in Little Britain played by the excellent Matt Lucas, when confronted by an Indian lady with an accent, I have no idea what he was saying. That nice lady decorating interpreter told me later that he is an expert in the culinary world. It seems that his particular speciality is the Haggis burger. I jest not. Whilst I was glazing over when listening to the guttural Glaswegian guests gob, that Nice Lady future haggis burger fabricator was taking notes and I fear that sometime soon I shall be forced to eat and pass comment on such an animal. I hope that I do not literally have to pass such a delight.

Lost Scotsman Departs

Back to some kind of normality with dinner at the house of Man Mountain, Peachy Butterfield in Valbonne. Also present was the Naked Politician who dropped the bombshell, he is no longer a politician. There was however no mention of any curtailment to the naked part of his epithet, although thankfully, and mainly because his "handbrake" in the lovely form of his wife Dawn, precluded any disrobing on this occasion, at least while we were there.

I was also introduced to a charming visiting plastic surgeon, chairman of BAPS (the British Association Of Plastic Surgeons; you couldn't make it up) Douglas "Mack The Knife" McGeorge who made a number of incisive comments, cutting to the heart of any discussions, and not putting the knife into anyone. Ok that's enough surgical jokes. He did look a little embarrassed when Peachy announced again that his penis reduction surgery had been a great success and that as a result he can now wear shorts. Perhaps Mac's "staff" had undertaken that particular short operation. By this time Le Peche Enorme was deeply into his stride, having spent much of the afternoon paying massive respect to a bladder of the freshest Macclesfield Malbec, still steaming from whatever vile process they use to produce the obnoxious liquid. Quite how the conversation turned to circumcision eludes me as I write this, perhaps it the presence of "Mack The Knife". Anyway, my notes are hazy as by this point I had managed a few glasses of a rather nice St Emilion Grand Cru that I had sneaked in when his back was turned. I cannot quite recall in what context but he contended rather too loudly (especially if any of our new friends were Jewish) that circumcision was a procedure designed to impede masturbation (although the mechanics of exactly how this might be achieved leave me a little mystified) but he said to be certain perhaps doctors should cut their arms off. As I say, I was a little hazy by that time.

Later he told an utterly tasteless joke about why a girl had two black eyes (because he had to tell her twice) and it became clear it was time to leave. We were sharing a taxi with Roly and Poly Bufton (their new names courtesy of Lucy Butterfield, who thought their real names were Roly and Poly Bufton. She is blonde, my case rests) and after being dropped off and whilst having a last nightcap under the stars on a balmy evening in the web, we heard the taxi return. Roly had left their gate bleeper behind and was incurring the shrill wrath of Poly, so beautiful when she is aroused. He did his case no favours when he fell over and made a Roly-sized indentation in a large thyme bush. Perhaps I should not have said "thyme to go home?"

I hear some underground rumblings from Peachy Butterfield yesterday (not unusual it itself) about my cutting remarks over the quality of the wine he habitually consumes. The emphasis in his household is on quantity rather than quality. Let me be clear, with most wines drunk by normal people one removes the cork to enable the aroma of the "crushed fruit" as Peachy describes it, to be savoured and enjoyed, but with Peachy's choice of wine it is important that it is uncorked early in order for the smell to be dispersed some time before intended consumption. Frankly, the longer the better.

Sunday in Valbonne in early summer is a splendid place to be. That Nice Lady Decorator loves a car boot sale and with the French equivalent (a vide grenier) spotted taking place in the village on the way to buy a paper, I thought I could settle into an espresso in Valbonne square with my Sunday Times in the full knowledge that she would spend a happy hour or so trawling over other people's rubbish, and thus leaving me in peace.

Today there may be an uplifting plan to have lunch on the beach on the way to the airport to see off Mac The Knife, our visiting token plastic surgeon. I would have said that I did not feel cut out for this after the weekend we have just had but that would have been the kind of cheap joke that I have been determined to slice out of this column. As I write, there is no certainty that the engagement is firm but I live in hope. Can I say I am putting on a brave face about it? Or could that be misconstrued by Mac the Knife? Juan les Pins for lunch on the beach is a bit of an extravagance on a Monday, but I contend that we are living (at least for the moment) amongst extravagant people and unless we join in we would look out of place.

A sharpener in the web was required before we set off for the seaside with Peachy Butterfield, his gorgeous well-stacked (sorry Lin but she does not like to be called statuesque) wife, Suzanne and "Mac the Knife". On the way we discussed his epithet in this column and he expressed a liking for it, saying it was better than "Plastic Mac" or "Placcy Maccy" as he is known in some circles. I could discuss this further but have drawn a veil over the subject, which should suit Peachy who has now added selling curtains in the south of France to his list of inactivity.

Once joined on the beach at Le Petite Plage by the Naked Former Politician and his lovely wife Dawn, the suitability of the conversation for inclusion in this column became sufficiently dubious as to be thrown into doubt. I dubbed it a case of back to the suture. A number of doctor's jokes and stories, some very funny indeed, unfolded but sadly most will have to be excluded. I would love for instance to have been able to tell you how best to numb nipples. One facet did occur to me though as we were talking. Although there seems to be very little difference between the spelling of hospitality and being hospitalised, there is clearly a great gulf in the meaning, unless you go private.

Flying Ipod

It is always a mistake when that Nice Lady Decorator gets her hands on the iPod and docking station. I try to keep it out of her sight, especially if she has lunched well, had a siesta, and then awoken determined to carry on in the same way as she had before everybody had left. The reasons would be obvious to anyone there in the pav last night. There are parallels with the concept of the perfect storm. Her superb decorating skills are neatly counterbalanced by her utter ineptitude with anything remotely technical. Her patience after a few drinks is, at the very least, not noted, and her dissatisfaction with things not going to plan means that those things that choose to offend her can get thrown around. Once I had won the battle for the music system not to be thrown into the garden and it was functioning in some measure, I was then treated to her utter certainty that by singing along to classics like "See Emily Play" and "Nights in White Satin" that she was somehow adding to the aural experience. If one is stupid enough (as I was) to throw the slightest doubt about the quality of this enhancement, she increases the volume exponentially until they see or actually hear the light.

Today then, once the ringing in my ears has subsided from shrill to dull pain, I have work to do before the Incomprehensible Scotsman returns this evening from the wedding in central southern France, if he made it, and if he can find his way back. Regular readers will already be aware of his inability to speak English properly, let alone French, and will be familiar with his cartographically-challenged nature. A map to him reminds me of another song which was butchered last night "I'm on the road to nowhere."

Whilst enjoying a very good value lunch in the sunshine, somehow the conversation tracked towards actors and lookalikes. I ventured the opinion that in my younger days I looked a bit like Russell Brand. To my surprise that Nice Lady Decorator agreed but then came the sting in the tail: she said that when I was young I acted like him as well. Becoming animated, she said that was why she had finished with me all those years ago, because she was worried about STD. "STD?" I said, and she retorted that she did not mean Subscriber Trunk Dialling (you have to be of a certain age to understand this). It dawned on me that she was alluding to Sexually Transmitted Diseases, or communicative diseases. I suppose writing this daily blog is some kind of communicative disease.

Lunch at Auberge de la Source did not start well. That Nice Lady Decorator loves an olive, so having polished off a plateful she decided that the pips should be cast into the river running beautifully alongside where we were sitting. Elvis Costello once wrote a song called "My Aim is True", however the expert decorator amongst us took no notice and proceeded to pepper some charming French people with olive stones. Luckily they thought it was funny, in different circumstances this act could well have brought forth a stony silence.

Inevitably, amongst our party was one Peachy Butterfield who was determined to exhibit his new iPhone app called "Fit or Fat'. It takes a picture of you and then analyses what it sees and gives you a rating between 0 and 10, 0 being fat, 10 being fit. I was the first to volunteer for the analysis, and whilst the app did its calculations, Peachy was heard to say that if I came out as " fit" he would show his arse in Burtons. Fate has a lovely way of punishing those that make silly statements, and although 6 out of 10 was a marginal pass, the app said "Fit" and that was enough for me to ensure that this ill-judged statement gets its just reward. It is official, I am fit and soon, when next I venture into Burtons I shall expect to witness a rather unpleasant unveiling.

Lunch was a little drawn out, and we were, as usual, the last to leave. However, a number of the party remained thirsty so regular readers will know what happened; we adjourned to the web in a vain attempt to satisfy that thirst. My picture today shows Peachy and Roly doing their very best to "enjoy" the afternoon. Quite why Roly is wearing a mink coat and Peachy is kissing him is not clear. Perhaps there are some secrets yet to escape from the closet?

Roly and Peachy after lunch, naturally and what is that dog doing there?

I would like to be able to report that the day ended here, by the pool with a glass in hand. However, it did not. The hardcore amongst us overcame conference calls and short naps to emerge from the afternoon and seek a curry. Once the Incomprehensible Scotsman heard that we have a curry house in Valbonne there was only ever going to be one outcome.

It is at this stage that I have to reveal that there was a surprising early casualty. That Nice Lady Decorator could not be revived from her power nap and did not come for a curry. We had half a plan to reconvene with Rupert Scott who had been with us for lunch but had left early to oversee his building team. He calls then the Communards, but probably not to their face. Tattooed and bald they may be, but gay? Perhaps not.

Talking of gay, it seems that Roly and Poly have decided to continue to employ a gay skipper to be captain of their boat. This is such a potential rich vein of material for this column that I think it could write itself for the next few days. My polite enquiry as to whether his name was Roger and whether he had a cabin boy will have alerted them to the literal danger that confronts them. At no stage should they ever address him in this manner: "Hello Sailor". Some of my dearest friends are gay but I have solemnly promised not to allude to any sexual orientation when (if) ever invited aboard again. For instance I shall not be making any comments about uphill gardening, shirt-lifters or nine bob notes.

In a desperate attempt to offset the physical effects of the profligate ex-pat lifestyle enjoyed (or would endured be a better word?) down here in the sunny south of France, that Nice Lady Decorator and I go for a walk every day. This is not a stroll but a full-on power walk up as many hills as we can manage. Without that counterbalance, I would be dead. The problem is that, like yesterday, one sets oneself out to have a day without a drink, in my case dedicating the whole day, well most of the morning, well certainly between 11 and lunchtime, to work.

The combined effects of old age and last week's man flu yesterday then sent me for a siesta in the afternoon. When I awoke, I was preparing for a little cycling but then Peachy arrived unannounced at 5pm.

His visit was on the spurious pretext that he had some stuff to deliver to us. Once unloaded it was inevitable. I tried to head him off at the pass with "Would you like a cup of tea?" "No, a glass of wine please" intoned Le Grande Peche and once again the foundations of good intent for a more healthy lifestyle crumbled like a dam trying to hold back an English drought.

It had been a lovely morning down by the River Brague as my picture today would have depicted had it not been invaded by the calamitous cocker Banjo. A pleasant siesta and then, 5pm, the sun going down, the temperature perfect, the provocation of a Peach and bang, back on the sauce.

Retail Therapy

That Nice Lady decorator is a totter at heart. The expression "totter" in this context has nothing to do with the wearing of high heels under the influence of alcohol. It is a term I learned in my teens when I was bringing my unique talents to bear on what I liked to call the waste disposal business. Yes I was a dustman for some time after passing my A levels (shockingly lucky result according to my pals at the time) and turning down a place at somewhere called "Swansea University" which is surely a contradiction of terms. But I digress, the term "totter" was used to describe those poor unfortunate people who cannot resist a good look at piles of refuse and collect items of supposed use from the steaming pile of garbage at the tip.

That Nice Lady Decorator cannot resist a car boot sale or a second-hand furniture shop, so it was with a sinking heart that I accepted and obeyed the command to hitch up the trailer and drive her to the second-hand store in Antibes, where she had seen a dining table she liked. "But we already have a big dining room table," I exclaimed, however it seems that we don't like the existing one and need a different one.

As if this was not enough to bring my day down, having loaded the bits of the new dining room table into the trailer, I was about to head home when I was apprised of a change of plan. She had decided that as we are now the proud owners of a new dining table, we obviously needed new chairs to match. "But we already have 12 dining room chairs", I whimpered.

So after visiting a second second-hand emporium and loading the 11 new chairs she had bought into the trailer (imagine, there were only 11, how will we cope?) it was back home to allow her to begin painting them all. Now call me stupid but if you want to have painted table and chairs, why not just buy them in the colour you want? Or better still paint the ones you already have? Why buy wooden furniture and then paint it all? Another question that has been lurking at the back of my style-challenged mind is why paint all the furniture in the dining room the same colour? I was sufficiently unwise to allow that question to leak out of my mouth. I do not want to talk about the consequences.

Anyway, after minor surgery and the application of some plasters, I needed to prepare for an afternoon with Tony "I invented the internet" Coombs to christen his new smart terrace. It is a lovely construction with far-reaching views over his estate, up to the perfume capital of Grasse and down to the Mediterranean. Well, you would be able to see the sea if the diving board had been built along with the pool he promised he would build in the last millennium. It is rather a sore point for his fiery but dazzling red-headed wife, Pat. I mentioned it once and I think I got away with it.

As it was Father's Day I contend that it was an honest mistake. I caught a reference from that Nice Lady Decorator about a good rubbing down and she said my reaction to that statement was a deliberate misinterpretation. Apparently I knew that she had to rub down all those new wooden dining room chairs ready for painting. It seems to happen to me all the time. Earlier this week for instance I had been talking about redirection of male, another misunderstanding.

Before she started all that nonsense we went for our traditional morning march in the woods nearby where I was able to take this picture. Quite what she was trying to do eludes me. Fans of Harry Worth may have some idea, but clearly that particular TV series was completed and aired a long time before either of us was born.

Spot that Nice Lady Decorator

We headed for Valbonne square in order for that Nice Lady Decorator to buy me dinner. As she was paying we went slightly up market to the Terra Rossa which backfired a bit as my steak was not very good.

One mis steak can lead to another and so it proved when I tried to tell the story of a friend of a friend who always had a different fugly (effing ugly) girl in tow. He was known as Sledge because he was always getting pulled by dogs. Now I thought that was funny but it was not an opinion shared by that unsmiling but still Nice Lady Decorator.

Watching Paint Dry

What is more boring that watching paint dry? Even more boring than watching a dour English football team grind out a victory against world beaters Ukraine? Answer: spending the afternoon watching that Nice Lady Decorator looking at paint drying. She loves to walk around and drool at cans of paint whilst stalking around a paint shop. This is worse than watching paint dry because whilst it is in the can it does not dry very easily, so the whole process takes longer, much longer.

Paint shops are of course the natural habitat of the decorating species, who get excited about things like oil-based derivatives and Elephants Breath (this is apparently a Farrow and Ball colour but my attempt at humour, that as a comedy duo they were crap, so why are they so good with paint, fell on deaf ears.)

She is painting everything that moves, and much that does not, at the moment in readiness for the summer rental clients that we do not yet have. Indeed I have to keep moving in case I get painted, which, in a very different way I have recently, with the competition to paint a portrait of me for the front cover of this book. It seems a "bring your own lunch" is taking shape for Monday July 2nd at Marina Kulik's Painting Studio in Plascassier where I shall be judging the entries and deciding on which work wins the prize. The prize of course is having the winning painting featured on my new book jacket. It is a prize that any aspiring artist would want, honest.

By the time we got back, with a skip load of paint, with names like Sheep Slobber, Snowgoose Snot and Parrot's Phlegm, it was hot. 30 degrees is enough to do two things: 1. to heat up the swimming pool to 25 degrees and 2. to ensure that the afternoon was entirely unproductive. The only activity that can be undertaken in these conditions is the rigorous testing of the garden furniture ahead of the rental season, should we get any clients. It seems a lot of people will be remaining at home despite the weather to "enjoy' the Olympics.

My pomegranate tree has suddenly gone mad and is festooned with flowers. Two years ago I had warned it that as it was so ugly in winter, being deciduous, that it had better start producing some flowers and fruit or it would end up as an addition to the log pile. With no discernible response at first I had sharpened my saw but on the day set aside for its cutting down to size it rained. Other jobs then crowded in on that nice old git gardener and it survived. Finally the tree seems to have got the message and is now playing ball and my little talk will soon, literally, bear fruit. A case of the prevaricating pomegranate perhaps?

At our irregular tennis gatherings on a Wednesday night, it almost seems to be a matter of honour for the public schoolboys amongst us (and by that I mean everyone but me) to be late. Regular readers will know that a unit of time known as a "Wingco" is a minimum of 7 minutes, so in different circumstances, his being late by 2 "Wingco's", and then spending some time on the phone during the usual desultory warm up, whilst undeniably rude, may have put us at a disadvantage, however as it turned out that was not the case. One of us was on time as usual, as befits a self-made organised man of commerce such as myself.

Quite how the MOGS, the Moustachioed old Gits, with a combined age approaching 120 could secure a victory over 3 sets in two hours in temperatures in the high twenties Celsius is one of those marvels that will be celebrated far and wide in this household, well, by me at least. Superior technique, superior strength and fitness, superior tactics all combined to ensure a famous victory. I am lying of course about the tactics bit. One of our (MOGS) quiet discussions about tactics when I suggested that the Wingco to play a little less aggressively was met with a particularly aggressive retort from the Wingco using the f word.

At the root of this event is fear. Our opponents, Dancing Greg Harris and Blind Lemon Milsted, frightened of defeat and the subsequent slagging they receive in this column, were finally coaxed on to the tennis court by the fear of the threat of receiving a white feather. Strange you may think that the fear of receiving the traditional damning mark of cowardice was outweighed by the fear of failure on the court.

At dinner afterwards it was noticed that Blind Lemon has recently had a haircut and it was mentioned that he looks a little like a geeky sixth former. I have a photo which I cannot show, taken in Valbonne square last week that reminds me of his hair pre-haircut. However, why he should have that hair planted in an urn in the middle of the village is open to question.

Post tennis dinner discussions at Capriccio at Pre Du Lac was the usual abuse of process, insults, accusations and jokes, with the non-public schoolboy element receiving the most abuse. I just think they don't like the idea of me being a successful author. It is a time-honoured tradition that we are the last to leave the restaurant and as you should know by now, I am a traditionalist at heart.

The annual French midsummers day festival "Fete de la Musique" was embraced by Valbonne for the first time last night, and although the square was buzzing, and that Nice Lady Decorator had to pull rank to ensure we got a table at the Cafe des Arcades, it did not have the edge of the music events staged in previous years in Mouans Sartoux.

I was however lucky enough to espy Dancing Greg Harris and able to ask him in front of a crowd of thirsty ex-pats how he got on at tennis the night before (when he lost horribly to the MOGS), but it seems amnesia has set in. Poor chap, I believe he is only in his early 70's, well at least that's what it looks like now that hair colouring seems to be part of his life, but I did not mention it in public, I have too much heart. Better that a small personal quirk, such as this emanating from a bottle, is revealed quietly in the best read blog and book in Valbonne. It gives people the chance to have a private chortle about him before they next see him. Laughing with someone is so much better than laughing at them don't you think?, and so much easier when one is forearmed with that knowledge rather than suddenly realising that his hair has changed colour when the chap is in front of you. I am so thoughtful and generous of spirit.

Let The Party Season Begin

A big party is taking shape at the weekend. Slash and Burn and child bride, the steely-eyed ice cool Lisa are having their leaving party in our garden on Saturday. This is a rather curious state of affairs as they left France for London about a month ago. What a good idea then, to sell your house, get the money and then requisition one of your friend's houses to throw the leaving party in the full knowledge that your own house will remain unscathed. Seemingly it allows one to attempt facets of culinary entertainment that one would never consider in one's own garden. A pig roast is apparently booked for Saturday.

The only people who seemed to know nothing about this until today were myself, and maybe the pig, but even he (or she, let's not be sexist about this) may have had more idea than I. They arrive from Muswell Hill this morning and will apparently take in the supermarket and the wine merchants before descending upon us.

A pig roast? In Provence? It is probably a fine decision if one lives in the frozen north of Britain, anywhere say north of a line between Bristol and The Wash, where people probably huddle around the burning pig fat in order to keep warm but Valbonne? It's in the 80s Fahrenheit now. At the time of writing I have no idea where this giant piece of bacon will be prepared. I am not even certain I have been invited. If I am then today will be overwhelmed by instructions from that nice lady porky party organiser for me to run hither and thither in preparation. It's a pig's life.

I have so missed her. Lisa Thornton Allan, not featured in my photograph today, is the blonde steely-eyed goddess and trophy wife of Slash and Burn. She is a very intelligent, articulate university-educated woman but just occasionally the blonde gene takes precedence and these are often moments to remember. They flew in from London yesterday to take charge of their leaving party today (despite the fact they left about a month ago), the responsibility for which until now has been left to that Nice Lady Decorator whilst they have been sunning (sic) themselves in Muswell Hill for the last four weeks. They have taken to long walks on Hampstead Heath to try to forget the weather in the UK and were out on the Heath when suddenly the Red Arrows aerobatics flying team scorched overhead on their way to a fly-past at Buckingham Palace for the Queen's Jubilee celebrations. Excited at this sudden explosion of spectacle and with no children accompanying her, she exclaimed to the dogs "Look, Missy and Berty, the Red Arrows." It is not reported if they were suitably impressed.

Her husband Paul, is a brilliant artist and has a design company called The Big Picture. OK, I have been nice enough to him now. Regular readers will be aware of my antipathy for all modern art and my certainty that all lovers of it are being fooled all of the time a la mode of the king's new clothes. Last night over a nightcap in the web after dinner in Valbonne Square, he revealed that his Art degree, which he achieved with Honours, was based on a piece depicting "man's impact on the environment". The work comprised a house brick tied to a piece of string and suspended in the middle of the room. Scratching your head yet? He went on to explain that as anyone entering the room would have to walk around his work, presumably to stop one banging one's head, his theme was clearly laid out (or tied up?). Thus his Honours Degree award. I think if I had seen it I would have been banging my head on the ground.

A story has reached me of a comment made about my first book "Summer in the Cote d'Azur", from "Plastic Mac" Douglas McGeorge, renowned plastic surgeon who recently purchased a copy. He said and I quote "it was as funny as "Wilt" by Tom Sharp." Impressed, I mentioned this last night to that nice Lady Decorator but deflation was immediate when she pointed out that he was sufficiently comically-challenged not to have realised that the British Association of Plastic Surgeons may have been shortened to BAPS.

As I write I am awaiting delivery of a huge porker in readiness for the pig roast, a gastronomic lowlight of a Provencal summer, which is intended to feed the 50 or so invitees to said leaving party, which commences at lunchtime today and will be attended by the great and good and many who have featured in this column in the past. I am expecting to collect a wealth of material to keep me going this week, so I must trot(ter) off now to help set fire to it or whatever they do. I have some petrol in the garage, which should give it a nice flavour. I do like a bit of crackling.

Party Over

The leaving party for Slash and Burn Paul and steely-eyed goddess Lisa Thornton Allan was a massive success, if measured only in terms if bottles of wine consumed. Some 40 people were present for much of the pig roast and some 80 plus bottles of wine had been emptied before I snuck off to bed a little before midnight. Lunch can be so drawn out don't you think?

Poolside before the arrival of the pig roast

As was to be expected a myriad of stories came to light during the day. Let's start with the lovely Lisa herself. She revealed that she had recently read an article about gangling and ungainly England footballer Peter Crouch. It seems that he was asked what he would have been if he was not a footballer and said "a virgin." She then added to the amusement by allowing those blond genes out of control for a second or so by saying "he has gone up in my self-esteem".

Slash and Burn took some great pictures of the garden before the onslaught, one of which I show here.

My style guru, Mr. Humphreys was free and arrived wearing orange shoes and a red T-shirt. It gave us all a lead on what we should be wearing this summer in the south of France. He told me that in the days when he actually had a job, working for a local council in London, his work involved running the LGBT scheme. I enquired as to what that might stand for. The Lesbian, Gay, Bisexual and Trans-gender building association was set up to help these four groups find work in the building trade in the area. Yes, the local "right on" local council was prepared to spend taxpayer's money to make grants to people who were willing to employ workers from these sexual groupings. The trouble was that his hands were tied (no not in that way) by being disallowed from offering any grant unless the hairy-arsed builders open-heartedly welcomed the concept of members from these groups into their teams of contractors. He was not allowed openly to ask them, they had to volunteer an open-minded approach. Now call me old-fashioned and perhaps it is an unfair stereotype, but I cannot imagine any builder I have ever met (perhaps with the exception of Peachy Butterfield) embracing the concept of willingly employing people from these particular groupings without some financial inducement. When I expressed this opinion to Mr. Humphreys, and asked him how many contracts were awarded he looked a bit sheepish (again nothing to do with the people he was trying to help) and he admitted they never placed a single contract.

St Tropez By Boat

Being a little late for the trip to St Tropez aboard the Master Mariner Mundell's L'Exocet, the wonderful sedate and thus inappropriately-named sailing boat, was perhaps understandable given the events of Saturday when a luncheon party finished a little after midnight. A number of our party was feeling a little shabby as a result and a tad forgetful. As it would be very rude, I cannot reveal whom among our party it was that tried, on a trip to a very expensive eaterie, to leave his wallet behind before revealing this fact, just at the point at which he thought I would not have time to turn back, but Slash and Burn may feel the colour rising in his cheeks as he reads this.

The trip along the Esterel coastline fuelled by beers, prosecco and rose was sublime. The Tahiti Beach restaurant is one of those providing its own tender to ferry customers from their boat to the beach. It was there waiting for us at Tahiti Beach and transported the sailing party to the restaurant and that's when the trouble started. I have a particular aversion to techno music at any time of day but at 4pm on a Sunday in a great restaurant on one of the best beaches in the world? It has cemented my hatred of the genre. Some old school rap would have been entirely acceptable.

Nick Davies gets a toe hold

It is true that I had a mild sense of humour failure until at last the cacophony abated somewhat. Amongst those accompanying us on the trip was Nick Davies, the man renowned for taking his clothes off on beaches in St Tropez. He is still barred from Cinquante Cinq after the last time, despite the rugby tackle performed on him by his lovely wife Lise just too late to avoid some impressionable children to be traumatised by this horrible spectacle. It is fair to say that whilst not wishing to witness such a spectacle myself, it would have been fascinating in a macabre way, a bit like witnessing a car crash. Anyway, this time unwanted nudity was avoided, probably because he is jet-lagged after returning from Bangkok. I have a picture of him today aboard the boat but quite what he is trying to do to that Nice Lady Decorator's foot is open to question.

Amongst those sailing with us in more ways than one was a young lady to whom I shall refer to as Dangerous Jackie Lawless. A charming and beautiful innocent slip of a girl at first I thought, but a few of her stories about running a building company and her life in general, including having once been married to the owner of a Premiership football club, revealed hidden depths and a complete grasp of colourful language. That's all I am saying at this stage as she has submitted a bribe to ensure nothing embarrassing need be revealed in this column.

The trip back was just magnificent. The Mediterranean sunset viewed from the sea has to be one of the best views in the world. With the moon rising (and by that I do not mean seeing any nasty crescents lurking beneath Mr. Davie's shorts) we managed to achieve a feat the Master Mariner Mundell had been convinced was impossible, we ran out of wine. Well it was after midnight before we parked in Porte de la Rague.

Calm Down

It just had to be a quieter day than the previous two. A massive party on Saturday followed by an even more massive boat trip and lunch at Tahiti Beach in St Tropez had to take its toll, and I knew for whom the bells tolled, it was for me. I know it was a Monday but there was no option. However it took 3 good Bloody Mary's at lunchtime to re-establish good humour.

But we are hardy folk down here in the Cote d'Azur and once the heat of the sun had abated slightly and a full siesta had been properly taken it just seemed right to have a couple of beers in the web just to cement the recovery. Almost inevitably there was an opportunity to trawl through the myriad of pictures that had been taken over the two days and you will not be surprised to know that I have featured one such animal today. Yesterday's picture featured an animal in the shape of ageing Lothario Nick Davies. Had I the space, he would have featured again today with a different kind of animal, a nice lady decorating pole dancing animal.

The case for the defence will, I suppose, contend that the mast of Master Mariners Mundell's sailing boat l'Exocet could have easily been mistaken for a pole, and with loud music emanating from the galley, mistaking it for a pole as in pole dancing is an error anyone could have made. Anyone, that is, who had consumed a skinful. Those who have had previous experience of party loving Nick Davies will also know that he needs little encouragement to join in, well, with anything at any time, with no thought of the consequences. Indeed, I do not believe he knows the meaning of the word. (Is that where one thing leads to another?).

It was at around 4am that I became aware of talking, laughing and yes, it has to be said, cackling disturbing the quiet summer night time peace of Provence. It seems that the nice lady decorating pole dancer suddenly remembered that she had a great deal to discuss with the lovely steely-eyed, occasionally blonde, Lisa Thornton Allan and Sprog 2 who arrived back home last evening. Such was the importance of those discussions that it could not wait until morning, and when she (finally) came to bed I asked her what was the subject but she could not recall. I do know that they were sufficiently well gone to have started drinking from the Peachy Butterfield 10-litre wine box which is left in the Pav for Peachy's private delectation and delight.

It's an interesting wine. During the day and before a party kicks off, one would not touch it with a barge pole, except for fun, but in the certain knowledge that if the barge pole comes into direct contact with the noxious liquid that it would be somewhat shorter when removed due to the abrasive qualities of the liquid inside. There is only one person whom I know can stomach it, hence the reason it is left in place for him. For the white-wine-loving girls to drink red is a rarity, to have dipped into the Chateau Bargepole was astonishing. However, Le Grande Peche leaves for his summer holidays in the darkest north of England shortly and there is only about 5 litres left, so it might just stand one more visit from him.

The Return Of Slash And Burn

There are phrases which you hear in the south of France that you may never hear in England. The phrase that was used at lunch yesterday by the as-beautiful-as-she-is-scary Lisa Thornton Allan at the Cafe des Arcades in Valbonne square was: "it's too hot." Indeed it was a little hot, 29 degrees is a bit too hot, so for the first time I am looking forward to getting back to England in mid-July for a bit of a cool down. I think I may be delirious.

The after effects of the big weekend were still lurking so it was a quiet lunch before, in the evening, I was dispatched the airport to collect Locust 1, aka Sprog 1, who was flying in for a couple of weeks in order to drink all my wine and beers and eat all my food. Sprog 2 arrived last night so the Locust Denudation has already commenced. Where did they learn to drink like that? I blame their mother.

So after a nice but rather expensive lunch, I felt it was a good move to embrace a siesta before heading to the airport to pick up the Principle Locust. Dragging the girls from the square proved a little difficult but eventually it was achieved, but not much before 5pm.

It was whilst we were enjoying a post prandial afternoon cap in the web, another story emerged from Slash and Burn Thornton Allan which occurred whilst aboard the boat on the way (or the way back, he cannot be certain) from St Tropez at the weekend. At some stage on the trip he lost a tooth, a titanium tooth implant no less, a shoe, probably a Gucci, and some Armani sunglasses. To lose one item might be considered unlucky, two items raises some doubts but to lose three items, including a tooth? What was he doing? Actually I know what he was doing but simply cannot discuss it.

When eventually his losses became apparent the next day, he was mortified. Normally he makes a profit on everything but these were losses that were hard to bear. He said that the repair bill for the tooth alone could run into thousands, but unexpected help was at hand, or rather at nose. It seems that fate was smiling upon him however because at some stage a little later in the afternoon he sneezed and then found his tooth. It almost took my eye out as it went past me at 200 miles an hour and tried to embed itself in my oak tree. We decided that a proper description of this miracle should be hitherto described as a corker snorker.

After Sprog 1's return, during the evening I was alerted to an expression I had not previously heard. He was referring to a friend who had a predilection for the larger lady, but I am not sure the expression "a chubby chaser" is politically correct?

Are inflatable balloons better than non-inflatable balloons? This was the apparent contention of Slash And Burn as we sat down to barbecue chicken at the home of the lovely Julie and the slightly less lovely, but still cuddly, Peter Bennett, last night. Slash and Burn seemed quite unaware that a non-inflatable balloon is, in effect, just a piece of plastic.

It was almost as if last night that, as they are leaving today to head back to London, I was deliberately being fed with material for this column by him, such was the range of snippets I was able to capture on my BlackBerry ready for today's missive. His mad professor countenance often conveys the almost certainly true perception that he is off somewhere with the fairies, arriving back into conversations after a little cerebral time-travelling in a rather disconcerting way. Often one can be talking about him and that vacant "the lights are on but nobody is home look" is on his face, but then suddenly he will make some incisive and pithy retort giving the wholly false impression that he has been with you throughout.

Last night there was a conversation about insomnia and I thought he had glazed over and entered a different astral plane, then snapped back to reality and announced that he had been awake for three hours between 3am and 5am. Call me pedantic if you like, but surely that is only two hours?

When I suggested he was slightly arithmetically challenged he accused me of picking on him, which I do not deny. As an example, he brought up the story in yesterday's offering, about how he lost tooth. I suggested that with the missing implant he looked a bit like a pirate, especially as he was tucking into some After-Eight mints at the time. I think he had eight pieces, or would that be pieces of eight?

Conveniently for an arch observer like my good self, he went on to complain about what he would have to go through before his tooth could be properly repositioned. Polygrip was mentioned and I asked if this might be the name if his parrot. Then he was gone again, with that mad faraway look we have all come to love.

Talking of looks, his steely-eyed goddess of a trophy wife, Lisa, who is rather too young for him, has one of those looks that I often receive from that Nice Lady Decorator. It is a sort of laser beam stare of such ferocity you forget who you are. I was the unlucky recipient of one such beam last night after she had said that she could count on her hands the number of times something or other had happened, certainly less than ten. I laughed at this mathematically-challenging concept but then the laser beam was tuned to stun. Suddenly I had a look on my face. "Rabbit in the headlights" sums it up.

A little like mosquitoes, but no less annoying, tourists are supposedly in short supply this summer, but whilst the spraying of the River Brague and the lakes, such as the Etang in Mougins, seems to have worked wonders in reducing the mosquito population, there is apparently not a similar treatment that is as effective on tourists.

There have been some worthy attempts to stem the tourist tide, the euro crisis which has reduced the comfort for them. The Olympic Games being staged in the UK has also stemmed the tide, giving them an excuse not to come over here, but nothing has been as effective with tourists as that spraying has been with mosquitos.

Don't get me wrong, some tourists are very welcome. As long as they have bought a copy of my book then they are very welcome. However, quite a large proportion of tourists have not done of this and I think a bit of spraying would in these cases be in order.

Aboard L'Exocet on the way back from St Tropez

Chapter 10

Irritating Tourists

Talking of irritating tourists, I must also prepare for the imminent arrival of Mr. Clipbeard (formerly known as Mr. Clipboard) on Sunday. He will be here for the whole of July, so I must be strong in the face of adversity. Actually that also describes him very well, "Mr. Clipboard, the face of adversity." He will want to lose to me at tennis and golf during his stay and I will be doing my best to accommodate him. He will, of course, be pathetically pastily-pallid having not seen the sun since last year but I think that makes him better looking.

Whilst that Nice Lady Decorator would support the catastrophic canine Banjo through thick and thin, contrary to my basic instincts, and frankly the instincts of any right-thinking man or woman, we do agree that the senior dog, the amiable springer called Max requires special attention. Thus yesterday, in the face of the injury he had sustained whilst out walking, that Nice Lady Decorator found some bandages and a bottle of the astringent antiseptic TCP in order to administer repairs. This should never been confused with PCP, or Angel Dust as it is known in some quarters.

Exhausted by this activity, and with the arrival in the late afternoon sunshine of Peachy and Suzanne Butterfield, who were on their way to the Mougins School Pass Out Parade, otherwise known as graduation, and who were in need of a restorative graduating glass of rose, a bottle or several were opened. It has been very hot recently, and in our house a couple of ice cubes are often dropped into the wine to ensure it does not get warm. What was a bit of a surprise was that the piece of ice that was assigned to my glass smelled of TCP. As I sniffed the wine, the overpowering aroma knocked me to the floor. "I needed a bit of ice to cool his foot," said that Nice Lady Decorator, but why she had to put that particular piece back in the freezer so that it could be served to me in my rose is a question to which I did not receive an answer. Had it been the lunchtime after she could perhaps have argued that it was the hair of the dog?

We stayed in. Just think of that for a moment, we stayed in whilst living in the Cote D'Azur in summer. It is such a rare treat not to have a social engagement that I really enjoyed it. We sat under the stars savouring a glass of red Roussillon wine from a tiny vineyard called Terrasous in south-west France that we discovered a decade ago and which remains one of our favourites, in the warmth and in complete harmony and at one with the world. That was until that Nice Lady Decorator attempted to alter the style of clothing that both Sprog 1 and 2 were planning to wear for the post-graduation festivities. She has never fully embraced the concept of the subjective or indeed of personal sartorial choice and she clearly has a monopoly on opinion, a monopoly that both Sprogs, in their infinite wisdom, chose to question. There will be blood.

My picture today, rather than being taken by Slash and Burn Thornton Allan from The Big Picture is actually a picture of the man himself. I snapped this earlier in the week in the web when he finally managed to find the golf tee he had been looking for. Quite why it looks like it has been burned at one end is a bit of a mystery. Perhaps that is why it had a rather evocative aroma?

When I spoke to him later, he claimed that the tee was burned due to the velocity of his swing through the ball. I think he has been smoking something funny.

Call me a tart if you like, but when the opportunity to spend the planned 70 or so euros on a round of golf with the Landlubbers was set against the late offer of revisiting Tahiti Beach at St Tropez aboard a private yacht, what can one do? It will still cost me 70 euros for lunch, but that will be after a cruise down the coast of the

Mediterranean, a nice lunch, a shed-full of rose, dancing with girls a third of one's age, drinking a great deal of, well, everything and the floating back.

So that's where my golf tee went

The alternative was to be baked on a golf course, spend a great deal of time looking for golf balls in deep forest, finding every bunker that Adolf Hitler ever invented and discussing the fact that trees are 90% water. It took a great deal of consideration but in the end I erred on the side of debauchery, and I don't mean the golf.

It all started when Master Mariner Mundell tacked into our garden just after lunch demanding beers and rose, and who am I to be contrary? He was after some pictures from our trip to the same place last Sunday, and had popped in on the off-chance, having previously ensured we would be in. These public schoolboys don't like to leave anything to chance. When the iPad was a tad uncooperative on the photograph front, there seemed no alternative but to do it all again today. The invitation was issued and immediately accepted by that Nice Lady Decorator and hence golf today was postponed.

Almost as the Master departed, Le Grande Peche and delectable slim line Madame Peche hoved into view, demanding similar treatment. Yet more rose and some Prosecco were pushed into service to accommodate said needs, brought about by their tenancy ending for summer and needing to store stuff in our garage for summer.

The lovely Suzanne raised the temperature a little by guiding me through some of the gardening tasks she had been required to undertake this week. She has an innocent look about her that can be deceptive. This is best illustrated by her pronouncement that she has a gardening bikini. Better than that, it seems it is a micro bikini, and is fuschia pink. Frankly, by the time I had considered the options it could have been rancid polecat pink and I would still not had enough room in my mouth for my tongue, but old age does that to you. Peachy refers to her as "the old coote" which coming from a fat northern git is a bit hard to take. I remonstrated with him that his description was a little harsh but he said that as a coote was water foul (not his spelling) such a description was like water off a duck's back. No, I do not understand either.

Mr. Clipboard received a warning (in triplicate) that we would not now be in Valbonne at the appointed hour this evening (bad show, on report no doubt) and this morning I must venture to local supermarket, Super U, now open on a Sunday for the next two months (hurrah!) to secure supplies for the intended voyage to St Tropez.

So rather delightfully, plans have been altered and St Tropez now beckons. As it is the weekend, I need not feel guilty about doing little for Currencies Direct, but then one never knows who else will be aboard L'Exocet, perhaps there will be a potential customer? Certainly when it comes to submitting the standard outrageous bill for lunch to my accountant, I do hope so.

Tahiti Beach, Again

Public school boys, don't you just love them? Yesterday, aboard l'Exocet, the 47 foot long sailing boat owned by Master Mariner Mundell was like a public schoolboy reunion. Apart from the Master himself, there were two other of this particular species on board for the trip down to Tahiti Beach at St Tropez for lunch. You can identify them almost immediately. They exude a misplaced sense of superiority and almost every conversation contains a reference to "school sports" as I think they like to refer to buggery.

Endless stories emanated, with beatings, homosexual acts and disdain for those amongst us (oiks) who do not share in their bizarre pride of, and in some cases, clear enjoyment of, the public schoolboy antics lacerating their soul to the fore. It started early with a chap called "Largy", who, given his ability to consume alcohol is clearly short for Lager, mentioning that he was about to go to Venice and wondering aloud if "man on man" would be possible in a gondola. He is an old Harrovian which is to say we was at school at Harrow. I wonder if former Borstall inmates are called Borstallians?

On the voyage over I accused Largy of being half cut, but he said as he was Jewish he was fully cut and that was sufficient for me to "end" that particular conversation.

Allo allo, what's all this then?

By the time we got to the restaurant, his loud pronouncements on his chosen theme attracted the attention of the local gendarmes as my picture above captures. I suggest that Largy, the chap who seems to have lost his hair, is exhibiting a love of men in uniforms. At one stage he even made the subject of getting tied up to a mooring boy (buoy?) sound a little tacky. His stated aim was to form the BBB party, a political organisation to Bring Back Buggery. I could go on as I have notes on my BlackBerry about "potage d'homme" and several other items, but enough is enough.

Art For Art's Sake

Now, let's talk about art. Today is the moment of truth for one aspiring artist who will no doubt be overjoyed to have their work selected to appear on the jacket of this, my second book which you now hold in your hand or on your Kindle. The judging will take place today at Marina Kulik's painting studio at lunchtime today. I do so look forward to any event that is all about me.

The decision was made. A painting of my good self by Sandra Seymour-Dale was the victor and is now on the cover.

It was the sort of lunch I love. It was all about me so what could possibly go wrong? Well, a thunderstorm at the exact moment the decision-making process came to a head could have been interpreted in two ways: either as a message from the gods to draw back before it is too late, or, the interpretation I favour, the ideal portent for the storming success that will overtake the literary world once the book sees the light of day.

If I had a criticism of the winning painting it would be the inclusion of a demon dog on the brim of the hat. I think it would have been more apt had the heinous hound Banjo (for it is an image of him) had been on my shoulder, much as in the expression "a monkey on your shoulder" which is sometimes used to describe a bad luck omen or something you are trying to get rid of. Need I go on?

Talking of getting rid of animals, I heard a story at the very convivial lunch that followed the momentous book cover decision. It seems that one of the ladies from the group had a neighbour who moved abroad to Germany. When they arrived at their new home, the first thing out of the removal van was their neighbour's cat. I asked what happened next. It appears that the neighbours did not much like the cat so it stayed with the family who moved. This gave me an idea. If any of you are moving soon, especially if it is a long distance away, please let me know, as Banjo enjoys long drives.

Opinion is split as to whether I chose correctly, but frankly I love being the bone of contention. Many people believe that the painting by the amiable Dutchman, Wim Teunissen, below, was the best. He did his very best to "lobby" me before the result was announced by giving me three fine Cohiba cigars having given up smoking himself, and I respect that. I am always in favour of bribery. He received many votes; mostly it must be said from people with suspiciously Dutch names. Surely that will be no manipulation of the vote? Perhaps we need some international observers to ensure everything is free and fair? Perhaps I should take his suggestion that a chap from Holland should be put in charge?

My image at the Wim of the painter

I thought it only fair to include all the other paintings submitted for the competition so here they are;

Painted by Fiona Biziouhttp://www.bizioufinona.com/

Painted by Cathie van der Stel who is happy to be commissioned to undertake portraits.http://www.cathievanderstel.com/

THE VALBONNE MONOGUES

Painted by Brenda Moorhouse

Painted by "Bevvy"

THE VALBONNE MONOLOGUES

*Painted by Sandra Seymour-Dale who would also painted the picture on
the cover and will happily accept commissions for portraits:
sandraseymourdale@yahoo.co.uk*

Yesterday's late afternoon solitude was disturbed by a rather
vulgar two-door convertible Mercedes, covered in bird shit, wheel
spinning up the drive. It was Master Mariner Mundell who was in
need of water. You would think he had enough water around him,
living mostly on his boat, but that was not the point, he wanted
mine. It seems that washing one's car in sea water when the sea
gulls have paid their respects it is not recommended and the port
authorities take a dim view of car washing in situ. Now you may
wonder why I am telling you this, and you make take the view that
this unannounced visit may be used as an excuse to break my iron
will to have a full day without a drink, and you would be right.
Having effectively irrigated all 2000+ square meters of my garden
with his unsupervised use of my hose pipe, he demanded beer
before setting sail. As a consummate host I complied, and a man
cannot drink alone, so, yes, that Nice Lady Decorator and I
backslid.

The Dream Scenario

I have invented the concept in tennis of the dream scenario. It is a rare animal that involves me serving to win the set. These are rare enough moments, but a double dream scenario is even rarer and is where I am serving for the set and the match. Imagine my delight then about the Moustachioed Old Gits, comprising myself and the Wingco, achieving a never-before-witnessed, unique, triple dream scenario last night against Dancing Greg Harris and his batman, Blind Lemon Milsted. Two sets up and with nothing more than pride to play for (and the Lord knows they have little enough of that), our opponents slumped to 0-2 down in the third set. It was at that stage that I worked out that if we won the next 3 games we would be 5-0 up with me to serve. I may have mentioned this to them, it may have been discussed, loudly, by me, and I may have predicted such a scenario out loud, repeatedly as we won each game in turn, and so it came to pass. A triple dream scenario, winning all three sets, the match and the last set 6-0 on my serve. I now know what Christians believe heaven will be like if it existed, which of course it does not.

Earlier I thought I had smelled fear. The Wingco is of course habitually late; indeed I have measured a unit of time also known as a Wingco which is approximately 7 minutes long. This is the minimum amount of time he is behind schedule. Last night for instance he was a full 3 Wingco's late. However when both of our opponents were similarly delayed I began searching in my tennis bag for that white feather, the traditional mark of the coward that I keep there for situations like this, in readiness for their eventual arrival.

As we sat with a beer outside the Vignale's now open bar, a very good early sign from the new owners, to discuss this momentous occasion, I sensed that our opponents were a little less willing to enjoy the moment. It was just a slight feeling, a nuance if you like. I can't quite put my finger on it but perhaps the expression "for f*cks sake shut up" was what enlivened my senses.

I changed the subject, well no, that is not strictly true, as it was once again all about me, to the painting competition staged at Marina Kulik's painting class. All present, with the obvious exception of the Wingco who refuses point-blank to read my daily column, "ghastly" he calls it, had seen some or all of the paintings, and whilst admiration for the artists was expressed, it seems that in some people's mind the subject matter left something to be desired. The general opinion, in which I did not share, was that they had all performed marvels with so little with which to work. Jealousy can be so destructive.

Mognipotent

I have invented a new word which I think adequately describes the MOGS superiority over all comers on the tennis court. Mognipotent somehow sums up the biblical scale of our omnipotence over any opponents who dare to challenge us. Yesterday for instance, we were challenged by Mr. Clipboard and Smouldering Nick Davies.

"Smouldering"? I hear you say? Sadly I was specifically forbidden to reveal why he has this new epithet, save to say that in his younger, I was going to say wilder days, a statement that is barely credible given current wildness quotients, there was an unfortunate incident involving fire. That is all I am permitted to reveal.

I cannot even say that he lit up the restaurant, as that may be misconstrued, or that after his tennis defeat he had to be hosed down. I am even precluded from going into the darker side of events that occurred in his childhood (in the late 1890s?) Instead I am asked to concentrate on his "lighter" side. I can say that he was no "match" for the MOGS.

Lunch then was taken at the Auberge St Donat; the French equivalent of a transport cafe except the food is very good. Amongst those present was the Master Mariner Mundell who has kindly invited us aboard L'Exocet for the Cannes Bay firework festival on Bastille Day, the 14th of July. I believe that the firework displays are best viewed from the sea rather than the crowded coast.

He is currently living on his boat and last week he came to our house in order to clean his car. I cheekily mentioned at lunch that I had expected him to come the next day with his washing. His retort, that it was in a bag in his car, was not quite what I expected, and I can hear our washing machine straining at maximum as I write.

Mr. Clipboard did not attend lunch, which was a bad show, merely partaking of a beer before leaving. His excuse; that he was lunching with his parents, was clearly a fabrication as I am certain that they left for Scotland last night. I believe that he hates being beaten (with the obvious exception of course of being beaten at his public school in that kind, loving, public schoolboy manner of his youth) at anything by anyone, least of all tennis by an oik like me.

Slash and Burn sent me a gloomy picture of life in England, where the sky is currently emptying itself of rain to be sure that it will be dry from late July when my exile commences. I felt the need to return the favour, so I took this picture illustrating the privations that we are experiencing at present. Can you see that there is no ice in my post-lunch, pre-siesta, glass of rose? Life is tough here as well.

Things can be tough here as well. The nearest ice is over 30 metres away in the fridge.

298

I was told, at the outset, that it was going to be a quiet pre-Wimbledon lunch. Of course it was a last-minute call, my finding out for certain that we had a luncheon engagement with Suzie and Norman Philpot barely an hour before lunch was convened at Auberge de la Source at Sophia Antipolis.

Quiet was the inoperative word, otherwise how could the quiet lunch have ended with us going back to theirs, that Nice Lady Decorator finding herself fully clothed in the swimming pool whilst I donned cricket pads and bat and faced a bowling machine set at 80 miles per hour? I have a picture of this as today's feature in support of my position. Surely every right thinking ex-pat should have a bowling machine for use on a boules court?

Boys with toys

The exact sequence of events is still a little hazy, and as I write I have no idea who won the ladies version of Wimbledon, or indeed if it actually took place. Norman and Suzie Philpot are dangerous and beautiful respectively. She was no less beautiful when laid on their hall floor "sleeping" in the early evening after boules, cricket and copious amounts of wine, and at which point departure seemed the best course of action. He is dangerous, full stop.

Earlier, we had partaken of the usual power march around the local forests, where we have found a plum tree producing the best fruit in the world, and from which we took strength in order to deal with the privations of lunch. As I write, that Nice Lady Decorator, who had a girly dinner planned for this evening, sadly now cancelled, at least as far as she is concerned, is snoring blissfully in a way she will utterly deny tomorrow. Sensibly, I have made a video recording of her snoring. You can never know when such evidence might come in useful in the defence of crimes I have not yet committed.

So last evening did not really start at all. Awaking from a late siesta at around 9pm was a privilege to which I alone was privy. That Nice Lady Decorator was, in boxing parlance "out for the count" and thus I was forced to feed myself. It is a fact that most men have no idea how the cooker works, and only a rudimentary understanding of something called a microwave, so an Indian take-away from Valbonne's Le Kashmir seemed the best course of action.

Being summer, and with the Indian besieged by tourists, I was informed that my order would take some 45 minutes to be prepared. Luckily, La Kavanou, the wine bar in Valbonne, is close by so I ventured in for a short while. I know that I am not very welcome there after an unfortunate incident after my book launch, for which I was not to blame, when Master Mariner Mundell and his arm wrestling antics pushed us down the list of desirable customers. So low down the list that we have been forced to avoid it since. Anyway, I was welcomed with open wallet and spent an interesting half hour talking to a wonderful chap about the meaning of life and everything.

Sprog's Defeat Dinner

Who would willingly have children?

I have made it clear to mine that they were their mother's idea and I had very little to do with their conception. Much as I love them now, having to reject an invitation last night to dine with the most stylish man to emerge from the sixties, Anthony "Dock Of the" Bay, and his impossible young and gorgeous wife, Amanda, because we had previously promised to take the Sprogs out for a meal, stuck in my craw. Anthony may have been wearing his bottle green crushed velvet suit, or maybe his silk Indian house coat, both undoubtedly fantastic photo opportunities for this column.

He mentioned that he had considered sending me an email expressing dissatisfaction about our non-appearance. It was to have taken the theme of "how dare a grammar school oik refuse a gracious invitation from a former public schoolboy", but had decided against it as he thought it might appear in a slightly edited form in this daily column, but nothing could be further from the truth. It would have been heavily edited.

Anthony was, of course, present at the lunch at the turn of the year at the Auberge St Donat when a number of public schoolboy bullies held me down and forcibly removed my luxuriant beard, and then claimed it was an accident. Indeed it was from this lunch that Mr. Clipbeard had his named changed from Mr. Clipboard. Anthony claimed that he never took part in this event but I was able to show him this rather grainy photograph taken on the day which forms the basis of the case for the prosecution.

The physical assault on my person on that day had very little to do with my beard, minor irritant that it was intended to be, but was in fact rooted in jealousy. My first book had just been published, to considerable acclaim at least in my daily column. Many of these chaps consider the whole idea of a self-made man like myself, from what they consider to be a lower caste, writing and publishing a book, to be an affront, which required punishment or at least a little humiliation. Mr. Clipboard had bought a copy and then proceeded ritually to torture and eventually destroy it. This would have hurt had he not paid for it, but a sale is a sale. The book, a living, vibrant commentary about the lives of the idle rich in Valbonne, was then the subject of an attack, which I felt as if it was my own soul being abused. Fire was used, a picture of one of my genitals (one of which they claimed was visible on the front cover - in fact it was my knee) was attacked and many pages were ripped out and used as paper planes. Anthony claimed that he did not involve himself, but when I found and showed him the incontrovertible evidence in this photo he changed his story, saying that he was merely passing the paper plane, shown in his hand, back to a fellow public schoolboy, but in the time-honoured "food fight" manner to which these chaps are clearly accustomed. It is a shaky defence and one that I intend to destroy in much the way my book was destroyed.

Imminent Departure Looms

The whole world is changing. I am having to move back to the UK for much of the rest of this year, banks can no longer be trusted, and neither can Mr. Clipbeard aka Mr. Clipboard, well-known as the pedantic timekeeping ogre who has, wait for it, both changed the timing of tennis at the Vignale today AND then cancelled. Is nothing sacred? It was something of a surprise then that he actually turned up at the Cafe des Arcades in a packed Valbonne square last evening having booked a table. I took up this point with him, that the two words with which I most associate him are "anally" and "punctual." It is fair to say that he was not best pleased by this observation.

A tirade aimed at non-public schoolboys (ie me) followed but I forgave him as he is currently living in a household of nine where he is the only male (although perhaps a chromosome test might be relevant just to be sure.)

The lovely Mrs. Clipboard was there and was excited about an invitation she had received, and extended to those present, to what seems to me to be an opportunity to watch paint dry. That Nice Lady Decorator gets all excited by anything to do with paints, decorating and especially a paint-making company called Farrow and Ball. Imagine her delight then to be invited to champagne reception at Raymond Blanc's Le Manoir aux Quat' Saisons in September to hear a talk about paint? She is already spitting feathers as it seems that oil based paints are being phased out and she needs an explanation of exactly what is being done to ensure that she can continue her decorating duties without recourse to water-based paints.

I was not aware that they are being phased out, and, like all right-thinking people, was not remotely interested, however I know she is very concerned and will have something to say to these people. Elephant's Breath (the ridiculous name of one of their colours) will be as nothing compared with the vitriol that they will be receiving if no alternative is forthcoming.

It is now hot here, so hot that even I, a confirmed non-swimmer, have had to seek solace in our swimming pool for extended periods in order to cool down. What is sometimes a little disconcerting whilst so engaged is to hear a loud splash and then find a spaniel swimming by with a tennis ball in his mouth as my picture today shows.

Dog with tennis ball, no this is not Wimbledon

This is Max, the fine old family (stone deaf) pet loved by all and he is welcome to use the pool at any time. There is however another dog who also uses my pool but he uses it without my permission. I have explained to Banjo, the calamitous canine who survives only due to the patronage of that Nice Lady Decorator, in words of one syllable, that he must not go in as he is not welcome but he feigns deafness and takes no notice.

Pink Floyd In The Pav

"I am tired and will go to bed early," said that Nice Lady Decorator as we took a late afternoon trip into Antibes on the train to buy something or other which was very important to one of us, but for the life of me I cannot recall what it was. As I write it is coming up to 2am and I can hear her listening to Pink Floyd in the Pav at neighbour-incensing volume whilst I try to get the earplugs to block out the cacophony. I like Pink Floyd in small doses and at sensible volume, neither of which I am hearing at the moment. In fact I cannot hear my own brain. The gendarmes will surely be here soon to put me and the rest of Valbonne out of its misery. Either that or I will have to bail her out again tomorrow.

On the way back on the train from Antibes, after a couple of pints of Murphy's and several Desperados respectively, at the Blue Lady, we decided to stop at the very French town of Mouans Sartoux for dinner, and very good it was as well, and at 50% of what it would have cost in Valbonne during this, the tourist season. It was at this point that she got the second wind.

Earlier, tennis had been postponed because try as I might, I could find no one willing to partner Mr. Clipbeard. That he is boring and a poor tennis player is not how I would describe him, although there are others who would. Another court has been booked for this evening and so far I have six rejections of the opportunity to partner him. Perhaps I can find someone who does not know him.

So now there is barely two weeks to go before the rain will stop in England as I leave the Channel Tunnel and land on English soil for the foreseeable future. I am certain that my arrival back will see the sun emerge from those pesky clouds and all will be well, in fact I predict more hose pipe bans by the end of August. I am often asked how I will deal with the enforced move back and I say "badly". There is some small solace in that Arundel looks beautiful, the Arundel Festival looks like a mini Edinburgh Festival and the house we are buying has a small garden with a gate into the next door pub's garden, so I don't even have to go off my property before I get to a pub. If it has wifi, or if my wifi reaches the bar, then I think I know where my new office reception area will be.

What sort of chap reneges on post-tennis dinner on the spurious pretext that his wife expects him back for dinner? Could it be the same kind of chap that decides, amidst another thrashing, that he does not like the surface upon which we are playing and whines to such an extent that we switch the match from clay to a hard court after he has lost the first set? I cannot reveal who was responsible for both these misdemeanours but I will say that Mr. Clipboard is a cad and a bounder.

It is a long-held tradition that, unless apologies are received in writing in advance, anyone selected to play tennis on a Wednesday evening is expected to partake of a post-tennis pizza. Simply dipping out of this arrangement without warning is an example of impossibly bad manners which, if I am honest, is a fitting description of the general behaviour of a former Wellingtonian public schoolboy whom I shall not mention, but he knows to whom this refers.

It is bad enough that our leader, Dancing Greg Harris had pleaded that he had a migraine or his period or something and had made his excuses (and had received the white feather for cowardice) not to play, but at least he did not let us down at the last moment. Thus the Wingco and Nick "Trousers Down" Davies and I took Pizza at the Auberge St Donat, newly open for the evening in summer.

It appears that all three of us, together with respective spouses, plus even a certain backslider, whom I have mentioned above but not named, are invited aboard Master Mariner Mundell's boat (the subject of my picture below) for the Bastille Day fireworks in Cannes this coming Saturday evening. I am reasonably confident that the three of us who did adhere to last evening's dinner arrangement will show up, but am less confident about the manners and reliability of the fourth.

The Master can take only 12 aboard L'Exocet, but has come up with a cunning wheeze to increase the numbers. By taking a RIB, a kind of dinghy, with us, which seats 11, we can tie it up to the boat and bingo -- we can have 23 aboard at anchor. The Wingco is bringing his guitar and Blind Lemon Milsted is expected back from the States where he has gone to see a man about a job; I feel an evening of ad-libbing musical firework nonsense may not be far away.

Fireworks aboard on Saturday

That Nice Lady Decorator flew back to London yesterday to help the unremittingly untidy Sprog 2 clean out her room at her digs in Kensington. She has taken with her the largest and most durable rubber gloves (called Marigold,) some industrial strength detergent and a paint scraper to see if she can return the room to a state in which we have some hope of retrieving the deposit. So last night there was no one at home to look after me, thus I had in mind a quiet nightcap in the Pav. Stupidly, I had forgotten that sprog 1 was at home looking after my beers and wine and he had thoughtfully invited about twenty thirsty teenagers to help in that effort. I know I should have retired to my bed and not spent at least an hour regaling them with stories about my career in the music industry. I just know when I am being funny. At least I think they were laughing with me, not at me.

One of the lovely aspects of living in France is the gourmet food available from any number of local restaurants, and the quality of the diet in general, with the emphasis on the lovely fresh local fruit and vegetables. So with the Nice Lady Decorator busy in the kitchen after returning from London, and with wonderful aromas reaching me in the web last night where I was nursing the first beer of the day, I was understandably salivating over whatever it was she was creating. She has been away over 30 hours and as I hardly even know where the kitchen is, let alone any of the machinery that does the cooking, I was hungry. So what was the treat? A tray of scotch eggs and some small pork chipolatas.

It seems that as we will be away for an extended period we must "eat the freezer." Apparently, as the freezer, well one of them, needs to be empty by the 25th July, our proposed leaving date, in readiness for when the summer guardian arrives, we have either to eat or trash its contents, so it looks like I am in for some gastronomic treats in the coming weeks.

For instance, I am not sure how I will react, with the temperatures hovering around 30 degrees during the day, to an unfrozen Christmas Pudding, which I happen to know is currently languishing in there. And who bought the frozen mince pies? At least it will be a period of rekindling my knowledge of English food.

Yesterday was too hot to do much and it looks like being much the same today, so what a sensible idea it is to play tennis today at 11am. There is a slight change of personnel today in that we have found someone who has not played with Mr. Clipboard for some time so may have forgotten what it is like. John Coward is a British Airways pilot who lives locally and is famous for being the co-pilot of the Boeing 777 that crash-landed at Heathrow a few years ago, just getting over the perimeter fence when the engines cut out. I do hope he has enough stamina to make it through the match without cutting out early. The usual jokes will undoubtedly reappear, for instance, should he hit the ball in the net, a cry of "up a bit" will be irresistible to some, such as me. The lob may attach "what goes up must come down" and the like. I think you get the picture.

There is just a chance that we will pop into the Auberge St Donat for lunch thereafter as another tennis quartet involving Milsted (Blind Lemon), Harris (Dancing), Bay (Dock Of The) and Mundell (Master Mariner) play at a similar time, and although the quality may be somewhat lacking, their enthusiasm is touching. Also, their commitment is open to question as they book just an hour whilst we shall have two hours. What is that expression about Englishmen and the midday sun?

On a slightly different note Roly Bufton called to ask what was the form for taking a boat into the Bay of Cannes as he would like to take his for the fireworks. There will be hundreds of other boats doing the same. He had previously sought advice from the naked former politician who advised him to anchor, and then stay anchored for some time until all the drunken boat parties had left, before returning to port. I do hope he was not referring to us.

Clipboard Speaks

As we sat at lunch at the Auberge St Donat, Mr. Clipboard was extolling the virtues of Le Clos De Pins a new restaurant at nearby Roquefort Les Pins. I am not sure if it was deliberate or not, but the Wingco mistakenly thought he was praising Northern Irish singer Clodagh Rogers, responsible for the UK's entry into Song For Europe several decades ago or more.

I mentioned that I had once been involved in Song For Europe some decades earlier as manager of Belle And The Devotions, the UK representative in the competition in, I think 1982, but I do not think they believed me

I am afraid that I have to report that one particular public schoolboy present was a huge fan of our Clodagh and admitted to his first sexual feelings, and it seems results, when confronted with pictures of Ms. Rogers in the 1970's. Of course, as he is my friend, I could never reveal publicly who was this love-lorn teenager but I would be prepared to bet that Mr. Clipboard is, as he reads this, experiencing some tumescence.

Lunch was, once again, all about me. The theme was how the public schoolboy bullies (as, except for me, all the other lunchers were from that ilk) could best punish me for my witty and erudite daily column and book (which, if I am honest, is not how any of them viewed either publication). I think it was when I mentioned that this week I will pass 70,000 hits on this web page that the trouble started.

As all present are invited aboard the Master Mariner Mundell's boat this evening, a litany of jealous ritual abuse aimed at me was discussed which I think was designed to try to reduce or "water" down my daily output. Keel hauling was mentioned, with special mention for the barnacles on the boat that might be able to sustain further physical damage, along with plank walking and, rather inevitably, buggery, cutting off one side of my luxuriant handle bar moustache, and one of them went as far as saying I was a cad. I am constantly amazed at how bullying has left its mark on these chaps. When I suggested that, in fact, what they were contemplating amounted to same, I was told that I did not understand what real bullying was all about, and that this was just a bit of fun. Real bullying, I was told, was much worse.

Further denigration of my achievement of leaving my poverty stricken roots behind and managing to drag myself out of the gutter by sheer hard work and ability (again, not how they saw it) was illustrated by one comment concerning the curriculum of Belleville School, in deepest south London which I attended as opposed to the very public school Wellington: "we had athletics, you had car theft".

Earlier, we had exhibited all the qualities admired around the world as Englishmen. We had played tennis at midday in scorching 32 degrees and unremitting sunshine, the only court of 11 in use, where an honourable draw was the result prior to lunch. John Coward, the BA pilot and Mr. Clipboard's partner was unable to clear that final hurdle to join us. Let us thank god his Boeing 777 did not suffer the same fate when he was the co-pilot when the engines on the plane he was driving cut out on the approach to Heathrow some years ago. That hurdle, the airport perimeter fence, was mercifully scaled, but only just.

Mr. Clipboard is an acknowledged nut when it comes to new technology. He is the first to buy a new bit of kit as soon as it comes out before it has been tested and shown to be useless. I bet he even bought a Sinclair C5. Last night as we sat on his wonderful terrace watching the sun go down over the Esterel hills, he showed us his latest retail triumph.

We were on the terrace, from where I took this picture, as the Cannes Firework display was postponed until Monday due to wind, and being a poor sailor and, with that Nice Lady Decorator a little under the weather, we decided not to accept the Master Mariner Mundell's kind invitation to what he called "plan B", which probably would have meant him having lots of fun sailing madly on a force 6 whilst his guests aboard parted company with the gallons of rose they had consumed before departure.

What is that wine glass doing to the view?

But back to Mr. Clipboard; Flying in last week on Easyjet, he had been attracted by one of their very worthy offers to buy an iPhone cover enabling you to use it underwater and take pictures. Basically it is a plastic see-through bag into which you place your iPhone and for which he paid a ridiculous 20 euros. I could have sold him something similar for 2 euros. Anyway he was very pleased with his purchase and was in his pool trying it out when he received a phone call. Sadly, that is when the design fault was revealed. You can answer your phone underwater but the bag is obviously sealed and no sound can be heard.

The Wingco and his lovely wife Maryse were also aboard the terrace. The gathering had been an impromptu response to the firework display being postponed, and the last-minute idea was to drink the wine and eat the nibbles that we had prepared for the boat trip. The Wingco, who still maintains that this daily column is "ghastly" despite claiming never to have read it, was determined to do his best to ensure there was no discussion about it because in his words "nobody reads it". I wish I had been able to capture his expression when his wife said "I read it" and then the equally beautiful Mrs. Clipboard admitted that she too read it and thought it was good. It was very rewarding for me and then the paintings created for my next book came up in discussion. Opinion was mixed but overall the feeling was that I had made the right choice. Anyway, I became slightly embarrassed that the discussion was all about me so I tried to change the subject. "That's enough about me" I said, "now let's talk about my blog".

Modern Art Is All Crap; Discuss

Tennis will reconvene this morning, and it will be very interesting as we have the usual bright sunshine as I write but a force 6 mistral is blowing. I am not sure if my usual lobbing game is best suited to playing in a gale but I am about to find out. Obviously, playing outside may be an alien concept for my UK readers who, it seems, mostly play their tennis inside huge hangars, another aspect of life in England to which I am not looking forward.

Having conceded the first set 6 – 1 in poor conditions on tennis court number 11 at the Vignale yesterday morning, where the position of the sun is a hindrance to quality play, Mr. Clipboard was chipper, claiming "the blog was writing itself". This is a comment that I often make when something funny and reportable in this column is or has just occurred.

On one level I was pleased to hear this comment as, once again, the subject of my daily writings was the topic of discussion, and, as you all know by now I love it when it's all about me. The Wingco, who has held a consistently negative view of this daily missive, at once attempted without much success to change the subject. As it turns out, Mr. Clipbeard was correct as, two sets later, having changed courts, the Moustachioed Old Gits were triumphantly downing a victorious beer having trounced our opponents by two sets to one and the blog had indeed begun to write itself.

Several beers were consumed during the post-mortem, or indeed the victory roll depending on whether one was a loser or a winner. After tennis, I adjourned to discuss this momentous victory with that Nice Lady Decorator and I am afraid that I have to report that she was less than impressed with my fulsome description of this famous triumph. I can still hear the words "who gives a fu*k?" Women will never fully understand tennis, or winning.

No, no and no

Dotted about Valbonne at the moment are a series of hideous sculptures of the kind beloved by the French and the kind of idiots who see merit in the entries for The Turner Prize. Modern art is of course a complete con, fooling all of its followers all of the time. The only reason I am glad to see such a beautiful village festooned with so much garbage is that it gives me something to write about and photograph, as I have here.

I was going to describe this piece as a" load of bollocks" but as

312

you can see, the bollocks are in the wrong place, above the penis. This is a measure of the lack of talent of the artist, getting a simple detail like that wrong. I have been told I am a Philistine, but I have no idea why the lack of appreciation for modern art might signal me as a man who would collect stamps.

No plans existed for lunch or any sort of entertainment until well after midday (try 5 minutes) when we received a call from Roly and Poly Bufton demanding that we join them for lunch. As it happened, I took the call and explained to them in some detail why we could not indulge them due to some gardening alterations, in which we were deeply involved, that had been imposed upon me by that Nice Lady Garden Designer. I described it as a fatwa, which I think meant that a fat bloke had to do a lot of digging, but once I handed the phone over to that nice lady lunch organiser, the day took on a different perspective.

She decided in an instant that their suggestion should receive an affirmative and so, with a silent prayer, I divested myself of my gardening apparel, took a shower and spent some time tending my luxuriant handle bar moustache, just to be sure that my adoring public would not be disappointed should they encounter me in Auberge De la Source. As it turned out, I need not have worried. There was only one admirer of this column at the table, indeed in the restaurant, and that was the writer.

Perhaps I am being disingenuous. The lovely Lesley (Poly) has admitted to dipping into the salacious delights of this daily missive, but had some words of warning. The theme of this was how I would be able to continue this labour of love, maintaining a newsworthy focus on Valbonne, when living in exile in Arundel, which I shall be forced to do in less than two weeks' time.

Gamesmanship

I want only to talk about the second set, as, during the first set the sun and heat seemed to get to the Wingco and he came over all aggressive, trying to hit the cover off the tennis ball. Once I had calmed him, normal "service" was resumed and an honourable draw agreed after two hours in gruelling heat.

Lunch at the much improved Vignale Tennis Club was good and Mr. Clipboard only mentioned this column in disparaging terms three or four times, which is a move forward. As he said recently, although in rather different circumstances, he cannot resist the temptation to have a go; "it's like peanut butter in the fridge, if you know it's there you just can't leave it alone".

That gastronomic delight reminded me of a conversation in which I had been involved in the day before with Roly and Poly Bufton. We were discussing truffles, those pungent pieces of mouldy fungus much loved by those gourmet types, of which Lesley (Poly) is one. Seemingly there is a restaurant, I think in Nice, specialising in truffle dishes. Now I don't mind a bit of rum truffle baba or ice cream from time to time, but I am afraid the evil smelling version leaves me a little cold. It seems these little blighter's taste only last about 3 weeks, hence the price. When partaking of a truffle at said restaurant last year, she had to send it back because "it had no taste". Frankly, that would have been a move forward for me, but no matter, in fact come to think of it I have been thrown out of better establishments than that for having no taste, but I digress.

The truffle was sent back and there was some altercation in the kitchen. I suggested that I would be wary of sending anything back anywhere unless it was accompanied by a hesitant attitude and at least a smile, as there are stories about waiters and chefs dealing with difficult customers by abusing their food. It was at this moment that the expression "truffle kerfuffle chuckle" entered my head. It made me smile but that Nice Lady Decorator gave me the look of a less than benevolent waiter.

Night And Day

It was important to get good night's sleep and go to bed early as I had been designated to undertake an airport run this morning to take Sprog 1 to catch his plane back to England. I say this morning but really it was late last night. 7am? What kind of time is that to be getting up?

Any sane person of my age knows full well that it is vital not to get up before 9am, and then only in extreme cases, weddings, funerals etc, in order to be on top form for the day ahead, thus about 10.30 am is the optimum, otherwise, one's normal bed time of 2 30 am is compromised.

That I agreed to make this sacrifice of getting up almost before I had gone to bed was really a stab at self-preservation. Once the two teenage lay-about magnets (Sprogs 1 and 2) have departed I will get my house back and will be able to end the patrols and spot checks necessary to protect the integrity of my fridge. I am not accusing my two darling children of being layabouts, merely that their presence attracts the cream of local teenage laziness, all of whom seem constantly to be thirsty or hungry or both. None of them seem to have homes of their own to go to.

I did consider not going bed at all and staying up until 7am but with the first cricket Test Match between England and South Africa commencing late this morning, and for which my complete attention is required, there really was no choice. Earlier I had hidden the TV remote to ensure it was not hidden from me when it becomes time to watch the cricket, to be contested by the teams ranked 1 and 2 in the world.

Last night, after some keenly fought tennis at the Vignale, we adjourned to the Auberge St Donat for a pizza. Traditionally this is a boys own evening, the kind of which is much beloved by the Wingco but I had decided to surprise him by inviting wives and children to join us. To say he was not pleased may be a slight understatement. The giant moustachioed one was bristling with indignation, muttering constantly about tradition, and girls and children should never be present, until the consumption of several carafes of table wine had calmed him after about 10 minutes. In this respect his ability to dispatch large quantities of wine in a very short space of time rivals, and even exceeds, the combined abilities of the aforementioned teenage layabouts.

Thus dinner for the normal tennis 4 became a rather unwieldy table for 12. In this context, the detailed analysis of the earlier tennis did not have its usual intensity, and I confess that I too partook of a little too much wine which is why I cannot recall the result. I do remember that it was a very good game of tennis between four chums in the sunshine and it is that which is the most important aspect. Winning or losing matters not a jot in these circumstances as we are all winners to be able to enjoy such an event.

As I sat in the web just before sundown I thought the beers tasted a bit odd. The bottles bore the legend " Pure Malt" but it was after the third one had no effect, that I had a good look at the bottle and found to my distress that they were alcohol free. What is the point of that? It's like unsweetened sugar, or bland curry, or soya meat, what purpose does it serve?

Apparently they were bought for now departed sprog 1 who had wisely declined to drink them and then in a misplaced sense of helpfulness, having inspired the drinking of all my real beers, he kindly filled up the fridge with bottles full of this filth. It is a cruel trick to play on a thirsty old man.

Pav Nights Coming To An End

Last night I slipped up to the Pav for some cheese and biscuits and a glass of les Pierres Plats, a favourite Roussillon red, whilst that Nice Lady Decorator flopped down exhausted and went to sleep watching Poirot. What a coincidence-- because that programme does the same for me. She has an excuse though; she is madly cleaning, boxing stuff and generally preparing for our move next week and is so tired she even rejected a last minute invitation to meet up with Roly and Poly, with whom we are supposed to be going on their boat for lunch in Villefranche sur Mer on Sunday.

Sprog 2 has taken to doing a fry-up for many of her friends on most mornings. These friends, who mostly look as though they live under stones are almost without exception from families far more affluent than I, and seem to delight in being entertained at my house at my expense. The expression "grinding the face of the poor" comes to mind. Anyway, recently I was able to photo this output and my picture today is the result. I think she needs a boyfriend.

There was half a plan to go for a pizza tonight at the Auberge St Donat, but in another fine illustration of the ability of the French to ignore the commercial world. It was shut. One may have thought that he word "entrepreneur" being a French word, we may hope to find the restaurant open as it is a Sunday, but no . They only open in the evenings for July and August because of the massive influx of tourists into the area and the evening warmth, so, French intransigence and refusal to adopt what they call "the Anglo-Saxon Experiment" in which the laws of supply and demand and a free market are central, seem to pass them by. Don't you just love it?

I think it is supposed to be two eyes?

The Final Week In Paradise

So now I have just received from that Nice Lady Decorator a list of jobs for today which include mixing more cement, lopping trees,

cutting lavender, cleaning the bar area, getting a Sunday Times, ,
mow lawn, pack clothes and clear garage. Does she not know it is a
Sunday, a day of rest? It's enough to make me consider becoming
religious (only joking Reverend).

With the sun out in England for about the first time this summer,
there was inevitability about yesterday's thunderstorms, the first
rain in two months. Actually it was quite refreshing sitting in the
pav watching the lightning and rain gradually reduce the
temperature to a more comfortable 25 degrees.

As I was sitting there last evening awaiting drinks after another
day of toil and trouble (I did the toil, that Nice Lady Decorator
supplied the trouble), I spotted the "Repulsive" container, featured
in today's picture, a spray designed to deter cats and dogs from
entering a particular area. It was purchased because some
neighbours' cats had decided the pav was a good place in which to
sleep overnight and something had to be done.

Pleasingly, the "repulsive" container featured a picture of a dog
that was the spitting image of Banjo, the name of the truly
unpleasant hound owned by that Nice Lady Decorator. Perhaps I
should not have written "Banjo" under the picture of him on the
"repulsive" spray in felt tip pen, but with him being allowed into the
pav on account of the storm, I could not resist the opportunity to see
how effective this product could be. Sadly, he seemed more
repulsed by the storm and rain than the spray, and just when I was
about to extend the experiment to a no doubt very satisfactory
conclusion, certainly for me, that Nice Lady Decorator arrived,
dripping wet but with a two Bloody Mary's in her hands and a look
in her eye. I admit I was torn. A Bloody Mary was very tempting
but on the other hand a wet and repulsed Banjo was also a great
lure. In the end one look at that Nice Lady Decorators' expression
and I chickened out and took solace with Mary.

Tomorrow morning we shall head for Ventigmilia, just over the
border in Italy to collect supplies of olive oil, parmesan, prosecco
and a cheeky little red that I have found, sufficient to keep out the
cold and wet of England until we are able to return. Frankly to do
that job effectively we would need a pantechnican with a trailer, but

we shall have to make do with cramming as much as we can into the 4 X 4.

He must have modelled for that picture

There is always a moment during the irksome completion of one's daily tasks in the south of France, when one dreams of lunch, even if time constraints look like they make such an idea impossible on paper. Such was the case yesterday when we had completed the so-called "booze cruise" across the border to Italy and back by 11 30. Consider this; 36 bottles of prosecco, 12 bottles of a decent red, 2 bottles of Absolut vodka, a bottle of Havana Club rum and a 5 litre can of virgin olive oil, all for under £200. With such success it seemed an obvious reason to celebrate, so we did, by going to lunch at Auberge de la Source at Sophia Antipolis, and, although the celebrations were somewhat muted by the attendance of Mr. Clipboard, this was offset in more than equal measure by the fact that the lovely Ashley, his wife, came too.

Amongst the very important issues discussed was a blog (not my own on this rare occasion) I had seen on Facebook called "50 sheds of grey". This seems to me to be a development of the wonderful

Monty Python sketch about Arthur "two sheds" Jackson, which if you were too young, and missed at the time is too difficult a subject to recount here. The girls amongst us became much more animated as this discussion developed, but I have to admit I did quite understand why. Grey sheds seems an unlikely subject about which to get excited, I guess I will never understand women.

Tennis last evening was postponed due to Blind Lemon Milsted acknowledging that his forehand was almost beyond redemption and pulling out on some spurious pretext, so spurious that it was not even revealed to his partner, me. However we all know that there is a problem here, and like the supportive friends we would like to be and are not, will do the best to expose this weakness when next we see him, this morning at 11.00am sharp unless he becomes even more spurious. On the tennis court, cool (forehand) hand Luke he is not.

Last night was a bit of a write off. It had started full of industrious intent. Our electrician had been jumping around to the commands of that Nice Lady Decorator, fixing a few electrical problems and as he finished in early evening I thought he deserved a beer before I got down to making another load of cement. I had my old clothes on, a barrow full of sand and was bracing myself for more hard labour when I got a call from Roly and Poly, asking if they could pop round for half an hour. That's when the trouble started. I should have known when they arrived carrying two bottles of wine, and they finally left around midnight. Had they arrived 10 minutes later, I would have had a wheelbarrow shaped lump of concrete to contend with.

One interesting footnote which I know will be of interest to the Reverend Jeff related to a discussion we had about some religious friends of Roly and Poly. At one stage I was told that they had "been to hell and back" with some issue or other. I suppose it is only the religious ones that are able to get back?

Journalistic Dreams

There are days that start badly but then improve to heights

undreamed of when wallowing in the slough of discontent. Such a day was yesterday. Let me start with the good news. A poorly-educated council house oik (the description of my good self regularly employed by a number of my public schoolboy friends) yesterday added the description "journalist" to the self-composed list of qualities, which include "successful author".

I think a celebratory cigar this evening?

In England, the leading conservative daily newspaper on a par with The Times is The Daily Telegraph. It is the newspaper of choice for those public schoolboy types. Imagine then my delight when they informed me yesterday that the very first article I had ever submitted to them, or indeed any newspaper, had been published. The small recompense that they will pay me is as nothing against the entertainment I shall glean over the coming days as my chums realise the enormity of the public relations coup this represents. I cannot wait to meet Mr. Clipboard this evening to discuss this triumph. I know he will be pleased for me.

It was just the kind of uplifting news to set against the increasingly depressing prospects of returning to England and there was something else that was depressing me. I have a hunch that it had something to do with tennis but, no, it's gone, but no matter, a new career in journalism, starting with one of the most prestigious publications in England, even the world, is sufficient to erase any disappointments that may or may not have occurred yesterday.

Even the prospect of the day ahead being littered with a string of tasks I have been set by that Nice Lady Decorator, most of which seem to involve me in furious manual labour in the heat of the day, is not enough to remove a smirk from my face, a smirk that will become a chuckle when I meet up with some of my better-educated peers this evening.

It was always going to happen. Public schoolboys do not react well when grammar schoolboy oiks achieve something to which they can only aspire. My having an article published by The Daily Telegraph, that bastion of conservatism, hitherto the reading material for the upper middle classes, landed gentry and those that were sent by their parents to schools with names like Wellington, was too much to bear, so to say I was looking forward to meeting up with a prime example of this ilk, an old Wellingtonian himself, to discuss this was an understatement of the highest order.

Thus, with a smirk on my face as wide as the Grand Canyon, I headed for Valbonne square for an encounter with chief fag toaster himself, Mr. Clipboard, to discuss the merits of said article. I had taken the liberty of forwarding the link to it just to be sure that he was fully aware of the public relations debacle that was about to engulf him.

His first retort questioned whether its publication in this very sober journal was a set up for "Jim'll Fix It", a popular TV programme from our youth in which Sir Jimmy Savile sought to give no-hopers a chance to live their dream (a description which he apparently applied to some young girls that turned into a nightmare). Magnanimity had, as I had expected, no place at this dinner table. His next line of attack was to ask who wrote it. Surely I had a ghost writer? he said, although this one I did not understand. What would Caspar have to do with it? But no matter, nothing he said could permeate that feeling of well-being that resides within me even now despite his continual attempts to belittle this achievement. I do hope it is such a bone of contention that he will continue his disdain at tennis this afternoon, then I will be certain it hurts. As soon as he calls me Boycie, a reference to the used car salesman character in another popular TV comedy series, I will know for certain I have got to him.

Yes, tennis, the very last game of which I shall be playing in this chapter of my life, as we leave tomorrow morning for a new life in the UK, with only a brief week's holiday back in Valbonne in late August. I have laid out my winter clothing because, despite a heat wave in England at the moment, there is a quiet certainty that I will be rained on at some stage the first day I set foot back there on Sunday. Two days to get back I hear you ask? It is perfectly simple. We have to travel through the heart of some of the best wine country in the world, so it would be a lost opportunity not to stop somewhere en route to sample the local delights, so where better than Beaune, the centre of Burgundy.

So there it is, over. My exile in England starts shortly and I will miss the south of France terribly. I shall be back though, hopefully before the new French president ruins the country with his tax the rich schemes which the rich will avoid. Also, I find it very difficult to drive past the magnificent Chateau Du Cocove, an oasis in the terminally boring and usually damp hinterland of Calais, so difficult in fact that I have decided not to drive past it at all, but to drive to it and stay on Saturday night for one last great culinary French experience before it is back to fish covered in batter, Cornish pasties, pork pies and other English delicacies.

Until then I shall hunker down in England and dream of Valbonne.

THE END